STRONGER

STRONGER

Changing Everything
I Knew About
Women's Strength

POORNA BELL

bluebird
books for life

First published 2021 by Bluebird
an imprint of Pan Macmillan
The Smithson, 6 Briset Street, London EC1M 5NR
EU representative: Macmillan Publishers Ireland Limited,
Mallard Lodge, Lansdowne Village, Dublin 4
Associated companies throughout the world
www.panmacmillan.com

ISBN 978-1-5290-5081-3

1 3 5 7 9 8 6 4 2

A CIP catalogue record for this book is available from the British Library.

Typeset in Warnock Pro by Palimpsest Book Production Limited, Falkirk, Stirlingshire
Printed and bound by CPI Group (UK) Ltd, Croydon, CR0 4YY

Visit **www.panmacmillan.com** to read more about all our books
and to buy them. You will also find features, author interviews and
news of any author events, and you can sign up for e-newsletters
so that you're always first to hear about our new releases.

Leela, you come from a long line of strong women,
who have always danced to the
beat of their own drum.

Take the sticks, make your own music,
be powerful.

We are with you every step of the way.

Contents

Strong *(adjective)*:

1. Someone who is **strong** is healthy with good muscles and can move or carry heavy things, or do hard physical work.
2. Someone who is **strong** is confident and determined, and is not easily influenced or worried by other people.

Prologue

It's 1986.

This is the year that the nuclear reactor at Chernobyl explodes. The first year of *The Oprah Winfrey Show*. Newspapers flutter with updates about Halley's Comet, which will appear like an ice-cream melting across the sky, a cosmic snowball reforming and burning briefly in our solar system, only reappearing again in 100 years' time. The M25 – AKA 'evidence for the hidden hand of Satan in the affairs of Man', according to the book *Good Omens* – is finally complete.

Along the M25, off junction three and a bit further on the M20, is a little primary school in Maidstone. The kids have been let out into the playground and the sun is out.

I'm six years old. The autumn light is reedy and weak; winter is tightening its grip. But it's better than being indoors where the smells of poo and plasticine are fighting for attention. (My classmate William sometimes inadvertently poos himself. He sits on his own table and all the kids tend to avoid him. No one explains to us why our behaviour is wrong and William is probably going through some serious shit . . . literally.) William doesn't come outside very much. But in any case, today is not about him, it's about Adam. Adam is the golden boy, the one that my friends and I fancy.

Because we are six and lack any type of language to articulate this, it distils into a very simple thought that out of

1

everyone, Adam is the loveliest to look at and I want to be near him. And it isn't the same as spending time with my best friend Elizabeth, who I make mud pies with.

Today we're playing kiss chase. This is where we run around the playground trying to track down the person we want to catch and kiss. This is way before conversations about consent and petitions to get the game removed from schools. Adam is the prize but given that I am six and I don't really know what kissing is, it's more like getting greyhounds to chase after a picture of a rabbit. It's simply a foil to get us moving.

Under that struggling sun, we hear someone yell 'Go' and my friends and I start running. We feel the breath in our lungs, hot but laced with the sharpness of the season. We laugh and giggle and feel good because our bodies aren't cramped at a desk but are doing the one thing they are supposed to do: move. I'm so caught up in running that I don't even notice Adam until I'm right up close to him near the shade of the wall.

I could kiss him right now and it would be OK and not at all embarrassing because this is kiss chase and that is what you were supposed to do. But I look at him and I don't know if Adam wants me to kiss him. So, unfettered by the angst and great burden of choice that comes with adulthood and romance, I decide running and laughing is far more fun than chasing after a boy. I don't know it yet but this is the most free I will feel in my body for a long time. It will take a lot of loss and a lot of healing to return to this place of wildness and joy.

But for now, in this formative mist, where I have the freedom just to let my body sing with movement, I turn my face to the sun, to find my friends, to keep running.

CHAPTER ONE

Diary of a Runt

In January 2016, eight months after my husband Rob died, I wrote this letter in my diary.

Dear Me,

I have not yet written a letter to you, I mean, the you after Rob's death. I'm scared of what you will think if I tell you how I really feel. But. Perhaps this is the year to stop being afraid.

You've had a really shitty year. Understatement. A bog awful, tit-twister of a year.

We lost the love of our life and we went through losing him twice. Once, when we thought we were going to be separated and divorced, which was a pain we never thought we'd recover from, and then when Rob died and we were lost, our heart ripped out, our days blacker than squid ink.

But what am I telling you this for? You already know this.

The reason for me writing this, darling Poorna, is because we are going to set out what we want from this year and what we want from life.

I think it's important to do this, otherwise we are just

*going to be travelling through the ether, adrift but not knowing
what is going on.*

*So what we are going to do is state our desires, our wishes,
our dreams and if not much comes out of it, fine. We tried.*

1. *We are going to leave England by October, latest.*
2. *We are going to take some time and spend it with our
   loved ones like Leela, Priya, Shabby, Mum and Dad.*
3. *We are going to travel. And get up early. And see
   sunrises.*
4. *We are going to be in love with Rob but also open
   ourselves to the idea of new possibilities.*
5. *We are going to get laid. At some point.*
6. *We are going to stop acting like work is life or death. We
   have seen death, and it isn't work.*
7. *When we get mad, we are going to remember that
   none of this really matters; what matters is love and
   kindness.*
8. *We are going to be the fittest we have ever been.*
9. *We are going to be strong in mind, body and spirit.*
10. *And remember, all things change.*

Twelve months after writing this, everything on this list had
happened, apart from point number one. And – I mean, you
probably already knew this – but this entire book is about point
number nine.

1995.

One warm morning in early September, when summer was
still clinging on by its fingertips and the air was starting to smell
of the sweet rot of dying flowers, a person walking along a certain
country lane in deepest Kent would have seen a strange sight
over the fence. In a corner of the empty green playing field of

the local girls' school, puffs of smoke were emanating like a chimney from underneath a gnarled collection of trees, accompanied by a sequence of splutters and coughs, like a bag of stones rubbing together in a sack. It would have been followed by some wheezing and 'Oh god, that was disgusting!' which would have been odd because trees don't smoke and they definitely don't talk. But little teenage shits do and this was the moment that I, aged 14, had decided to try cigarettes for the first time. I'd put more organisation into that moment than I did with my homework. I woke up one day, decided I wanted to smoke and put a plan into action. The first step was procurement.

Despite having the chutzpah to take up smoking independently of any peer pressure, most local corner shops were run by fellow Asians and I did not feel confident in asking a random auntie for ten Silk Cut, most likely to be met with a shrivelling death stare. (With South Asians, any stranger above the age of 50 is given automatic auntie status even if they only met you five minutes ago. This allows them to critique your relationship status, life choices and appearance.) Since purchasing was a no go, I resorted to crime, stealing a couple of loose cigarettes from my uncle Ashok's corner shop in London on our last trip to visit him in the holidays. Even if he noticed them missing, I reckoned, I'd be long gone, on a train back to Kent.

The second step was recruiting a willing accomplice because if I got caught, it would be infinitely better to do detention with a pal. But also, I needed a witness to my new adult, cool status as this was a time before smartphones, Instagram, TikTok, Snapchat.

The third issue was location, location, location. My smoking virgin foray was not going to be conducted in Smokers' Alley – the dodgy wooded area that connected our school to the bottom of the hill – which was frequently raided by teachers.

So why the playing field, also known as the manor green?

It was one of four areas we did physical education, P.E., at my all-girls grammar school. The first was the gymnasium – a large, light-filled room with a shiny wooden floor used for gymnastics and dance. Gymnastics was the least terrible, given that it involved a trampoline, which is pretty impossible to fuck up unless you spring off it and splat onto the floor. Dance was the nadir, because we had to run around with sky blue t-shirts tucked into sturdy, burgundy gym knickers (more unresolved angst on these later).

The second was the tennis and netball courts that sat next to the main school building – a place that should have been my domain given that I used to play tennis. But we didn't play tennis often at school and, as I was five foot three, people were not clamouring to have me on their netball team.

The third was the vast hockey pitch near the next-door high school and a fairly fraught location. This was not only because hockey was terrifying, given that we were whacking around a ball that could easily knock out your front teeth, but also none of us had ever forgotten our P.E. teacher losing it at a student and throwing her hockey stick across the pitch.

The fourth, the manor green, was where we did the more niche sports, such as javelin, shot put and long jump. In theory they were fun – because javelin and shot put were effectively weapons that you got to throw as hard as possible – but the reality is that we weren't very good at them and while none of us were under the illusion we were training for the Olympics, neither were we given any specific goals.

Once a year, we would have a sports assessment in the gymnasium and, among other drills, the most dreaded challenge was the rope climb. This was where, despite no training or guidance whatsoever, as well as having the upper body strength of a noodle, we were expected to climb up a battle rope that stretched upwards about 20 feet into the ceiling.

These spaces didn't just make me feel useless and inept, they also made me feel powerless. As if the inability to do these activities and do them well was due to some inner failing. In the classroom, I could try to at least think my way around a problem, whether it was memorising the periodic table or slogging through Shakespeare. The solution to failure was just working harder. But in these arenas of physicality, it wasn't a question of studying more. The way we were taught – or rather not taught – made us feel like our bodies were failing us in some way.

Consider the rope climb assessment: it's an incredibly intense activity even if you have been doing strength training, let alone as a 13- or 14-year-old who hasn't been trained to do such a climb. But this is exactly what you're being assessed on. Can't do it? Well, you're probably a weak little runt. No good at netball? You're probably not trying hard enough. The subtext of that lack of achievement can be deafening, especially when, as a girl, you aren't exactly swamped with positive reinforcements around your body anyway.

Very few of us entered those places of physicality and felt belonging. Or power. So popping my cigarette cherry in the very place where my self-esteem was often flat on the floor? Hell yes. Up yours, javelin; suck it, shot put. As childish as it sounds, it was a tiny, feeble way of redressing the balance, of reclaiming that space. The next time I had to trudge onto that field and stand in line and be told what to do, and then be yelled at for not doing it right, or dismissed because of my physique, there was that tiny piece of defiance buried at the base of those trees.

It didn't occur to me until around 25 years later, when I was 38 and finally stood in my full power of what made me feel mentally and physically strong, how damaging those school years were to my understanding of physicality and my ability. How, if I'd felt a sense of belonging in those arenas, I may not have felt so disconnected and estranged from my own body. More importantly, being empowered in those spaces may well have made me feel more prepared and less vulnerable when it came to all of the things that eroded my self-esteem and self-worth in the intervening years.

At a time when our bodies were going through an unprecedented transformation, like a werewolf's first shift, a time for nurture, love and reassurance, most of us were not taught about moving our bodies in a way that felt joyous in an environment that felt safe. Few if any of us learned about the mental benefits of moving our bodies. On the contrary, many of us exited girlhood forgetting that it was meant to be fun and instead carried around the weight of comments, bullying or just believing we weren't 'fitness people' because P.E. was a torturous bag of shite. Even if you loved P.E., or were good at sports, it certainly wasn't considered to be a 'cool thing' at school as it was for boys, and you certainly weren't immune to comments around your body. From there, off we went, defenceless into a world where fitness is thereafter almost always reframed within the scope of weight loss.

So if this is you, too; if somewhere along the way you lost the part of yourself that felt you could do anything, be anything; if there is a part of you that doesn't feel strong or doesn't know how to begin, that doesn't feel you look the way you 'should' or feels ashamed in your own body, I am here to tell you whatever you have believed in the past does not have to determine your story.

None of us start out believing we can't do something. As babies and children, we always begin by believing we can do anything – until someone or something tells us we can't. The question is: how do we stop ourselves from losing this belief? And how do we get back what we lost? If you are the girl, the woman who feels like she is never enough, that she will never be as strong, as good, as capable, I am here to tell you that you are enough. I am here to tell you that while it shouldn't have been your burden, you can write a different story.

Teenagers are a bit like golems in that, during this time, a script is being written and built into our clay that will guide us in who to be, how to view ourselves and what we can come back to as a touchstone for strength and guidance. Most of us will take this well into our adult lives, so what it says matters.

That script could be teaching girls how movement isn't something to be embarrassed about. It could show role models – many different kinds – who can demonstrate that strength comes in all shapes and sizes and abilities. It could show how what a body *does* and how that makes you feel should always come before how it looks. But that is largely not our experience at a younger age.

My story, however, is only one of many, and so in order to get a deeper sense of our different experiences around physical activity as girls, to find out how that had shaped us as women, and what continues to influence us emotionally, mentally and physically around fitness, I wanted to speak to other girls and women. I ran a survey with 1,043 girls and women, aged between 12 and 71+, and pushed it out across Twitter, Instagram as well as closed Facebook groups for women of colour. I wanted to know about the things that negatively shaped their experiences with fitness, what gave them joy, what had been the biggest blockers – from self-confidence to low income – where they liked to exercise, where they didn't like to exercise, and what made them feel strong. I also wanted to know about the blind spots – women who had been neglected and failed by mainstream fitness – and wanted to speak to women who had been dealing with physical and mental illness, hidden and visible disabilities; women from different cultures, races, religions; older women and the LGBTQ+ community. I wanted to know about guilt and how they felt about their bodies, and what led them to a place of trust and love. I also wanted to know where and how it was going wrong for girls, because this disconnect around physical activity and girlhood seemed like such a missed opportunity to me.

'I was picked on at school and P.E. was one of the lessons where that was really a problem,' says Beth, who took the survey. 'I developed early and was a bit chubby and the sporty girls picked on me outside of class anyway, so P.E. just gave them an arena where they had permission to chase me, throw things at me and shout at me. I carried all that bullshit with me until I was almost 30. Then I decided enough was enough and I wanted to make a change.'

When I think about my script, I think the belief that looking slim was more important than being strong acted as a chloroform, knocking out my connection with my own body. I went from being the little girl who ran in the wind and sun and felt the sheer pleasure of being an animal to a creature trapped in a cage designed to keep me as small as possible.

It took an earth-shattering event to make me rewrite that script. The reason you are holding this book is because I went from someone who utterly hated P.E., believed she was terrible at sport, felt a sense of disconnection, shame and distrust around her own body, to someone who in their late thirties lifts weights competitively, experiences joy and self-assuredness in movement, and is grateful for every day her body powers on through grief, anxiety and illness. Through this journey, I realised that what girls and women have been taught about strength is mostly wrong and that we have been held back from fulfilling our potential around being strong, whether it's weight-lifting, cycling, swimming, running, boxing, yoga, martial arts, climbing, fencing – you name it – in many different ways.

Pursuing physical strength gave me purpose when there was none. It required mental strength to start the journey, but once undertaken, became a vital part of keeping mentally well. It gave me worth when my entire schooling told me that when it came to physical ability, I was worthless. It made me feel seen when the entire fitness industry told me that my version of physical ability was not worth seeing.

It took something unusual and immense to make me break free and finally look at the bullshit that I had lived my entire life by. But it isn't necessary to go through something earth-shattering like this to find your strength and hopefully this book will be the shortcut for you to be able to do that for yourself in a kind and compassionate way.

But first, here's what happened.

I am not saying that knowing the truth better prepares you for when bad things happen but I think if we were more truthful about what life actually is, and how there is no one way of being, we'd have more realistic and manageable expectations of it.

For me, the biggest lie was thinking that all I had to do to step onto the road to never-ending happiness was to meet the love of my life, get married and have children. I am hardly a traditionalist and I didn't have my dream wedding sketched out but somewhere along the way, I had absorbed this dream into every fibre of my being. So when I met the love of my life, a Kiwi named Rob, I thought this would happen. Our lives slowly entwined together – he was endlessly curious about my

Indian background, I was fascinated by this man who was born on the Lost Continent and we poured the same amount of love into each other.

But four years into our marriage, something catastrophic and world-ending happened. Rob – gardener, birdwatcher, science nerd, punk rocker – died. He had been struggling with addiction and depression and took his own life while in New Zealand.

People describe a suicide as a grenade thrown into your house. I think of it like napalm. In order to burn, napalm sucks in all the oxygen in the vicinity. Its chemical nature makes it so effective in what it does. It can attach itself to anything usually impervious, like a bunker or a tank, and violently burn through all of it. Rob's death was like that. It burned through everything – our past, my future, hope, my will to survive – until almost nothing was left.

In the first few months after he died, I was dimly aware that something was awakening inside of me. I imagined her as a creature that lay dormant in the inky depths of my existence. She rose up to meet a need because my conscious, everyday self was being flayed by grief, piece by piece. I'd lost a piece of myself the moment I had answered the call from my mother-in-law to tell me that Rob had been found by the police. I lost another when I saw him in the funeral home. Another when we buried him. Coming home and seeing his side of the bed. Seeing his clothes hanging in the wardrobe. A pair of his shoes tucked under his desk.

The world felt so raw; everything hurt. I didn't know how I was going to wake up the next day and do this all over again. Every breath, every action required so much. Most of the time I didn't want to do it. I sometimes found myself paralysed in reverie, where I'd lie under the covers and pretend Rob was in the kitchen making coffee and if I moved more than an eyelash, it would shatter the illusion. I just wanted to go to sleep and not wake up. And when I felt like this, like a lightbulb that just wanted to be switched off, this dormant part of me would awake. She would make her way from the depths and swim to the surface, encircling me in her wide embrace. And somehow she would take over. I'd find myself in the shower. Preparing food. Talking to another person.

But even grief couldn't rob my body of its urgent need to move, to escape. When I felt able, I'd go to the gym or run, which was my favourite activity at that point. Runners often describe that sequence of movements as feeling as if you're flying, a liberation in your own skin. I would grab onto any moment when my body didn't feel weighed down or exhausted.

A month after Rob died, I signed up to do a 10K for the men's suicide prevention charity CALM and that propelled me out of bed three times a week to go running by the riverside. It became a shield against the relentless flow of the thoughts about what I should have done, and what I perceived I didn't do around his death. Near the river, I felt peaceful. I'd see birds paddling near the water's edge and they'd remind me of his fondness for birdwatching and the many books that occupied our bookshelf.

I'd catch eddies and swirls in the water and they'd mesmerise me, allowing my conscious mind to drift to a place of white noise for a while. Sometimes I'd see someone who looked like him walk past and I'd stop jogging. I'd pretend to catch my breath against a tree when really I was summoning every bit of strength to stop more pieces splintering off my already broken heart.

I loved running but, if I am being honest, it was a complicated thing. I saw the river and it told me that oblivion could be mine too, if I found things too hard. But, rather than do that, I told myself that every day I jogged past that river and didn't jump in was a day that would make me stronger. One day turned into two, two into three and soon it became weeks and I used that knowledge to climb further and further up and out of that pit of grief.

For a time, I just stayed as still in my life as I possibly could.

I stayed in the same flat that we had lived in together, everything more or less how it had been before he died. The pictures he put up stayed where they were. I slept in the same bed, kept his pillow, couldn't bear to give away his things which were kept in the loft. He was like the last remaining bottle of a precious perfume: from the wisp of cigarette smoke on his jacket to his fingerprints on our saucepan handles. For a brief time, our existences overlapped even though he was no longer a part of the mortal world.

After a year of this, I realised that though staying in the same place had given me immeasurable comfort, it was also now the thing that was holding me back. I was living in a ghost home, lost in the memory of what had been, unable to think about what could be. The first thing I understood was that our big, beautiful bed had to go.

When Rob and I first met in early 2009, much was made of the bed. 'It's a super king,' he said proudly. Having crammed in with previous partners on single beds and double beds, I couldn't understand what the big deal was, until I spent the first night in it. It was like a spaceship – a huge, comfy place where we could both sleep at respective ends of the bed in peace and cuddle up when we wanted to. Our dog Daisy loved to sit on it and stare out of the window waiting for us to return. (Even though it was CLEARLY forbidden.)

After he died, I slept on my side of the bed during that whole year, as if he'd just gone away on a trip and hadn't yet returned.

But things of the dead – especially inanimate objects – are talismanic in their power. This bed represented the polar ends of our life together: the blossoming start of our relationship, the scene of a thousand kisses, and also a place I started to resent when Rob was in bed, ill with depression, then sick with withdrawal from heroin that ate away the latter years of his life.

After he was gone, I would lie under a fold of sheets and look over to my right. I would call to him across the ocean of grief that now lay between us and will his form to pool into the slight dent his body had made in the mattress. But all I ever saw was emptiness and I could feel how it held me back.

When I finally went to buy a new bed, the saleswoman started rabbiting on about the mattress I was about to buy. 'It has a wool blend, so it's more hygienic but you'll have to turn it over every two months or so.' I just nodded. I didn't care if the mattress was filled with unicorn dust, I just wanted my old bed out and the new one in, and I paid extra for the delivery men to handle all of it. I couldn't bear to look at the bed as it was being carried out. It felt like yet another goodbye, another part of my life that had chipped off.

When the new bed was in, I felt better than I thought I would. Mainly because my first thought was: *this mattress is amazing and bouncy and WHY didn't I do this earlier?* But two months later, it was mattress-flipping time. And what followed was an absolute shambles.

Until I moved in with Rob, I had only ever lived in rented accommodation with friends and the bed was always already set up. Shortly after getting married, I decided I wanted to get a new mattress for our bed but it arrived when I was on holiday with friends in Mexico. 'I'll get it sorted out before you come home, honey,' Rob texted me. And he was true to his word.

Now, I faced my brand new, heavy mattress in a world without

Rob and I tried to flip it. It was heavy and wouldn't budge. I tried to attack it from different angles multiple times and ended up sweaty, exhausted and unable to do anything more than get it on its side. As the sweat pooled around my neck, a lightbulb moment occurred.

During our whole relationship, I had relied on Rob's strength to get things done. Hell, I was even attracted by it. When we first met, his physicality was absolutely something I fell for. He was six foot with broad shoulders, massive, calloused hands and thick, brawny forearms. When we moved house, Rob took charge of the physical aspect of that. 'I'm the donkey and that's OK,' he once said. He moved the washing machine, the dishwasher, bookcases. He assembled the bed, lugged the pot plants around. Before him, I had always relied on my dad, male friends or other guys I was dating. It was a given that if I had a suitcase heavier than I could physically carry, then a man would carry it.

Why had I not realised this? As I sat there, sweat dripping down my face, there was a hardening of something inside me. I was no longer sad about my old bed. I looked down into the corridor of where Rob had gone; he was not coming back.

'You are not here,' I said out loud, angrily. I have never been angry at Rob for the way he died but I was angry at how hard life had become. I was angry that I'd been left to deal with all of this and, yes, I was angry that he wasn't around. I was angry that he'd broken a promise to be there. And it was easier to focus my anger on something small like Rob not being around when I needed him to flip a mattress, versus something big like not watching my niece grow up. Just then, I missed him with a rage that pulled itself into 20-metre high waves and thudded against every part of my life.

But I also knew that I was no longer going to be the type of person who would spend the rest of her life relying on the strength of men. Flipping a mattress was only going to be the start of it. I had already started to think about moving house. I would start going on holidays that meant I'd need to carry my own luggage. I didn't want to wait with my suitcase at a train station hoping some well-meaning man would help me carry it to the top of the staircase.

You left, I thought. *And so now I have to figure this shit out. Myself. Like I had to do in our relationship when you stopped talking to me about what was wrong. Like I've had to do every single minute of the day since you were gone.* That anger burned so bright and with such fury, I felt like it could blow out the windows of the room. There was no alternative. I grabbed the corner of the mattress and painstakingly used every advantage possible offered by gravity and leverage to try and flip it over. Twenty minutes later, following a couple of scraped elbows and a lot of grunting, it eventually happened.

'YES! Omigod, yes! Yes! YES!' I screamed. (I think my neighbours must have thought I was having very exciting sex.) Afterwards, there was a sense of achievement. The surprise of being stronger than I had given myself credit for. The relief that I hadn't had to ask someone for help. But what struck me was the small glow of potential and positivity I felt in my physical accomplishment, and how it had cut through the chaos I felt around grief.

If I could do this once, with grit and determination, what else might I be capable of? There was so much I couldn't control, I thought, but I could control this. And maybe at some point, the accumulation of what I felt physically capable of doing could help and heal the parts of me that the grief had blasted apart. I knew in that moment that the previously separate circuit boards of my mental strength and physical strength had just been soldered together. The next day I went to my gym around the corner from my office and I asked for a personal trainer.

'I don't like to be shouted at,' I said, 'so make sure it's not one of those overly peppy types.'

'Let me see who we have,' said the receptionist, looking at the screen. 'Actually,' he added absently, 'it might help to know what you're after. Like is it toning, weight loss and so on?'

'None of that,' I said sharply, and my tone made him look up. 'I want to get strong.'

Those five words may not sound like much but it was like walking between worlds. It had taken me 34 years to utter those words and really mean it. I wish it hadn't taken the decimation of one world to forge another but we don't always get to choose the thing that remakes us.

My journey in going from runt to Strongest Version of Myself is just one story in the vast galaxy of what comprises women's physical and mental strength. Each star shining bright in it represents a different history, a journey, a story and when viewed from a distance, the sight of all of that achievement and strength is dazzling. But the world we grow up in cloaks that brilliance, and teaches us that there is only one source of light in the darkness of the cosmos, and it comes from the pursuit of a very narrow idea of fitness – the one we have come to believe through reading fitness magazines that only ever feature young, slim models, seeing picture-perfect influencers and dramatic celebrity weight-loss transformations and fitness DVDs.

Once I knew I was going to write this book, I wanted to talk to other girls and women and hear their stories of what had held them back, but more importantly, I wanted to find out what they loved about physical movement and the emotional qualities they associated with it. I wanted to know how it strengthened them mentally to paint a more accurate picture of the way physical activity and fitness can make us *feel* when we don't just view it as a mechanism to lose weight.

I've read a lot of great books about physical strength for women and a lot of great books about mental strength for women but the premise I am putting forward here is that the two things are synonymous. That's not to say you can't have one without the other. But together, they unlock an incredible reserve of mental and physical strength that has a bedrock stronger than diamond. This will give you a foundation from which you can operate at full strength in every aspect of your life.

However, it's not just a question of moving more while learning some skills to help with mental resilience. There's a lot of work that needs undoing first because what most of us have been made to feel about our bodies, and about female strength, has been experienced and perceived through an incredibly narrow, shrinking lens. We can't access that reservoir if we are still holding onto a system and a structure that demands we make ourselves as small as possible – whether that's physically or mentally.

It's time to take up some damn space.

The survey I ran is split between the 91 per cent those who do some form of physical activity, and the 9 per cent who don't do any at all. I know I should start with the biggest numbers first but I'm actually going to do this backwards.

I'm very interested in the 9 per cent. It's not an insignificant number – that's nearly one in ten women who took the survey. Even though they said they didn't exercise, they still felt compelled to fill out a survey about it, indicating that they weren't indifferent but most likely had had a negative experience. In fact, nearly half (41 per cent) of the 9 per cent said the reason they didn't exercise was because they felt self-conscious. A third of them said they didn't enjoy it. While 21.6 per cent said they worried they would be bad at it.

All of which points to a massive problem women have around confidence when it comes to physical activity. In 2019, Sport England ran a survey looking at 130,000 children and found that, from age five to seven, girls were far less likely to take part in team sports even though they said they loved being active.[1] The biggest thing they cited that got in the way? Confidence. That might stem from bad P.E. experiences, unconscious bias around boys being 'better' at sport or fatphobic comments from other kids and adults. But my survey also highlighted the lack of a roadmap for women in terms of redefining their relationship with fitness after a major life event such as illness, disability, trauma, having a baby or menopause.

There have been significant moves to change this. One of the biggest is This Girl Can, the ground-breaking campaign from Sport England which first launched in 2015. They identified that, despite increases in people being active within the UK, women were still persistently less active than men and then went about building a campaign that highlighted the reasons why this was – which wasn't just about the physical aspect of it, but tackled emotional and mental blockers. As a result, they have inspired millions of women to be more active, which shows that when handled right, change can and does happen.

Many of us in our thirties, forties, fifties and beyond still cling onto the goals we may have had as teenagers or in our twenties because we live in a society that lionises youth and the women we see on social media and advertising campaigns are mostly young and slim. But it is madness, given that the *only* certainty in life is that our bodies change, and that older bodies are capable of as much bravery and achievement as a younger body. If we could embrace this positively, we'd be unstoppable. In fact, almost all of the older women who took the survey spoke about how empowering being active made them feel and how it taught them that what we'd been told about ageing and ability was nonsense.

Out of the 91 per cent who did exercise, there were some interesting findings. Although 63 per cent said the reason they started exercising in the first place was due to weight loss – no surprises there considering the enormity of diet culture and how fitness is continuously framed in that lens – there were positives to take away. Over 67 per cent said it was very important for their mental health, 78 per cent said physical activity had helped them when they were struggling mentally and 69 per cent said they exercised because they enjoyed it. The top three feelings most strongly associated with physical activity were mental wellbeing, feeling strong, and over half said it made them feel empowered.

But there were some undeniably grim, consistent patterns of experience and behaviour. The gym emerged as the least popular place to work out in; 18 per cent said they had felt some form of fatphobia around their presence in the fitness space. Over 65 per cent of women said that comparing themselves to others was a major blocker to working out, while over 50 per cent said that feeling self-conscious had at points prevented them from working out, citing reasons ranging from not 'looking fit enough to work out' to people staring. For some, that pervading sense of self-consciousness is a double-edged sword: you can't reclaim that space because you don't feel you look like someone who is fit. The reason you may think someone who works out in a gym looks a certain way is because of all the images we've been fed, mixed with the lack of confidence or negative associations we likely had as children.

'I was overweight as a child,' said Katrina, who took the

survey, 'and that had a huge impact on my confidence as a whole and stopped me from exercising at all until the age of 19. I remember going swimming with school in year 6 and intentionally forgetting my swimming costume so that I wouldn't have to do it. I just felt that exercise wasn't applicable to someone like me who wasn't skinny and didn't have a good base level of fitness.'

Negative associations with fitness at a young age might be for a variety of reasons – and certainly fat-shaming came out from the survey as a common factor in cementing shame around fitness. Another thing that was also clear is that different layers of identity such as race or sexual orientation make things much harder.

Bhavna, who also took the survey, said: 'I was a fat kid who didn't like to exercise but was told I had to because I was fat. I was fat-shamed at primary school and secondary school and, as the only Asian girl in an all-white year group, I stuck out enough without that as a limiter. My husband is the only reason I turned a negative relationship with fitness into a more positive one but I still have a long way to go.'

I have never had to deal with fat-shaming but I am aware of how it has affected some of the people closest to me. It's something that crops up frequently in the stories of women via direct messages and comments on the fitness inclusivity platform I created on Instagram called See My Strong. The idea for the account came to me when, in June 2019, I had reached a boiling point around mainstream fitness – from the endless slew of white slim models on the cover of women's fitness magazines, to the types of fitness accounts that were hugely popular on Instagram. By that point, I had started competing in powerlifting competitions and had seen first-hand how varied women's bodies and abilities were, and I knew that mainstream fitness was not representing the majority of women in fitness. I also knew I was fed up and done with waiting for them to change, and so I decided to create a space online that allowed for the stories of women and girls to be told in an honest and inspiring way. It was also rooted in the emotional and mental health aspect of physical movement, and designed to help other women realise that fitness isn't just an aesthetic, and that no body type, age or race has the monopoly on it.

Yet it speaks to how slimness is a leprechaun's pot of gold as far as body goals go, because despite having a body size that society deemed 'acceptable', I still was made to feel like I was never slim enough. A mixture of race, culture and gender meant I don't think I felt like I ever belonged in those fitness spaces as a teenager, and definitely not in my twenties and early thirties. It took me 30 years to wear a swimsuit or a bikini in public and not feel red hot shame – which definitely stems from being Indian, the conservatism that comes with our culture and being worried about the male gaze – but it was also from a self-consciousness around my own body that was embedded when I was a girl.

But I certainly do not feel like that anymore. When I draw a line between my earliest experiences in the gym to how I felt just before I turned 39, the two could not be more different.

The first time I joined a gym was at the age of 24, weighing barely 52kg, and I only did it because my flatmates went. At the time, I was living with my three oldest male friends from university in a flat in Surrey Quays, south-east London – Niaz, Kumaran and Ahmed – they were still studying as medics while I was in my first year of journalism. Our kitchen was generally crammed with tuna and tubs of cottage cheese which the guys would chow down after working out. 'PROTEIN!' they'd say, while I'd stifle the urge to barf.

We would all arrive at the gym together in Ahmed's car and the guys would head to the weights section while I would stick to two spots in the gym – the cross-trainer and the stationary bike. Sometimes the treadmill, but this was more problematic as I remember feeling hyper-aware of people looking at how slow I was running or seeing things jiggle. Which was laughable given that I literally had nothing *to* jiggle. Not to mention that the clothes I wore were so baggy, I could have been the three-boobed alien from *Total Recall* under there and people couldn't tell. Which was sort of the point. If someone hopped on a machine next to me, I'd pretend I was finished and move away from them. And if I sensed that someone was looking at me, my skin would grow hot and it felt as if a layer had peeled off and they could see how truly worthless I was. Half the time it would turn out they weren't looking at me at all, rather the TV screen. But that flood of shame would take a while to dissipate.

Compare this to me on the cusp of 39.

It's December 2019 in a huge, draughty weightlifting gym in the depths of north Devon. A powerlifting competition is taking place, which is where you do three attempts of three lifts: squat, bench press and deadlift. The goal is to lift the heaviest you can possibly handle. Clustered in front of the deadlift platform are the spectators and the judges. Behind the platform are the competing women and girls lined up in order of the weight they are going to lift. I am one of them. Our hands are white with chalk and we look nervous yet determined.

Most of the competitors are ordinary people: we fit training in around our day jobs which range from working in accounting to being full-time students. We all have different shapes, different proportions, different aesthetics but are united by one thing: we lift heavy. On that platform, the only thing you can hide behind is your hair. Your body is clad in a one-piece singlet – similar to what you might see on a wrestler. Or a baby. Not only do you have to wear this piece of clothing, you do your lifting in front of a crowd.

I look over on the screen and see that I'm shortly due to do my third attempt deadlift – the final lift of the day. My trainer and one of my closest friends, Jack, has been looking after all the other women in my team, giving them words of encouragement. Now he comes over to me. He looks straight into my eyes and starts speaking. 'You've got this. This is yours. You can do this. Attack the bar.' He understands how much I want this lift. It's 130kg, over twice my own body weight, and I've failed it before.

Just before I go on, I tunnel down, deep down into the core of everything that makes me, me. Everything I have overcome, all the loss, all the love, all the strength. Every door inside me is open and it floods with the sense of being limitless.

My name is called. I step onto that platform to the roar of my teammates and friends calling my name in support. All of that fades to white, stillness and calm. Like a lightning bolt connecting me to earth and sky, that strength is summoned, and I bend down. My hands grasp the bar and I pull upwards.

I know this isn't a clean lift. I can feel it hitching up my leg and know almost certainly that it won't pass the judges. But this is not about them. This is about determination, and will, and belief. My physical strength begins the work but my mental strength takes over halfway through. It is like a relay and I grasp the baton. Slowly, that bar goes up and up. I cannot, I do not, accept anything less.

And then finally I pull the bar up and get my legs to lock out, and, just for a moment, though it feels far longer, a door opens to a place of serenity. It is calm, it is light, it is infinite. It is the point at which my mind, body and soul are utterly connected in unison and it is the purest form of freedom. In that moment, I don't care who is watching. I don't care that I'm wearing a glorified BabyGro. I don't even care that technically I have failed this lift. This is the song of my body and my mind, and it is strong, and it is vast, and it is powerful.

The only reason I was able to break away from the cycle of shame – worrying about what I looked like in Lycra or concerned about putting on weight – is because of two big life events that jolted me outside of my reality.

The first was a hole in my heart, which I was only diagnosed with at the age of 31, despite having had it since birth. It changed my entire relationship with my body because the surgeon told me that once I had the keyhole surgery required, I would probably be able to do more than I could before. And he was right. I started running and my body felt like it had been upgraded to a race car. I remember holding onto that feeling like a beam of light and vowing I wouldn't take my body for granted again. The second was losing Rob and realising that I didn't just want to be mentally strong, I wanted to be physically strong. Also because I was searching for anything that would lessen the absence of him.

Both of those types of strength were born from the need for survival but my wish is that girls and women tap into their own sense of strong without needing to experience trauma. Our individual and collective ability to endure and cope and be resilient is so vast, but we are also physically capable of so much – whether it's creating life, grieving, holding that love and loss and pain in our body and still carrying on. What if we connected that point of physical strength to our mental strength with one straight line? What if, rather than pockets of strength, we melted it down so that it occupied an ocean of power that flowed through every corner of our lives?

Few people put it better than the author, journalist and mental health campaigner Bryony Gordon, whose work I had followed for a long time and then we became friends. She's extremely candid about her own mental health and speaks often about the benefits of movement and exercise. She's known for running the London marathon in her underwear to dismantle stereotypes around body image and exercise, and has inspired and empowered so many people to accept their own bodies just a little bit more, as well as take control over certain aspects of their mental health. She has also made running accessible for countless people who may have thought it wasn't for the likes of them.

'Exercise generally was something I thought you had to be good at to do it,' she said to me. 'It's ridiculous when you think about it because it's like saying only people with Michelin stars can cook. So it scared me. I thought exercise was always about me making myself smaller and thinner, and was about losses.

'I realised exercise was about gains and clarity and also the knowledge that your body is really strong and can carry you through long distances. With running, you don't have to be training for a marathon to achieve those gains. But you're giving yourself opportunities for your brain to go, *oh my god my body is amazing and it's not this piece of shit I thought it was for so long*.'

What I hope you gain from reading this book is how to release some of the baggage we might be holding onto when it comes to our bodies and physical movement. It's about working out what your story looks like in the here and now, not shackled to the Ghost of Shite P.E. Experiences Past. It's about setting fire to the comments from people who didn't give your body, the respect and reverence it deserves.

It's also really important to say this is not just about making yourself physically stronger, or to suggest that this is the only way you can get mentally stronger. When I started writing this book, I was the most physically strong I'd ever been – I could squat twice my own body weight. But by the time I finished writing the book, I had caught covid-19 during the 2020 pandemic, and experienced longer term symptoms, now known as 'long covid' which led to a complete shut-down of energy and strength for many months. I could no longer rely on being physically active to manage my mental health, or use my physical ability to give me confidence. Truthfully, it almost made me unravel because the thing about long covid is how slow recovery is, but also with it being such a new illness that even experts don't know much about, it prompted an unprecedented level of me needing to listen to my body, but also my mind, to see what it needed and how it wanted to move. The almost overnight loss of strength led to me needing to work out what else made me feel strong, and how I was able to define that in a way that was beyond what I could physically do. It struck me, as I worked through it both physically and mentally, how this adjustment around ability, self-worth and capability, is something that we do over and over again in our lives, and how vital it is to fully appreciate how strong we are in a multitude of ways.

In terms of figuring out what makes you feel physically strong, well, weightlifting may not be your thing at all. It might be running, like it is for Bryony, or one of the other many different sports and activities that will be mentioned along the way. It doesn't matter. It's about connecting to physical activity in a way that is right for you, which is something only you can decide – and that stuff is *soul-deep*.

For me, being able to lift heavy weights was something that once upon a time would have seemed impossible. I had a bad time of it in P.E. I had a hole in my heart and then I lost Rob.

I'm not saying this because I want pity or a pat on the back. I'm saying that I am not exceptional but I managed to change my story. I went from a scared little girl to the strongest, fiercest version of myself. Like many of you, I spent most of my adult years beating myself up for the food I ate and believing that the main purpose of stepping into a gym was ALWAYS to lose weight and shrink, and thinking that making myself smaller was an achievement.

Being your strongest self has got nothing to do with how far you can run or how much weight you can lift. It's about freeing yourself from any and every limitation you have silently ingested like poison over the years. Do you want to know how to be that fierce warrior that walks the earth with your head held high, and every atom in your body humming with power and strength and wisdom?

Well, there's no time like the present. Let's go.

CHAPTER TWO

Death to Gym Knickers

We all have different journeys, different strengths and different traumas. Being physically active, for instance, is not a quick fix for mental anguish. You wouldn't suggest someone with depression could 'cure' it by going for a run every day, would you? But physical activity can be part of the weaponry you use to battle through the tough stuff in life and it can be a huge generator of joy, confidence and capability.

But while this sounds great in theory, there's one small problem – many of us didn't have the best experiences with physical activity as girls or in school. Unless you were naturally brilliant at it, you probably thought P.E. was a shame onion – layer after layer of experiences designed to make you feel embarrassed, self-conscious or wrong. Even if you were brilliant at sports, it likely still didn't make you exempt from comments or critiques. The England rugby player Abi Burton, for instance, was a star pupil in sport when she was at school and captain of her rugby team, but was bullied by other kids for her size and told she looked like a man. I'd venture to say that a lot of the baggage and hang-ups we have can be traced to that time – and/or the things we heard about our bodies or other women's bodies while growing up.

Learning why we hold shame around our bodies and where that came from – because it wasn't just something we made up ourselves – is important in order to let go of that shame. It is very hard to change or move forward until that happens. I think we have such an all-powerful shame narrative around what's considered to be good (slim bodies) and what's considered to be bad (plus-size bodies) that it makes it hard for people to remember that physical activity isn't supposed to be punishment, it's meant to be fun. When you then couple this with bad experiences as a kid, particularly at school, it is tough to break out of that. As for people not being the 'exercise type' – that's like saying birds don't like to fly. Exercise doesn't have to be 100 burpees and vomiting behind a tree, but you are an animal, hence – physical abilities withstanding – your body wants to move, even if that is a short walk in the park or going for a swim in the local pool.

People who routinely think: 'I'm crap at fitness', 'I'm just lazy', 'I'm not good at it' or 'I'm useless' didn't just wake up one day and think that. Out of the 9 per cent of non-exercisers who took my survey, 33 per cent said they 'didn't enjoy exercise', and while I don't have data as to why this is, I strongly believe it's linked to this negative internal monologue and shame we feel around our bodies and abilities. If you are someone who thinks you aren't the exercise type, or that you're just not good at it, it's most likely because of all the external stuff that shaped and moulded you, from diet culture to a society obsessed with celeb bodies and abs. Many of us, at some point, have held shame around physical activity, whether that's based on what we feel we look like while doing it, feeling we aren't doing enough, feeling like we should do it to lose weight, feeling like other people look better than us – and none of that comes from thin air.

Will Parry, who is a quantitative social scientist and data scientist, told me there were three leading theories as to why someone might have psychological barriers around physical activity, which are: motivation theory, achievement goal theory and self-concept.

Motivation theory is split into two main parts – intrinsic and extrinsic. Intrinsic, he says, is doing something because you want to do it, perhaps you enjoy it and find it rewarding. (Let's say this might be something like going out and dancing with friends.) But extrinsic motivation is when you do it for an external reason, such as to lose weight or when you are obliged to take part. (So this would be like training to hit a certain weight target or having to do dance class at school.) 'Intrinsic motivation,' he says, 'is often very stable (if you enjoy something, that will tend to be true long term). Extrinsic motivation tends not to be – failing to reach a particular standard or being forced to participate might affect your future motivation.' That might explain why, for example, you may have loved physical activity in your spare time as a child but if you went to a school where you had to take part in highly competitive sports, you might end up hating it.

Achievement theory is also split into two and is about how you structure your goals when you're physically active. The first is task-orientated, and is where you're competing against yourself or trying to master a skill, so your goal might be a running PB, swimming lengths or accomplishing a difficult yoga position. The second is ego-orientated, which is where your goal is to be successful against others, such as being the best in a team or winning a race.

Extrinsic motivations and ego-orientated goals can undermine consistent participation in physical activity, because they tend to be less stable over time and depend on other people's performance. The reason why I love powerlifting, for instance, is because it is mainly about the effort you put in and how you build your strength in a stable way, beating your own previous lifting totals.

The third part is self-concept, which focuses on how you view yourself, something that is mainly developed in childhood. There is a strong social comparison element, says Will. So, if you were the type of child who didn't love P.E., experienced bullying or comments about your appearance, or had an encounter that made you think you weren't great at sports, you may then take that resulting sense of fear and comparison into adulthood and that may prevent you from walking into certain spaces, like a gym or a fitness class. Many of us in adulthood, says Will, gravitate towards physical movement that isn't anything like what we were taught at school, for the kind of reasons described above. That definitely resonates with me. I know that I will never ever do any of the sports that were taught to me in P.E. But I know that lifting weights is something I will do either until I die, or my body gives out. There is no cap, no limit on something that gives me that much joy.

For my entire childhood, I was fairly small – always one of the shortest in a class. I was also pretty skinny despite eating a lot – which now, looking back, may have been because of the hole in my heart.

'Are you sure it's not worms?' I remember a family friend saying when I was about eight or nine, because I didn't just look slim, I looked underweight. After spending the week anxiously trying to look down my throat for signs of worms, let me advise that, should you suspect an eight-year-old has worms and you are not a doctor, perhaps don't vocalise it.

I may have looked scrawny, but my personality did not match my diminutive physique. I had – to quote the *Saturday Night Live* sketch – Big Dick Energy. In other words, chatty, loud, with swagger.

My childhood until puberty was split into two very different experiences.

My parents had been based in England for a number of years but decided they wanted to move back to India and set up a life there with myself and my older sister Priya. And so at the age of seven, I left kiss chase with Adam behind and settled into life at an Indian school in Bangalore.

One of my strongest memories – probably because it was the first and last thing I ever won in sports as a child – is running in a relay race. We had only recently moved and I was enrolled in a temporary school which was co-ed while I waited to join my sister at her superior all-girls school. It was sports day, though I didn't really know what was going on, beyond being told that I had to run with a baton and pass it on to the next kid. I was the only girl in my team and I remember running along the dusty track as fast as I could once that stick was pressed into my hand and then afterwards being told we had won the silver medal. The surprise and pride I felt at winning still stays with me and somewhere there is a picture of me smiling, gap-toothed, next to my three fellow runners. I don't remember being remotely aware that they were boys and I was the only girl.

The relay race was the spark of something small: a tiny belief that I might be good at being physically active. That spark was enough to make me try judo – although, in truth, I mainly wanted to do it because I liked the outfit. At the time, *The Karate Kid* was HUGE and although judo wasn't karate, the outfits looked similar (to me, anyway). When it became clear to me that I liked the uniform more than I liked judo, around four or five sessions later, I quit.

My most prized possession at the time was my climbing frame – a six-sided metal structure that had bars you could do roly-polys on and clamber over like a little monkey. My parents had bought it for me when we were in England and it was so adored that it was one of the items packed up and shipped over to India. No mean feat when you consider my parents were not well off and the cost of sending our household belongings as freight meant everything we took was precious. I spent hours on it and there is a picture of me turning upside down, flashing my knickers and not giving a shit, my face showing pure joy.

A few months after arriving, I settled into my new school with my sister Priya, where sports day wasn't something I ever excelled at but I remember it being fun, and we weren't made to feel bad if we weren't good at it. Around this time, there was a pretty pivotal moment when it came to women in sport, at least in my tiny world. I grew up in a time before social media and when satellite TV was something only the wealthy could afford, so exposure to inspiring women in sport wasn't as common back then or as easily accessible as it is today. But two sporting events were big enough to break through the void and reach me – the 1988 Olympics and the 1989 Wimbledon Championship.

It was a time of big female sporting personalities and three in particular stood out for me and commanded my attention. The first was P.T. Usha, who was such a massive deal at the time because she was doing so well at track athletics and was representing India in Seoul. She was remarkable because she came from a small village and was often sick as a child, and her parents had no idea about athletics. But she was asked to run for her school and she went on to win race after race, becoming the youngest athlete at the 1980 Moscow Olympics. She was from Kerala, a neighbouring state to our state, Karnataka, so there was something about her that was more reachable, more tangible.

Then, the following year, it was all about Martina Navratilova and Steffi Graff at Wimbledon. Fierce, strong women. They made me want to try tennis and when I saw that the rackets came in turquoise, white and pink, I wanted one immediately. Once a week, I'd go to the clay courts near our apartment for tennis lessons. The heat was often searing – contrary to what an 'Indian summer' means in the West, with iced coffee and warm weather, an actual Indian summer will blast the skin off your face.

I started to get 'jokes' and comments about how dark I was from being in the sun all the time. In India, as it is with many other Asian countries and parts of Africa, the Caribbean and Middle East, colourism – the bias towards fair skin over dark skin – is alive and well. Dark skin was, and is, viewed as unattractive and devalued your beauty, and was therefore an additional blocker to being outdoors and playing sport. While boys and men are by no means exempt from colourism, there is an overwhelming importance placed on girls and their beauty, framed in terms of their marriageability, which underpins their worth and reason for existing.

But I loved tennis so much that the enjoyment of it won out over the comments. It was a space I felt was mine; one place where I felt free and in control, and it wasn't home, school or my relatives' houses.

Outside of school and tennis, when I was at home, I played with the kids in my neighbourhood, which at that time, were two boys who I loved – Ajit and Krishna – and felt very safe with. We all lived in a development on a newly created road that barely even had tarmac on it and there were still a few undeveloped pieces of land and empty houses. We'd poke around the building sites, read comics, play board games, observe ants in the garden and ride our bikes around. People would use the word tomboy as I tumbled around with them but I really didn't see any distinction between us. I mean, yes, I was secretly in love with Krishna but it was a baby love, where all I wanted to do was hold hands and be around him.

When I was ten, there was a flicker of something that would be the beginning of the end of this kind of innocence. One day, Ajit, who was the oldest of all of us, couldn't come out to play. Krishna and I went around the houses to see who was up for playing hide and seek. By the time we finished, we had a motley group of about eight – six boys and one other girl apart from me, all around 10 or 11 years old. I didn't know the rest of the kids that well but we needed the numbers.

The girl and I were paired up together and we chose to hide on the top of the garage. I was wearing a dress that day. I didn't think anything of it. When we were discovered, the group of little boys crowded round. Something in the body language of a couple of them made me a bit hesitant. There was something feral snapping in the air. 'I bet you can see her knickers!' I heard one of them yell.

I remember the feeling more than I remember the sequence of events – instantly there was a hot flood of shame and self-consciousness that I had never felt before, with a dark vein of fear snaking through. I looked at Krishna – the boy I had loved and played with every day for a year – and saw that while he didn't egg them on, he didn't stick up for me either. In that moment, I felt incredibly sad, as if something had broken between us, something fragile and pure, and I knew that when

I inevitably got down from that garage, it would never be the same. Eventually, the boys got bored, wandered off and we clambered down.

Around a year after that, my parents decided they didn't want to settle in India and started the move to relocate us back to England. In 1992, we moved from our apartment, from a place of blazing sunshine and fat pearls of rain, from the embrace of our cousins, from moving freely in our bodies and skins, to Kent, which was all green hedgerows and children who stayed behind their front doors.

I kept up my tennis lessons for a year when we returned but with less enthusiasm and eventually they tapered off. I wasn't good enough to progress to the next level because I couldn't sprint fast enough, unknowingly due to the hole in my heart, and I started to lose interest in it.

By the time I turned 13, I did not play with the other kids in the street. I did not do anything that was extra-curricular in sport. I did not really move my body beyond what was expected in P.E. and I HATED P.E. Without realising it, the anchors connecting my self-worth and my body in terms of what it was capable of snapped one by one. Desperately seeking validation, I looked in the wrong places: my friends and in the measure of how attractive boys found me.

When I was 15, I wrote some words in my diary that I still find uncomfortable to read: 'Sometimes I really despair that I am so ugly, I won't ever meet someone.'

Not only did I not have a way of building self-esteem healthily I was looking to get it exclusively from people, which can be extremely problematic. And so began the erosion of all that bedrock of strength I possessed as a child, which would eventually disconnect my body and mind so success-fully that I fell into that whistling void, the gap that a lot of girls do, believing that I would never be enough, and that I wasn't worth much.

The gap for girls is an actual, real, thing. This is the point between where they believe they can do anything, be anything regardless of gender and when they stop believing it. When this happens, we start to see things like self-esteem and confidence levels drop.

Whatever your views are about Barbie, the brand's owners, Mattel, ran a solid piece of research that defined a critical period when this gap occurs.[1] They called it the 'Dream Gap' and they found that it could start as early as five or six, when girls start to think they aren't smart or capable enough to engage in certain activities.

Dr Jennifer Hartstein, a child psychologist based in the US who wrote a piece off the back of the research, said: 'When girls begin to think, however subtly, that they "can't" do something, very often, they "won't". This thinking creates the "dream gap": the gap that comes between girls and their dreams. If they hear that something is for boys, they internalize that, creating a narrative of not being as good or capable as their male counterparts.'[2] In their book, *The Confidence Code for Girls*, authors Claire Shipman and Katty Kay describe a Ypulse poll they took looking at 1,300 girls between the ages of 8 and 18 that demonstrated that confidence levels fall by 30 per cent during this time. But critically, when internal self-belief plummets in girls, boys are still 27 per cent higher.[3]

That gap also widens when we then start to factor in things like social media. While I'm not a fan of social media being blamed for all the ills affecting children and teenagers (mainly because I think it blinds us to other things that are also responsible, such as structural gender and racial inequalities), there is a case for how it contributes to poor mental health being more common in girls than boys. A 2019 study from the University of Essex and University College London looked at 10,000 14-year-olds and found a strong correlation between those who spent the most time on social media and poor mental health. The study identified that this might be for a range of reasons, including poor sleep (heavily using your phone, for instance, has been known to affect the quality and amount of sleep you get), poor self-esteem, online bullying and poor body image. For those who used social media for more than five hours a day, there were higher depressive symptoms in 50 per cent of girls as opposed to 35 per cent of boys.[4]

Another study in 2019 from York University in Canada, found that young women – out of every demographic – were more likely to feel worse about themselves if they were asked to look at social media pages of people they perceived as more attractive than them.[5] (Which then gets even more complicated for girls and women of colour because attractiveness globally is framed in terms of proximity to whiteness and European features such as button noses and light-coloured eyes.)

This Girl Can found in 2020 that nearly a quarter of women follow a fitness influencer who makes them feel bad about their bodies.[6] If we, as adults, follow people online who make us feel bad about ourselves (also referred to as the 'hate follow' on Instagram), imagine how much more deeply that must affect girls who don't have confidence-building and resilience in their emotional toolbox, or the ability to sift what's real out from what's not.

The fact that images on social media impact girls and women more is a symptom of the underlying problems around how we do (or don't) boost self-esteem in girls. We can't just look at those gender differences and go 'Oh, that's just how girls are.' If there is disparity, where one gender is being more nega-tively impacted than the other, then there is a reason behind it. Understanding that reason is important because girls aren't naturally more fragile or less resilient than boys. So it probably means that they are going through a different life experience which is creating this negativity.

In puberty, the number of girls engaging in physical activity and sports starts to drop off in a way it doesn't for boys. From the ages of 8 to 15, boys spend twice as much time doing sport activities as girls, according to the Office of National Statistics (ONS). A survey by St Mary's University in Twickenham looking at 40,000 women in 2019 found that almost 40 per cent of women in the UK decreased their phys-ical activity during puberty or stopped altogether. Globally that figure is 25 per cent.

So how can we look at that massive difference between girls and boys doing any physical activity in puberty and then say that gender isn't important or hasn't got anything to do with girls feeling more confident and at home in their own bodies? And, more to the point, why are we persisting in teaching girls about physical activity in a way that clearly isn't working?

Will Parry confirmed what I believed, that policymakers have been trying to increase the levels of physical activity in the general population without much success.

'Historically,' he said, 'they have tried to intervene by making children do traditional, competitive sport at school but this hasn't worked. Typically, children from active families tend to enjoy school sport, while children from inactive families tend to have poorer P.E. and sport experiences at school, essentially doing little to tackle inequality in participation.'

P.E. wasn't just terrible for me because I was bad at hockey and rubbish at rounders. P.E. was terrible because it was a hell stage designed by Beelzebub himself, where at a time when your body was changing and you were most self-conscious of it, you were forced to wear clothes that displayed the most of it: shorts, short gym skirts and the devil's undies incarnate: gym knickers. (Told you we would come back to this.)

'What was it that you hated about P.E.?' I asked my school friends Sonia and Alice.

'The gym knickers,' Sonia replied without missing a beat. Our gym knickers were these sturdy, burgundy undies that left nothing to the imagination and we were frequently told to tuck our t-shirts into them. 'Leggings, shorts – anything would've been better,' she added.

We had operated in a big wolf pack throughout secondary school and I didn't remember any of us enjoying it or either of them doing sport as an extra-curricular activity outside of school. On sports day, we hid behind a cluster of trees near the games field and sat on the grass talking about boys and yanking up daisies.

When you are already embarrassed by your body, being made to wear a garment that amplifies that embarrassment is bad enough, but also it creates a deeply unsavoury connection with exercise. If the goal is to get more girls to be physically active, why make it harder for them by making them wear kit that their bodies feel uncomfortable in?

'I didn't mind the knickers,' Alice said, 'but I didn't like the changing room and the attitude of some of our classmates in there.'

The changing room was an unofficial weekly inventory of whose boobs had come in, whose hadn't, who smelled of body odour, who had a cute crop top, who didn't, who had hair on their legs and arms, whose thighs wobbled, and so on.

The researchers who did the St Mary's study found the

reasons girls were disconnecting from physical activity ranged from the powerful, life-altering arrival of periods to body changes such as breast growth and body hair. Embarrassment and low confidence were also factors. It's not to say that boys aren't subject to seismic body changes including hormones, but no one beyond the changing room is scrutinising their sweat production or penis size when they are on a playing field.

Clothing aside, the average P.E. experience wasn't just damaging because it made girls feel self-conscious. It was damaging because it created impossible expectations (being able to competently throw a javelin after a handful of classes, for instance), which then determined whether or not you thought you were good at it, and for many of us, affected our confidence around physical activity. It was also such a huge, missed opportunity for teaching girls other secondary skills.

An amazing example of getting it right is the charity Street Games, which helps people from disadvantaged backgrounds engage with sports, because participation is so much lower than for their affluent peers. 'The gap,' says Jane Ashworth OBE and CEO of Street Games, 'widens when gender and low income are taken into account.'

She explains that young people in high-earning homes are more than twice as likely to take part in sport than kids from low income households, and when you consider that sport helps with confidence and leadership skills in adulthood, that places one group of kids at a massive disadvantage. The world is already unfairly stacked against them, given that getting a foot in the door of a number of industries can be down to nepotism or which school you went to, and that's before we layer on additional blockers like race and gender. Programmes like Street Games are therefore vital. They work by offering help and programming through existing networks in the community, whether that's in leisure centres or community centres. But more importantly, they actually use common sense and work alongside girls rather than forcing them outside of their comfort zones.

Their girls' programme is called Us Girls and it's designed for girls who aren't naturally sporty. 'What they tell us,' says Jane, 'is that they really value being able to go somewhere with their friends to improve their own fitness levels. Friendship was critical. We call it the three F's: Fitness, Fun, Friendship. It's about providing an active outlet for their social life that was important.'

When Jane told me this, it was a thunderbolt moment because, until that point, I had been struggling to remember why I disengaged from physical activity as a teenager. A big reason was because none of my friends were particularly interested in it either. It just wasn't what we did for fun. In suburbia, you made your own fun and that was often smoking cigarettes on the sly, drinking booze siphoned from your parents' drinks cabinet and hanging around shopping centres waiting for boys.

Jane said at the beginning, though, they got it completely wrong. They were trying to appeal to girls who weren't sporty, but they used sporty images and colours such as red and black, that didn't resonate with the girls. 'I'm a football fan,' she says, 'and another key person running this was a county tennis player. At first, we assumed that it was an access issue, so if we just made normal sport available to the girls, they would come. And they didn't.'

They had to change the colours they used to magenta and alter the type of activities. 'There was a lot more table tennis, more music, moving around to different fitness stations, trampolining,' she says. In other words, it matches what Will said about the barriers to physical activity around enjoyment, achievement and working with each other rather than being overly competitive.

Jane also found the girls preferred it indoors where they couldn't be scrutinised. 'They wanted single gender,' she said. 'They liked the music so people were distracted and not looking at each other.'

Us Girls wasn't successful just because it offered girls the opportunity to exercise. It's because it directly acknowledged that girls and women feel self-conscious around their bodies and adjusted the programme to accommodate that. Rather than making all girls do competitive sport, they were allowed to enjoy movement and achievement in an environment that made them feel good about themselves.

There is also a strong case to be made for how physical movement can help girls dealing with other health issues, as well as mental and emotional difficulties. When Hannah Corne's daughter Florence was three years old, she had selective mutism, which is a phobia of speaking. Florence couldn't talk to anyone who wasn't her mother, father or brother. Hannah started to notice, however, that whenever Florence was in the park and running around, her mutism and anxiety seemed to be at its lowest. Hannah herself struggles with anxiety and finds physical activity helps, and wondered if the same might be true for Florence.

She searched for some type of programme that joined physical movement for kids with mindfulness and empathy and came across an initiative called Mini Mermaid Running Club. Founded in the United States by Megan Tresham and Heidi Boynton, it was a curriculum to help kids find the joy in movement and also teach them about emotional and mental coping tools. Hannah decided to start the UK branch of Mini Mermaid Running Club, which is for girls aged 7–11, in Leeds, where she is based. The idea is that teachers and school staff take girls through 12 sessions which lead up to a five-kilometre challenge, and along the way the children learn about resilience, compassion and learning from failure, alongside physical movement.

'We introduce the girls to the concept of their inner critic, who is called Siren,' says Hannah, 'who tells them all the things that are wrong with them and pulls their confidence down which directly affects their participation in physical activity. Our inner cheerleader – who is called Mini Mermaid – is the voice that builds us up and tells us how amazing and unique we are . . . much like a best mate. We focus on teaching the girls how they can turn a Siren voice into a Mini Mermaid voice. It's changing the "I can't" into "I will try"'.

There are two important things here. The first is that the solution to bridging that gender gap can't just be all focused on physical movement – there has to be a mental and emotional piece there too. The second is that boosting the self-esteem and confidence of girls can't just be telling them they are great all the time – it's about teaching them how to handle those negative thoughts and work around them.

For Florence, it has been life-changing. 'She grasped the concept of Mini Mermaid and Siren really easily,' says Hannah. 'It has helped her in so many ways to try new things and to continue being active. She is a climber and started climbing even when she couldn't talk to any of her coaches. She is the epitome of resilience and belief in her own ability and she understands how and why she is active, participating in "sport" however she can.'

Florence's story shows that while physical activity doesn't magically solve your problems, it can add a lot of benefit to your life. 'State of the Nation: Teenage Girls and Sport Quantitative Report' was a major study commissioned by Lidl in 2017. It showed how sport can have a massively positive impact on the mental health of girls. Researchers spoke to female teens and their parents and found that it could boost girls' happiness and confidence among the 12–17 age group. Given that mental health disorders in children are rising, affecting girls in older age groups in particular, to the point where a fifth of 14-year-old girls self-harm, this isn't to be sneezed at.[7]

On the flip-side, 61 per cent of girls who played sports said they had high body confidence. Girls who didn't play sport were four times more likely to have low body confidence than their peers who did. Girls who played sport were less likely to feel lonely, to get depressed or to feel bored – 68 per cent said they felt happy on a daily basis as opposed to 48 per cent of girls who didn't play sports.

From all this information drawn from the various studies, there are some obvious conclusions which give a roadmap for plugging the gaps and giving girls their best shot:

1. The confidence and ability gap for girls is real and tangible – and has far-reaching consequences in our adult personal lives, careers and mental wellbeing.
2. There is also a sports and physical activity gap which is felt far more acutely by girls – but is also compounded by negative experiences in P.E.
3. Poor mental health in girls also starts becoming more prevalent when they become teenagers and affects them more than boys.
4. Girls also start to become hyper-aware of their weight and appearance.
5. Doing sport and exercise can help instil a sense of confidence and girls who do sport and are active have

reported feeling more confident with better mental well-being.

While in some ways it's depressing to know that girls today still have the gauntlet of impossible beauty standards and inequality to run through as my generation did, it's comforting to know that groups such as Mini Mermaid are around to make it a different experience for them.

'The world is full of mixed messages around how girls should look and act and it is really hard for them to navigate their way through,' says Hannah. 'If they have the tools to be able to think about what makes them feel confident, content and valued then they can go through life being much kinder to themselves. If they feel valued and love themselves regardless of their shape or size, then they are more likely to understand the benefits of being active rather than looking at it as a negative thing that they have to do to conform to whatever body shape and size is deemed to be in fashion.'

CHAPTER THREE

Role Models: the Good, the Bad, the Non-existent

'My dad is cleverer than your dad,' my boy cousin with the Friar Tuck fringe said.

A bunch of us, aged between six and eleven, and our parents, were in the back garden of our terraced house in Maidstone and we were bickering.

'Well, my dad is a doctor,' I replied, going back to making my mud pie and thwacking on a layer of wet sludge.

'So what? My dad is bigger than your dad,' he said, with his hands on his waist.

My face grew hot. 'Well, my dad is stronger than your dad,' I said. And, upon seeing him open his mouth to answer, and to settle the argument once and for all, I yelled: 'AND HE HAS BIGGER BALLS TOO!'

There was silence. Friar Tuck didn't know what to say.

'Poorna!' said one of the adults, as they all tried to suppress their laughter.

I must have been about six. I don't think I even really knew what balls were, but I knew I had a strong dad. My dad Ashok was someone who had muscles and lifted weights. Not everyone's dad did this.

'He's a bodybuilder,' I heard my mum Jaya proudly tell someone and it became part of conversations at family gatherings when we'd all clamber into one room and serve ourselves from big pots of dal and mutton curry placed on the dining table.

When we did our big move to India when I was seven, our dad stayed behind in England trying to sell the house we owned there. But the recession of the late 1980s meant that this dragged on, and one year became two, and soon we had spent five years without him, save for a visit once a year. As a result, he became a deified figure during this time – crystallised and defined by things like his quietness, his gentleness and his physical strength.

After we moved back to England just before I turned 12, I often saw his weightlifting belt lying around. I knew that there was a special gym he went to, where men would go and huff and puff and lift weights. (I'm not sure how I picked up that women didn't really go to this particular gym, but I knew.) It seeped into my consciousness that I had a strong dad and he lifted weights and that was why he was strong. And that strength was admired.

His physicality became a shorthand for safety for me. One of the things I loved about Rob was his quiet physical presence – he was a broad-shouldered, tall man who was naturally muscled and when all five foot three of me bopped along next to him while walking down the street, I loved the feeling of safety I got from the proximity to his strength.

Where we lived in Home Counties suburbia, Dad was also a runner and, after work or at the weekends, he'd step into these horribly small running shorts and head out for runs either by himself or with friends, and that also cemented his status as a fitness dad.

As far as parents went, mine were loving and supportive. It wasn't all sunshine and kittens but as an adult, I realise how lucky I was that I came from a good home and always felt safe. Before they retired, my mother worked as a civil servant, and my dad worked as a doctor. We lived in an area so boring and drama-free that I wore fishnets, black lipstick and batwing dresses to try and liven it up.

While my parents didn't come from wealth and sacrificed a lot as immigrants trying to make it here in the UK, by the time yours truly came along, we were financially comfortable. While we weren't wealthy, when it came to education, they were willing and able to spend money on extra classes. Given what I now know about girls from low income households and how P.E. is often the only access they have to physical activity – so if it's bad, they may disengage completely or simply not have time if they are working part-time jobs or if there are people at home they are caring for – I see that I took this for granted. If I wanted to try something and it was part of my education, there was no question: my parents would let me, within reason. Tennis lessons were replaced with guitar lessons after I decided I wanted to be in a band and play electric guitar. (I was terrible, and the dream died after I reached my pinnacle of musical achievement – a grade two certification.)

Having a dad who was into fitness undeniably gave me a basic foundation as to why physical activity was important. It's why – although my motivations were not the right ones – I eventually did join a gym in my mid twenties and working out became something I did fairly regularly. But the irony isn't lost on me that despite having a father whose identity was so framed by weightlifting, it didn't remotely occur to me that this was something I thought I could try.

I don't blame my parents at all. Female strength at that time was seen through a very specific lens. Being South Asian was an additional issue because, in the main, women were just not seen as sporty and there was an overwhelming focus on academics and marriage.

When I asked Mum about it recently, she agreed. 'I think South Asians have never given priority to physical activity because of a cultural issue,' she said. 'The Asian attitude is that their standing in life is judged by how well their child has succeeded and inevitably that is linked to the child getting better jobs than their parents had, making more money, marrying into the right family, etc. So from a very young age, children are pushed into studying so that they get excellent grades to go to the top schools and become doctors or engineers. That does not leave any time for sports. It is only now with globalisation that things are improving.'

Most South Asian women – regardless of size or ability – aren't made to feel that fitness is a space for them. In fact, the idea for this entire book began after reading a statistic that South Asian women were the least physically active out of every demographic in the UK. I was shocked. I knew this wasn't due to laziness but additional bindings around culture and the pressure for women to behave in a hyper-feminine way. I mean – how do you encourage girls to play sports outdoors but at the same time tell them that if their skin gets darker because of the sun it's unattractive and no one will want to marry them? You can't. The only way a girl or young woman who wants to play sport can ignore it and carry on is if you relinquish caring about your marriage prospects or your family's approval. That requires exceptional strength and mental gymnastics within an Asian family, where everything pivots around those twin ideals.

I knew that, among many things, if we removed some of

these cultural blockers, had more relatable role models and encouraged girls to be physically active (the same way boys are) that the number of women being active could go up. That applies to anyone – not just South Asians. When it comes to overturning gender roles and getting girls to see what's possible, role models are essential. But it takes more than seeing professional women in sport. While their visibility is crucial to dismantle gender stereotypes and to encourage more women into sport, the average non-sporty girl or woman needs to see women in our families and communities doing this kind of stuff.

For me, my old childhood hero P.T. Usha is a great example of this. She was a brown, professional athlete and I was so proud of her. But beyond playing games in the park and yelling: 'Come on fool! Run like you're P.T. Usha!' I didn't think it was remotely possible to do what she did. It wouldn't have even occurred to me just to go for a jog, even though there was P.T. Usha, even though my own dad was a runner.

What would have worked was the sight of a brown woman in our neighbourhood, jogging down the street. It would have done more than any flashy, expensive ad campaign designed to get me to move more. I remember my mother going to the gym when I was a teenager, but gyms didn't seem particularly interesting or fun, and I don't recall making that connection that it was something I should do. Although in the last ten years she has pivoted to boxing and handheld weights, back then, a lot of the gym-based exercise she did was on the treadmill and cross-trainer which held no attraction for me. Now about to turn 70, Mum inspires a lot of younger South Asian people especially when she trains in the gym in India, because it's unusual to see a woman of her age working out, let alone lifting two 8kg dumbbells. It's why I feel really strongly about women of all races, sizes, abilities and religions being empowered to feel confident enough to post pictures of themselves on social media being physically active or being vocal about it in their communities.

The absence of good role models in physical activity can pass on the negative message that 'fitness isn't for the likes of us' from generation to generation. Reshma, who took my survey, said that women in her family just didn't do any form of fitness and that had a life-long effect on her. 'I was never taught to respect my body and think of myself as strong. It was much more acceptable to be seen as weak and in need of a man. In my family, there are no physical role models and the relationship with food is based around reward, it's so very toxic. Even though I know the right thing to do, I find it very hard to break a life-long familial habit of not exercising and eating badly.'

No one's blaming our families or our communities – that's just how it was. Plus, it's not like school was any better. Even schools gendered the type of sports and activities we did as girls, so trying certain sports didn't even occur to us in adulthood. I remember talking to my friend Jesse, who was Rob's best friend, about this when I went to visit him in New York. We're the same age, and he had taken up CrossFit at around the same time I took up powerlifting. He was telling me how liberating it was as a Black gay man, to re-enter that space, given that the weights space in his school was a place steeped in fear, where little gay boys most likely got bullied.

'YOU HAD A WEIGHTS SECTION IN YOUR SCHOOL?' I yelled so loud the pigeons in Central Park took flight.

It didn't even occur to me that some boys' schools would have had weights sections, let alone used these spaces to shame each other. Talking to Jesse made me think about the gay community but also trans and non-binary children growing up within such binary ideas of strength.

While cisgender women aren't shamed around a lack of physical strength – instead we aren't even presented with it as an option. No one told me I couldn't lift weights like my dad. But no one told me I could, either. The fact that I was only able to once my entire world shattered tells me how powerful, how absolute and horrifyingly efficient the machinery around keeping women's strength contained and small actually is.

I'd venture to say a lot of us didn't have attainable role models during our formative years. Caroline Kings, co-founder of a movement called We Are Girls in Sport, says that even though she grew up in a sporty household and loved watching it, she wasn't sporty: 'I realised that as a young girl, there hadn't been many role models for me. My mum was active but I didn't take to the sport she played.'

Caroline and her co-founder Jo Wimble-Groves set up the movement to help bridge that sports gap for girls and believe that the gap begins at home. 'Girls and boys, on the whole, are raised and, therefore, programmed differently. The way that many girls are raised puts them off sport and physical exercise and so P.E. doesn't really have a chance.'

For Caroline and Jo, a big part of what they do is showing grassroots examples of girls who have continued with their sport of choice and how they have benefitted. 'Psychologists tell us that real-life, grassroots, amateur examples are really important as girls and young women will be able to relate to them better,' says Caroline.

In trying to figure out where my relationship with physical activity dropped off and then became all about weight loss, I drew a timeline through my life and charted my relationship with fitness. Then, I drew a secondary line to show how I felt mentally alongside that.

One thing was very clear from my list: the gaping lack of role models.

Ages 0–6:
God tier. I genuinely thought I could be anything, do anything, from being an astronaut to cycling on a tightrope between two mountain peaks.

Ages 7–12:
What I did: Played tennis, had a climbing frame and spent time outdoors with friends riding bicycles and playing hopscotch. Loved being active.

Role models: P.T. Usha, Martina Navratilova, Steffi Graff, Joyce Griffin Joyner, Monica Seles. Didn't know anyone in the family who was physically active barring Dad, who wasn't living with us at the time.

Blockers: Was made fun of when I got darker in the sun while playing tennis outdoors due to colourism. I was also scrawny for my height and age and this was a constant source of teasing (my nickname was Mowgli – I hated it).

Overall message: Shame linked to beauty standards. Girls could do sport as long as they didn't get dark. And I was too thin.

Ages 12–16:
What I did: Mandatory physical education only.
P.E. involved:
Hockey (terrible)
Netball (bad for anyone short like me)
Javelin, shot put and high jump (abysmal)

Indoor gym rope, pommel horse, general gymnastics (really abysmal)

Trampoline (really fun but still terrible as it was undertaken in The Knickers)

Tennis (the least terrible, and dependent on seasons)

Role models: None.

Blockers: Terrible teachers who didn't seem to care about finding out what we were good at, made us self-conscious, no encouragement to join any sporting clubs, friends weren't interested in it, more exciting things going on, e.g. boys and booze.

Overall message: Don't bother trying because you'll be terrible and no one cares about making you better anyway.

Ages 16–24:

What I did: Let's keep it short and sweet – I didn't do any form of physical activity whatsoever.

Role models: None – this was the *Friends/Sex and the City/Desperate Housewives* era of women being super skinny, no South Asian women in fitness ads or visibly undertaking mainstream sports in the UK.

Ages 24–31:

What I did: Joined a gym to maintain my weight; took up kayaking on holiday when I was 28.

Role models: None.

Blockers: Overwhelming messaging that fitness was to lose weight and stay thin. I was no longer skinny, as my metabolism had changed. I didn't feel comfortable in Lycra so I wore baggy £1 Primark jogging bottoms and Dad's cast-off t-shirts because I felt incredibly self-conscious in the gym. Didn't know how to use the equipment and felt too embarrassed to ask.

Any movement that could be deemed even remotely sexual – e.g. the thigh machine, which I called the fanny flapper and hip thrusts, which I called air shagger – made me want to crawl into a hole and die. I was hyper-aware of my body and didn't want people to look at it.

The weights section in the gym was off-putting and, though I hired my first personal trainer when I was 29, she didn't show me anything in that section of the gym. I remember going into activewear shops like Nike and JD Sports and the women's sections were always much smaller than the men's.

Weightlifting – not even on the radar.

Swimming – too embarrassed to wear a swimsuit or bikini until I was 28.

Running – was scared I'd start running and then end up too tired to run back (yes, I realise how mad this sounds).

Yoga – did this intermittently but worried I was being judged by more flexible people, also everyone was white, and it seemed beyond weird that we said *namaste* at the end of the class.

Hiking – this I loved doing and went on a hiking holiday to the lower Himalayas.

Overall message: Fitness equals weight loss.

Ages 31–present day

What I did/do: Back to god tier. Diagnosed with a congenital hole in the heart at 31. Recovered from surgery and started to take up physical activity. Started running outdoors and ran two 10ks. Then took up weightlifting. Currently power-lift and compete internationally with my federation.

Role models: Innumerable thanks to Instagram and athletes telling their own stories about identity and mental health, e.g. Serena Williams, Simone Biles, women in my own community, my sister, my mother and father, my trainer Jack and my powerlifting team.

Blockers: Overwhelming message from people I know and reading comments online, that doing weights will make me muscular or bigger and that's a bad thing.

Overall message: Strength-orientated goals give me focus and transferable skills such as confidence in myself. People have very weird, fixed ideas about strength and what women's bodies should look like. Fuck them.

'Women are strong' is a message I've had my entire life and I've been privileged to know and be surrounded by strong women. But female strength is almost always exclusively used as shorthand for emotional and mental strength. Rather than the miles they have run, the lengths they can swim, the weights they can stack, women's strength is measured in survival of trauma: lost husbands and children, escaping violent partners, beating the legal system, surviving sexual assault, battling illness. Of course surviving that *is* strength but it is also endurance, and women's strength is much more than that.

Strong female role models – and by that I don't mean just women who are emotionally strong, but women who physically look strong – are important if we are to change the notion that physical strength belongs exclusively to one gender. Even someone as famous as Serena Williams, who has won countless championships and four Olympic gold medals, has been body-shamed for her muscles with people saying she was 'born a guy' because she looks so strong, a comment often levelled at muscular women, which is also offensive to the trans community.

The world does not recognise female physical strength in the same way that it does with male strength. Our physical strength is belittled, defined and used as a measurement for weakness. Our language is littered with it; 'like a girl' being the ultimate declaration of weakness. One of the clearest examples of this is a ten-year-old girl called Anna who does freestyle football tricks as well as playing 'panna' football, which is one-on-one football where to score a goal the ball must go through an opponent's legs. It requires incredible skill and is usually played on the street as part of challenges people can get involved with.

Anna belongs to Yo Street Zone football crew and posts videos of her playing panna on her Instagram account. One video of her beating a guy twice her size in Margate went viral, but more tellingly, the guy she beat stomped off, and his mates jeered at him. None of them congratulated her on the win save for a random passing tourist who high-fived her. Her skill went ignored, and her win was framed as a way to emasculate the guy who lost.

For me, the ultimate test to show just how effective society has been in teaching women that we are weaker, is to ask yourself if you have any problem with gaining muscle or 'bulking up'. If you do – as I did for many years – that is the sign that society has done its work on you. Because there is and should not be any reason to fear gaining muscle because all muscle ever does is help you to physically *do* more, whether that's lift your own luggage or lug heavy things around the house.

The comedian Jessica Fostekew wrote a brilliant, hugely popular comedy show called *Hench*, which was inspired by her love of weights and tackled the weird double-standards of feminism when it comes to strong women, diet culture and the policing of women's bodies. 'It's so important to get girls to think about physical strength because it's literally empowering, to feel physically strong,' she said. 'The stronger we are the more we can physically do, the less easily overpowered we are and the better we feel. What's not to love? There is no earthly modern justification, outside of bare-faced, old-school sexism, to argue that women should literally be weak, or weaker than men, or small or quiet. I challenge anyone who isn't already a self-confessed sexist to justify that, intellectually.'

The simplest reason to get physically stronger is to be more capable and to be able to do more. That's it.

But the world has convinced us that female physical strength is not desirable, and that is compounded by an absence of role models, or not being shown different varieties of female strength. This type of thinking is so ingrained and is so perfect in its systematic and structural bias that not only is this told to us in messaging from TV, films, books and everyday language in schools and the workplace and home, but we believe it and buy into it even if we consider ourselves to be rational feminists.

The classic example I often think about is chivalry. Chivalry has always made me feel slightly uncomfortable and I've never really understood why, until Dr Pragya Agarwal, a behavioural scientist, explained it in her book *Sway*, which is about unconscious bias. 'When someone talks about chivalry or that "women are more deserving of respect", in some cases this can create a sense of wellbeing for women,' she writes. 'However in other cases, it reinforces the idea that women are defined by their biological sex, that they need to be taken care of and looked after by men because they are somehow weaker than men.'

And that for me is it in a nutshell. I didn't realise until Rob died how much of these gender roles had shaped my life, had constrained me and how I luxuriated in some of it. I thought there were certain household jobs that were Rob's jobs because he was the man. I liked it when he paid for dinner when we first started going out. I even liked it when people said, 'I'm so glad you've found someone who can take care of you.'

But the subtext around all of this was that I, the woman, was inherently weaker and needed looking after, and I didn't even realise it. In all my years, I had never realised how much of my physical strength I had deferred to men. And by giving away that power, I had allowed other people to limit how strong I was.

Stories matter. The right dialogue matters. Because, as the trope goes, you really can't be it if you can't see it. Most of us didn't grow up seeing women's sport on national TV channels in the same way as men's sports. Even now, men's sport is just called sport, women's sport is well, women's sport. When the UK entered a second lockdown in November 2020 due to the coronavirus pandemic, men's football academies were allowed to stay open while women's were not. Those tiny seeds, once sown, take root in the back of our thoughts until we don't even notice they are there. It often takes exceptional circumstances to overcome unchallenged, ingrained beliefs and they don't just affect people like me, who were always going to be crap at P.E. within the UK's education system, but even girls with the potential to be professional athletes.

Lisa O'Keefe, who is the insight director at Sport England and a former Scottish rugby international who competed in two world cups, embodies this. She was an integral part of the This Girl Can campaign which was unprecedented because, for once, it wasn't a campaign banging on about why girls and women should be more active. Everyone knows they need to be more active, said Lisa, but this was about emotionally connecting. It featured women sweating, jiggling, addressing the self-consciousness, not looking perfect and talking about the liberating joy of movement in a way that was right for you.

Back when I was working as executive editor at HuffPost UK, the news of the campaign fell under my remit of reporting.

As the women in my team and I watched it for the first time, we all had a lump in our throat. We had lived it, we breathed it. We had been that girl, that woman worrying about her body and being stared at. Not a week would go by when one of us wouldn't have a story to tell in our team meeting about being catcalled while going for a run or cycling to work. Until that campaign, many of us hadn't realised that we weren't in the minority in terms of how we felt and what we'd experienced. And, long after it aired, whenever we were exercising alone, or felt small or slightly scared, we'd feel the arm of that campaign and all those other women around us, and remember we weren't really alone. It gave us that tiny spark of courage.

Though people like Lisa, from a sporting background, worked behind the scenes on it, the campaign used everyday women – those who didn't do it professionally and didn't look like fitness models – for a reason. I find it hard to instinctively relate to people who played sport throughout their childhood – mainly because it wasn't my own experience and possibly because I'm a little jealous of the confidence they seem to exude. But I called Lisa to ask her about her own experience and how, as a professional athlete, she had managed to create a campaign that resonated with so many girls and women who weren't.

Lisa grew up in Scotland and was a rugby fan from a young age, but despite all the matches she had watched, it had never even entered her consciousness that she could play. When she was at university, she went to watch a men's Scottish Premiership league match with her dad. During half time, they were standing in the clubhouse looking out over the pitch when, in the far corner, they saw a group of women throwing a rugby ball around and doing some training.

Her dad was transfixed looking at them and, at first, Lisa wondered what on earth he was thinking. He turned round and said to her: 'You could do that.' Stunned, her first reaction was 'Er, no,' because it seemed impossible. But he persuaded her to go over and talk to them.

'I remember that whole thing like it was yesterday,' she says, 'and I ask myself: why is it still so vivid? I think it was because in the early 1990s it was still so unusual for women to play rugby. So even though I'd been a rugby fan from the youngest age, I had never expected to play. It was never in my consciousness. So when I had that conversation with my father, who was saying "you can do that", it completely shook my thinking in a way that has never happened before or since. It was a defining moment. I realised how much I'd been conditioned to think in a particular way and hadn't questioned it. I question everything now.'

What Lisa's story shows me is that even if you didn't have a negative experience at school around P.E., the limitations and gendered messages around what girls can do are so restrictive that we don't even think of some sports as something we can try. Big realisations tend to occur when there is some sort of catalyst to take you outside of yourself. Sometimes that is a person like a parent and sometimes that might be an event or a trauma that has radically altered how you view the world and your place in it. Or other times, it is a person, a group or a community who see the potential of so many girls who are falling through that gap and hold out a hand and say, 'You are worthy, you can do this, I've got you.'

I may not have had the most obvious fitness or sporty role models when I was growing up and in my twenties but the fact that I had a mum who went to the gym every Saturday meant that it trickled into my consciousness that this was a space I could occupy. Mum wasn't an athlete who did performance-based sport and, like a lot of women of her generation, she did talk negatively about the size of her body, but there was something about the regularity of her going and taking that time for herself that seeped into my brain.

My big sister, Priya, who remains one of the most influential people in my life, has also had an impact on me trying new things even when I was adamant at the time that they weren't for me. For instance, I remember when she started investing in good sportswear. It's a tiny thing but can make you feel so much more confident in male-dominated spaces, and yet I was so sure it was a waste of money. But eventually the example she set filtered down to me and I thought, *why didn't I do this sooner?*

But, more than that, they both gave me the belief that I could go anywhere I wanted and be anything I wanted. It prepared me for dealing with any hostility I might encounter in that space and, more importantly, helped me claim the *right* to be in that space.

Being at an all-girls school, and not being someone who played male-dominated sports like football or rugby, I didn't really encounter the whole 'you're a girl and you're weak' mindset when I was younger. But I did experience it in my mid thirties when I decided to try boxing. Women had been allowed to compete for the first time in boxing in the 2012 Olympics and Nicola Adams, who won gold for Great Britain, was relatable and fierce. Which probably helped to influence me when I saw an advert for a ladies' class at an old-school boxing gym in London Bridge. It seemed like something that might be fun for my best friend Mal and me to do once a week after work, and meant we could catch up and grab a drink afterwards.

The gym smelled like the bottom of a laundry basket; the mats were often damp with what we hoped was water and the ladies' changing room resembled something from a penitentiary.

But weirdly Mal and I liked the grossness of it – it somehow made it seem more 'authentic' and gave us something to laugh about over a glass of wine. Though I can't say it sparked a deep passion for boxing – mainly because I was so crap at remembering the sequences and almost always forgot to guard my face – it was a good, all-round workout.

One week, Mal couldn't make it, so I decided to go alone, and went for a mixed class rather than a ladies' class. At this time, I had already started training with weights so my physical fitness was pretty good and I had tons of stamina thanks to some new muscles. But my heart sank when I saw I was the only woman as I knew that when it came time to spar, whatever guy I was paired up with would not be pleased about having to spar with a woman. The instructor, Dave, was known to be cranky and sometimes borderline inappropriate with his comments, and that day was no different. But usually I had Mal with me and we could laugh or roll our eyes at him.

Dave put us all in a circle and did one-on-one sparring with us. When it came to me, he mimicked my jabs as feeble girly play-fighting – you know when girls sort of slap at each other's hands. He didn't do this with anyone else. I pulled my mouth into a tight line and just carried on, ignoring it. I didn't want to be the one who made a fuss – which is always the fucking way and how they always manage to get away with this stuff. But then Dave couldn't help himself.

At the end of the class, we usually closed with a circuit that involved sprinting, burpees and press-ups. I was keeping up with the guys and, for a moment, allowed myself to enjoy the power and strength of my body. Until Dave bellowed at me: 'Wow, you're really strong you know.' The subtext was deafening. He didn't say this to anyone else. I knew what he meant. Strong for a girl.

But then he yelled: 'Guys, this girl is really strong you know.' And instantly I felt like I was plunged into fire. Singled out. Humiliation. 'Come on guys,' he yelled even louder, 'she's beating you, she's doing better than you.'

I stopped what I was doing. I got up and I shouted so everyone could hear me: 'STOP BEING SO SEXIST.' And then I carried on doing what I was doing. Dave mumbled how it wasn't sexist, but it shut him up.

If my mother and sister hadn't been the kind of women they were, I would not have had the courage to stick up for myself. But it is telling that I never stepped back into a boxing gym ever again. We can have all the role models we like, but we also have to be able to equip girls to survive in spaces where our strength is not recognised or valued by boys and men.

There's perhaps an irony that the country's most popular sport, which didn't resonate with me whatsoever because it seemed to be the most hyperbolic version of masculinity, is now also the sport being used to empower a lot of girls and young women.

I'm talking, of course, about football.

My only real exposure to football was as a young woman when I was at university, when I was living with Kumaran, Ahmed and Niaz for the first time. They'd go to our local manky boozer and take me with them to watch it because they didn't want to leave me out. To try to keep me entertained, Kumaran would point out the players he thought I'd find good-looking. I'm ashamed to say it worked, but not enough to make me properly take an interest in the sport.

Although I still don't watch it, I'm no longer dismissive about football – and the only reason is because of the rise in profile of women's football. Part of that is to do with the English

Lionesses coming to prominence and the other part is due to Megan Rapinoe, captain of the US football team, who led them to World Cup victory in 2019.

Megan grabbed my attention when I saw photos of her on social media – one photo in particular. She was standing on the pitch, her arms outstretched as if she was blasting out every bit of power she had, a tidal wave of force, determination and confidence. I didn't even know footballers could look like her, be like her. To me, it wasn't just about the little girls watching, it was also a message to boys that this is also what a footballer looked like.

The Lionesses embody what football should always have been about – dignity, strength, teamwork and humility. I remember first reading about them in 2015, when they came third in the World Cup, and the reason they caught my attention was because they seemed so starkly different to the stereotype of male footballers. But also, seeing everyone support them – men and boys too – felt important. We can't just role model to other girls and women because we don't grow up in a single-gender world. That role modelling has to be relayed to all genders so that spaces are made safer and less hostile for everyone who isn't a cisgender, heterosexual male.

One young person who knows how painful it can be being a girl who likes to play football is Olivia Hancock, who is just 14 and won the Diana Award for her campaigning efforts to get boys to respect football-playing girls. In 2019, she was punched by a boy while playing football. When asked why he did it, he told a teacher he didn't like the fact that a girl was better than him. While that is Olivia's worst encounter, it is sadly not the only time she's received abuse for playing football – and shockingly, not just from other kids. A parent once called her a lesbian as an insult. My brain can't even fathom it.

'An important but lesser-known reason for gender imbalance in football is the shame, bullying and insecurity of girls that is created from a young age,' wrote Marva Kreel, on a blog post called 'Why Girls Stop Playing Football'. Marva is a twenty-something artist manager and sports journalist, and came to my attention when she tweeted that some teenage boys had verbally harassed her while she did kick-ups in the park. 'It was the same park I used to get mocked in as a young girl. It hurt me that nothing had changed.'

I asked her about what it was like when she was a girl. She said it dampened her love of playing. 'Whenever I would play with boys or even with boys around, I knew they were watching and sometimes judging or worse,' she said. 'It definitely hurt my confidence and my willingness to just go out and practise on my own or with a female friend, or join a kickabout with other kids, which could have really helped my development as a footballer. I also still have that chip on my shoulder as an adult.'

Marva plays for a women's team, as well as a group of men made up mainly of her brother and cousin's friends. 'But even with those men,' she said, 'if I do something wrong I'm much more paranoid than if I do something wrong when playing with women because of how those early experiences shaped my confidence.'

When you then layer on race, the numbers of girls who get involved in the sport are bleak, because the number of role models are low or non-existent. In *Sway*, Dr Pragya Agarwal talks about the shocking discovery that there had never been a British Asian female footballer in the England team and very few at club level, despite the fact that British Asians form 7.5 per cent of the UK population. She said that the general consensus from women she spoke to while researching for an article she was writing, was that 'football wasn't for people like us'. 'The lack of any role models,' she wrote, 'creates a self-fulfilling cycle where the absence of similar others in a domain is itself a signal that one does not belong or would not be welcome.'

In Cardiff, that's slightly changing thanks to people like Ayah Abduldaim, a 19-year-old Muslim footballer who moved to Wales from Libya when she was 11. She said that sport helped rebuild her life, and her presence on the football pitch has encouraged other girls aged 14–16 to play, and, more importantly, has meant their parents allow them to play.

Goals 4 Girls UK is a brilliant organisation run by Francesca Brown. A football development programme for girls aged 11–16, it aims to raise their 'aspirations, confidence and motivational skills by breaking down social and personal barriers, through sports and education,' says Francesca and for her, that has to include focusing on girls from under-privileged and/or disengaged communities. It's also successful: in 2018, they had a retention rate of 87 per cent of the 400 girls who took part and 90 per cent said confidence, resilience and ability to make friends had improved.

The future of sport, says Francesca, is one where stereotypes regarding gender roles, race and equality are no longer a topic for discussion. Black women, for instance, only make up 10 to 15 per cent of the Women's Super League in comparison to Black men who make up a third of the Premier League. 'Marketing and advertising must show women of all sizes, ethnicities, cultures and ability,' she says, 'as without this, a young girl who does not look like the poster girl will never imagine that sport is also for her.'

I'd go one step further and say that this is applicable to the entire fitness and wellbeing industry. How many of us have thought that fitness, physical activity or sport wasn't for us because we didn't look like how we thought a fit person should?

Unravelling this stuff is important. Not just for ourselves. But because without thinking about where these limiting and even harmful stereotypes come from, we pass them on to each other, and to our girls. It also brings me to the biggest reason why, for so many years, I went to the gym and worked within such a narrow expectation of myself. Role models that I could relate to, in different sports, would have given me the confidence to try different activities. But, just as importantly, role models with different body sizes and abilities would have been enormously powerful in overturning the societal narrative that fitness is an aesthetic, and they would have been an antidote to physical activity always being framed in the context of weight loss.

My sister Priya and I can be the best role models for my niece Leela. She will, without question, have two very strong women in her life: mentally, emotionally *and* physically. Between us, Priya and I have covered more life experiences than most people, from divorce to widowhood, chronic fatigue to heart disease, motherhood to singledom. But I also know that it's not enough for Leela just to see us being strong – she has to learn how to generate that strength for herself.

I know that, at some point, all it will take is a comment about her beautiful body or some snotty little shit singling her out for being a girl, to make her question her place in the world. She is lucky to have a mother who is aware of what negatively shaped her own self-image and therefore so attuned to how to help Leela navigate these murky waters for herself. But I also desperately want Leela to know her own strength and know her own worth, and to carry that like a shield and sword into places that try to cut her down to size.

All of us have been subjected to diet culture and, by extension, the message that physical activity is about weight loss. It is a belief that is really, really hard to root out – but it must be. Never doubt *why* we are made to feel like our bodies are the enemy: it is done to keep us from realising our strength.

If we think back to the role models who profoundly changed our lives and moved us, what they looked like had zero bearing on why they inspired us. I'm willing to bet they were inspiring because they were brave, courageous, possessed a sense of freedom and self-confidence within themselves – and no size, shape or gender has the monopoly on that. When it comes to fitness, some women feel they need to look a certain way, or be a certain size before they can inspire others around them. But it isn't true. Simply by being visible and showing the joy that movement gives you is being a role model.

After all, isn't that what you would have dearly wanted for your younger self?

CHAPTER FOUR

Your Body Is Your Land

When you consider that your body is the only land you arrive with in this world, no one has ownership over it but you.

You may have lovers who lay claim to it, your parents may believe they have a say over it, you may experience the dark horror of people trying to violate it, but never once do you stop having autonomy over your body.

From a very early age, people will come to your borders. They will shout things across the fence. They'll remark on what your land looks like and the things they believe should change. Over time, they make you believe it is not your land to own. They make you look over the fence at what is happening with other people's territories and compare yourself to them.

But here's the thing: it doesn't matter if you do *everything* these people are telling you to do. It is never enough. You will never reach the place where *you* are happy and *they* are happy. Because people who shout those things, who make those comments, don't actually want you to be happy. Even people who have undergone massive weight-loss transformations for health reasons will almost certainly find that some of the same people who criticised and belittled them will find other ways to make them feel bad or insecure about themselves. Consider the culture around celebrities' bodies and how they are treated in the tabloids – one minute the papers describe them as being bloated, and the next feign worry about them looking gaunt.

The reason why the conversation around women's bodies needs to change isn't because weight loss is a bad goal in itself. Sometimes people may need to lose weight for health reasons – for instance if they are pre-diabetic, with the guidance of a doctor. Others may be dealing with long-term weight-related issues, or may be deeply unhappy about their weight – which can have a significant impact on their mental health and it would be remiss not to acknowledge that, or just brush off their concerns and say they should love their body no matter what. But the problem is when weight loss is the only goal, and is framed as the route to some sort of nirvana where they feel self-acceptance and happiness. When women are made to feel bad about their thighs or bum being big, or their back being broad – rather than celebrating how those attributes mean they might actually be amazing and genetically pre-disposed to being excellent at some things (for instance, doing squats or flipping over a tyre) – it's because we have a deeply embedded narrative that shames women into shrinking themselves and making them do things they don't want to do.

I realise that as a woman who has always hovered between a size 10 and 12 there is a shitload of body privilege I carry. I don't have to worry about whether I'll find something in my size when I nip into a shop, endure unsolicited advice from people who assume they know how healthy I am just by looking at my physique, get tutted and stared at when I get on a plane or a bus, or laughed at because I dared to wear a swimsuit. So for clarity, when I talk about this personally, it's in relation to my own experience and insecurities as opposed to saying it's like this for every woman. However, while I've been writing this book, I've interviewed and chatted to plus-size women to learn more, as well as represent the experiences around body image more broadly using their voices.

Before I write about how I unplugged myself from the I-need-to-be-slim matrix, I have to describe the matrix itself. It helps me to visualise it like a spider's web but if that creeps you out, maybe think of it like a *Mission Impossible* room criss-crossed with loads of crazy lasers.

When I refer to the matrix, it's the general system that is in place to oppress women because we don't have the automatic privilege and power that come with being born male. But also, it acknowledges that the system doesn't affect every woman in the same way and that for some – depending on factors from race to sexuality – it is a lot worse. Black women, for instance, are adversely affected more than white women in every area of life from pay to mortality. Also, side note: I'm not saying that boys and men aren't affected by this system, but I'm saying that it affects women more.

So here goes. My life as it relates to body image, strength and fitness goals is divided into three parts.

1. Everything before my hole in the heart operation.
2. Everything between my heart getting fixed in 2012 and Rob dying in 2015.
3. Everything that happened after Rob died.

Until I took up weight training, I never felt like my body was enough, or the right size. Despite being the size society said was 'fine'. What my body could *do* was irrelevant, since what it *looked like* was considered more important, framed within how slim it was or wasn't. The reason for this is because, like most people, I grew up through the weeds of diet culture. Diet culture, according to anti-diet author, dietitian and counsellor Christy Harrison, is 'a system of beliefs that: worships thinness and equates it to health and moral virtue, which means you can spend your whole life thinking you're irreparably broken just because you don't look like the impossibly thin "ideal".'

If you feel like you can't trust your body around food, if you've grown up listening to your mum or aunts fat-shame themselves, if you refer to foods as 'good' and 'bad', if you have 'rules' around what you can and can't eat (e.g. not eating bread or chocolate), if you feel you need to exercise to work off what you've eaten – all of those are hallmarks that you've been affected by it. You may have normalised it by saying, 'Well, everyone does it,' because the thinking and language that support it are inescapable, but it isn't normal. If it was, babies would do it, and they don't because they are the purest examples of intuitive eaters.

There are two main approaches that I think can help untangle some of the disorder we feel around eating – intuitive eating and mindful eating. Intuitive eating is described as a 'self-care eating framework' that invites people to reject diet culture completely, identify their emotional relationship with food, do away with rules and instead listen to their hunger cues. The way it was explained to me was regaining trust in yourself around food. Until it was pointed out, I didn't even register that I didn't trust my body around food, and if you feel like that, it may be because you restrict yourself in some way, which makes you overeat it, which then makes you feel ashamed, which you then use as evidence that you can't be trusted, and the whole shitty cycle starts again.

Ultimately, intuitive eating is meant to help you to have a

better relationship with food. For instance, if you're an emotional eater, it doesn't mean that you need to beat yourself up if you get comfort in food but it does mean recognising that, in addition to food, there need to be other things that comfort you emotionally. And then in time, food becomes an occasional coping mechanism rather than the default one.

There is a ton to say about intuitive eating but the best way to learn about it is by reading *Just Eat It*, a book written by one of the leading UK experts on it, Laura Thomas. Another great person to follow on social media is Ruby Tandoh, who addresses a lot of the shame around food. In her book, *Eat Up: Food, Appetite and Eating What You Want*, she charts her own journey with eating disorders.

Some people struggle, however, with intuitive eating and can find it overwhelming, so in the first instance, mindful eating can be a good approach. Mindful eating also falls under the umbrella of intuitive eating as a method of eating, but as a standalone practice it's essentially about being mindful and aware of the food you are eating while you're eating it, and how it makes you feel. The idea being that when you're consciously aware of what you're eating and listening to your hunger cues, you self-regulate better. It is quite remarkable. The first experience I had of it was during a mindful chocolate eating session, which I initially laughed at. The teacher gave us two squares of chocolate and took us through various things like paying attention to the texture and smell of it, and really slowing down the act of chewing. Before the class, two squares would have seemed paltry, but by doing everything the teacher told us to do, it turned out that it was actually just the right amount. That session still stays with me several years later. One of the leading registered nutritionists in the country who employs this approach is Rhiannon Lambert who told me that food can often be used as a tool to cope with difficult emotions, and that weight gain can sometimes cause psychological and physical distress. Mindful eating helps, she says, because 'when we deliberately direct our full awareness to our bodily sensations, thoughts and emotions arise and disappear as we eat, which suggests that slower and more thoughtful eating can help with weight problems and poor food choices.'

The reason I mention intuitive eating and mindful eating is because our approach to food is also inextricably tied into our approach to fitness. 'Diet culture is probably the biggest culprit in terms of fucking up our relationship to food, our bodies and ourselves,' wrote Laura Thomas in *Just Eat It*. 'It demands thinness no matter the cost on our mental and physical health. A simple way of thinking about it is the culture that upholds the thin ideal as the standard of beauty. Sometimes it's obvious: an advert for a slimming club. Sometimes it's more insidious: as absence of body diversity in the media, a diet masquerading as a healthy "lifestyle", even the "war on obesity".'

Intuitive eating is thought to have started as a concept in the mid 1990s and, more recently, has extended towards thinking about fitness intuitively. Personal trainer, podcaster and author Tally Rye wrote a book about it called *Train Happy*. 'The dominant narrative within fitness,' she told me, 'is that we do it to lose weight and change our aesthetic. It's totally understandable that many people come to fitness with that goal because that is what is marketed to them (particularly women) and you don't really hear much discussion of any other options. Many of those external reasons to work out are born out of diet culture: the desire for a "bikini body", slimming for a wedding, getting your pre-baby body back, getting "little black dress ready" have all been marketed to us, whether that's on the cover of magazines, before and after photos as you get on the Tube or by some of social media's biggest fitness stars who are selling their 10- or 12-week transformations.'

Why mention all of this in a book about girls' and women's strength? Because the belief that slim and thin automatically equates to fitness and health is not correct. Sure, some slim people are healthy but some are not. It definitely doesn't mean they are fit. Some plus-size people are healthy, some are not. And it definitely doesn't mean they aren't fit. The point is that everyone, whatever their size, has the right to move their body and not feel self-conscious or ashamed.

'Growing up,' wrote Rochelle, who took my survey, 'I was always the "curvy", or "fat", friend and although I had enjoyed things like dance and swimming as a child, when it came to exercise as a teen and adult I always felt like the big one. Even now there are some friends who, if we exercise together, make it very clear that they believe they will be fitter than me because they are thinner. It took a long while to get over the idea that exercise wasn't for me because of that.'

This outmoded, over-simplistic way of thinking big is bad and small is good means that some people feel they can't go to the gym or exercise outdoors because they are ashamed of their bodies or think they don't look fit enough and this holds them back from getting physically strong. It causes serious problems if we starve ourselves trying to look like some fitness Instagrammer because they look the part but who may be dealing with an eating disorder or taking supplements. And it's definitely an issue if your biggest fear is becoming bigger and that's why you won't do strength training.

'The problem,' writes Laura Thomas, 'is that we become so obsessed with reaching this arbitrary ideal that we put our lives on hold until we get "there". Diet culture keeps women suppressed both financially and emotionally by seducing them with claims that they will be happy once they reach a certain weight.'

Your body is a living thing. It changes, it expands, it keeps you alive, it protects you, it rises up to meet a need when there is one. It doesn't just contain a heart that pumps 2,000 gallons of blood around you a day, or a brain that has 86 billion nerve cells. When you think about all the amazing things your body can do, how efficient a machine it is, the huge potential it contains, that it is capable of fighting off disease, and then you think that our chief preoccupation is how small it is, doesn't it sound laughable?

But like many women, I believed this, fervently. I believed that a flat tummy was more important than how far I could run or anything else that I could physically do. And that pre-occupation robbed me of so many opportunities to engage with physical activity in a healthy, positive way.

When I turned 21, my body started changing and putting on weight. I remember the first time I became aware of this. A group of friends of mine, boys and girls, were going to a cricket match. As long as I could remember, I'd always worn crop tops. When I think about this now, it almost feels like a different lifetime, a person lit with a confidence that was unshakeable and pure, because I didn't feel self-conscious at all while doing so.

That all changed on this day, however. I wore a crop top and I remember one of the guys – who I didn't particularly like – pointed at the flesh poking between my top and the waistband of my trousers and said: 'Wow, you've, er . . . grown, haven't you?'

I looked down and saw my brown skin rounding over my waistband and a kernel of shame planted in my belly. Soon after, I stopped wearing crop tops. At the same time, my changing body was subject to commentary whenever we visited family and friends in India. As in other parts of Asia, it's seen as a cultural norm to comment on people's weight, but it also probably gave me the biggest dysfunction I felt around my body. My size would be the first thing someone would comment on. And I was never slim enough. Given that in my early twenties I was a size 8–10, I would still receive comments such as 'you've put on weight' and 'remember how slim you used to be?'

I didn't realise it at the time, but they were comparing my woman's body to my child body. Because when I look at photos of myself from my twenties, I think: 'What were they talking about? Why did I let it affect me so much?'

The next decade would see this endless pedalling towards maintaining slimness or trying to cut down to be slim. Maybe if I cut out bread, sugar or caffeine, or maybe if I did this type of exercise . . . I never had a specific idea in mind, just that I was always one step from being fully satisfied with how I looked. And if only I could work a bit harder, or resist that piece of food, then I'd not only get to the hallowed gates of self-acceptance but, most importantly, everyone would say how amazing I looked and how I'd finally made it.

However, I know despite the 'carbs are evil' years, I am lucky that my body has never been mined and consumed by an eating disorder. And I also know that my journey is nothing compared to the journey of plus-size people who have been made to feel conscious and aware of their bodies all the time to the extent that it has shaped so much of their lives.

Stephanie Yeboah is one of my favourite influencers and an author and activist in the fat acceptance space. Fat acceptance is a social movement designed to change bias and part of the movement is to reclaim the word 'fat' and use it as a neutral identifier or descriptor, rather than it being an insult. Fat accept-ance and body neutrality is different from body positivity, or 'bo-po', which is about 'loving yourself'. Bo-po is also viewed by some as problematic because the message has shifted from initially championing Black women, such as Stephanie, to predominantly white women and other women who Stephanie describes as 'acceptably fat', such as those who are a size 16.

The bias against fatness is so strong that none of us are immune to it. We've grown up in a world where we automat-ically assume it means you're unhealthy or lazy and we base our attractiveness and self-worth on the perception of our own fatness and slimness. But these beliefs are wrong, because they are rooted in bias, not scientific fact.

When I tell someone this, they often say something like, 'Oh, but what about the higher health risks if you're obese?' But do you do this with *any* other group of people? Do you do this with people who drink more than the recommended amount a week, or smokers, for instance? If you don't, then why do you immediately conflate fatness with 'oh they must be unhealthy?' That's fat bias.

We make assumptions that someone is slim because they made 'responsible' choices whereas someone may be slim for a whole host of reasons – maybe they aren't eating enough, maybe they are orthorexic and over-exercising, maybe it's genetics, maybe they have thyroid issues, mental health prob-lems or drug and alcohol issues. We mostly can't know for sure, which is why making positive or negative assumptions about how 'healthy' a person is just by looking at their body is plain wrong.

An important way of tackling fat bias, and to prevent it from blocking people's path to physical activity, is to just see more plus-size bodies in the fitness space. For it to be neutral and something we just naturally accept without feeling surprised by it. When Nike made a ground-breaking move by unveiling plus-size mannequins wearing fitness wear, it was so refreshing to see different bodies represented, and they've also featured people like Stephanie in their Instagram ads. Yet, the Nike mannequins prompted criticism that it was 'promoting' obesity. Stephanie pointed out the distinction in an interview for the *Guardian*, saying: 'We're not promoting obesity, or telling people to be fat, we're just saying, if you're fat you don't have to hate yourself.'

Stephanie is a vital voice in this space and her journey is heart-breaking but, I would venture to say, not dissimilar to many stories of people who take to activism. She was put on a diet when she was 12 and was told that she'd be so much prettier if she lost weight. It ended up making her bulimic. In 2014, she found bo-po but then switched to fat acceptance. I sought her out after seeing her featuring in a Nike sponsored post and she spoke to me about her views on the difficult relationship we have with working out: 'While there are very valid reasons for using working out as a way to aid weight loss [serious health reasons, for example],' she said, 'I personally don't think it's healthy to frame weight loss as the sole reason to work out, unless one has insecure, fatphobic views towards their bodies. The diet industry will have society think that you can tell someone's health by their body shape and this is absolutely wrong, with countless reports and studies to support it. Before I started my self-love journey, I would equate weight loss with success, beauty and high self-esteem. However, eventually, when I did go on to lose four stone, I achieved none of those things, and did not feel any more healthy than I did when I was five stone heavier.

'I love working out because of the endorphin rush, because

I'm competitive, and because I want to build on strength. I stopped looking to exercising for the sole purpose of weight loss and instead now see it as an inconsequential by-product of exercise. If I lose weight, fine. If not? Also fine.'

When I was in my twenties, social media wasn't a thing. But I knew from magazines, TV and other people that the gym was a place where you went because you wanted to be slim and you didn't want to be fat. That was it. It was as one-dimensional as that. I stuck mostly to the machines – so for years I'd do short stints between the treadmill, the stationary bike and the cross-trainer. I'd go on the mats sometimes to do some work with a swiss ball and medicine ball and that was about it.

The first time I hired a personal trainer was when I was 29 and wanted to get 'toned' for my wedding. Rob was a soppy git known for thinking I was the most beautiful thing in the world so this need to transform didn't come from him. Rather, I knew, without question, that when you got married, you needed to be your thinnest possible. How did I know this? Because that's just what everyone else did. When I asked a friend getting married recently why she wanted to lose weight for her wedding, she said to look as good as possible for the pictures. Because slimness is associated with what looks good. It's never-ending.

I did not enjoy having a personal trainer, even though she was perfectly nice and most of our work was focused on moves to get me moving and sweating. We didn't step into the weights section once.

On my wedding day, I realised I had lost slightly too much weight and my dress kept slipping down. I remember feeling petrified that it would drop all together and my first act as a married woman would be to flash my boobs to my nearest and dearest. I didn't feel bad that I'd lost that weight but I definitely know I didn't feel good. It wasn't an achievement. But I still carried on like this for a while, always favouring exercises that seemed most strongly associated with weight loss, such as running or the stationary bike. Until Rob died, when I realised that all of this hadn't prepared me for anything.

The ever-present goal of weight loss had been a distraction. I mean, genuinely, what had it ever given me? How did it actually add to my life in any way? How did stressing about eating a bacon sandwich and then feeling the need to pedal away on a cross-trainer – the most boring exercise machine known to humankind – ever achieve anything? It didn't help me flip a mattress. It didn't even make me feel satisfied or happy. When it was really important, when all of life was held in the balance and I stood at the crossroads of my survival, all of that counted for nothing.

When Rob died in 2015, my life disassembled and reverted to primordial goo.

I carried on running throughout the first year after his death, my steps on the pavement a steady reminder that I was still alive. But when I decided to make a change and become strong it wasn't because I thought, 'Hey, I know what will help with this unending vortex of sadness – lifting weights!' It was because I knew I needed to get strong for practical reasons.

Although I was lost in an ocean of grief, this plan to get strong was something I could do, that had purpose and direction. Slowly, life started to take form and shape.

The gym was a minute's walk from the HuffPost office, where I was still working at the time, and had it been further away or more complicated than that, I don't think I would have made it there. A couple of days after I walked into that reception and said I wanted a PT, someone called and said: 'We've found you a trainer, his name is Tyrone.'

Before my first session, I already decided I was going to hate Tyrone. First, I didn't really want to be trained by a guy. Second, I don't like being told what to do or barked at. On my first day of training, I walked into the gym and there he was, sitting in a chair with his clipboard and an open and easy smile. Tyrone, it turned out, was a young, Italian-Australian strength trainer who'd moved to the UK with his wife, lifted heavy himself and was calm and likeable. But more than that, he carried himself with an air of neutrality. He wasn't patronising. He just asked me what I wanted and then made suggestions. And he made it really hard to hate him.

For once I didn't say I wanted to be 'toned'. Toned is a nonsense word because what it actually means is to show muscle but also have less body fat. But because of our social conditioning, women have a problem with the word muscle, so we use toned because it's more acceptable. Cassie Smith, an American professional lifter and coach said it perfectly: 'Using the word "toned" instead of "muscular" to describe a goal or a woman's body reinforces the notion that if a woman picks up more than an eight-pound dumbbell, she'll somehow look like Hulk Hogan, moustache included.'

I had no idea what exercises to do but I told Tyrone I wanted to get strong. He put together a programme that had moves like squats and deadlifts which I had never done before in my life. I worked out with him once a week and on my own twice a week and filled out the weights I lifted on his programme sheet. After a while, I noticed how the number of those weights steadily increased and I could feel something tangible taking shape from it. Although I was a bit scared at first going into the weights section without Tyrone, I'd been there with him enough times and watched him shoo people off equipment. Eventually, it made me feel confident enough to do the same. No matter how bad my week was, Tyrone was a reassuring presence at the end of it. I didn't have to tell him my whole back story and he temporarily filled that gap of male energy where Rob had been – but as a friend.

At the time, I was still fairly small in size. Grief had eaten me from the inside out but as I went back every week, I noticed my body changing and becoming a bit stronger. Less wraith-like. Because the gym was so close to the office, I'd usually see a colleague in the weights area – always male – and we'd exchange watercooler chat. They'd say positive things about me lifting weights but not in a patronising wanker way, more like mutual respect. It was a completely foreign feeling but a good feeling, nonetheless. I noticed that I was able to do more around the house. I could move Rob's plant pots and carry them up the stairs with ease. I could carry my own luggage up and down the steps at train stations without looking pleadingly at a man to help me out.

'We're going to get to the 100kg deadlift,' said Tyrone and I laughed at him. 100kg seemed impossible – I couldn't even conceive of it, even when I hit the milestone of 80kg.

In the middle of my training with Tyrone, I went to India for a holiday with my parents, where they had an apartment in which they spent three months of the British winter. Normally I wouldn't have bothered with the gym while holidaying but because I wanted to continue with my progress, my dad and I would go for sessions together. I loved that it was a little bonding moment for us – making sure we had our breakfast before leaving, grabbing a few mini bananas to snack on, chatting away in the car on the way there.

When we got to the gym we'd go our separate ways but I

remember being the only woman in the weights section at the time. As I prodded and felt my way around this newfound strength, I realised that it gave me the confidence to be in spaces I normally would have avoided. I also loved being in the same space as my dad and that being something we shared.

When I came back to England, I continued my sessions with Tyrone.

The more I lifted, the more I ate to fuel my workouts. I remember worrying about my body getting bigger as clothes started to get tighter in certain places. I didn't realise it at the time but I was approaching a crossroads. Should I continue down this path of strength training, which had given me an anchor to hold onto in the waves of darkness, but was unknown and scary? Or should I go back to the familiar place that was socially acceptable? I wasn't aware at the time, but I was being pushed against a glass ceiling of women's strength and ability. You can be strong, but not too strong. You can be strong as long as you don't get bigger.

With most strength building, you tend to spend periods eating a bit more and lifting a bit heavy to put on muscle which is a process called bulking, and it means you may look a bit heavier than you usually do. Then you may have periods where you are getting lean, which involves shredding a bit of the excess body fat that you've acquired to make your muscles more defined, and that might involve lifting lighter weights but doing a lot more reps. It's totally normal, then, to have a different physique at various points over the year, but it took me a few years to learn this. When all you see on Instagram are fitness influencers who seem permanently lean with six-pack abs, it then creates a strange dissonance because you're seeing your body getting bigger but not understanding this is a whole process around building muscle. It can be really disconcerting.

Women who do ironman, strongwoman, ultra-marathons, expeditions, open swims – any kind of endurance- or performance-based strength sport – have all probably stood at this same junction, asked to choose between their potential and social acceptance. I was talking to Kelechi Okafor, the actress, podcaster, founder of Kelechnekoff Fitness Studio, and one of the sharpest minds on modern-day racism and feminism, about this. Born in Lagos and raised in Peckham, Kelechi had been an air cadet at school and used to run for the South-East region in the 200-metre sprint and relay. She was also captain of their football team. But despite all of her sporting achievements, she'd get comments from friends who'd tell her she was 'just so muscular' and overhear people saying, 'Why does she look like that?'

'I remember when I was 16,' she said. 'One of my very first boyfriends would say: "I just don't like that you do sport so much because it makes you look really muscular and you can't look more muscular than your boyfriend." I loved sport, so somehow that didn't quell the fire to keep going but when people start saying things to you about your body at that age where you're impressionable and you're insecure, you maybe then shy away from it. And I think that's often what happens to a lot of young girls or young women growing up – they think they have to choose. And I guess mostly they choose the opinions of other people and I understand why they would – it is not an easy choice to make.'

Even when we are older, as I was when I came to weight-lifting, we are given the scissors to clip our own wings and it takes exceptional courage to put them down and take flight instead. Although the weekly sessions with Tyrone made me feel sane and safe, although lifting that barbell made life solid when all else seemed so transient, although it gave me a flicker of joy in that unending grief, I couldn't do it. I didn't trust my own body, I couldn't see the way forward, and I didn't want to risk the acceptance I already possessed.

The defining moment was when I saw my weight approach the heaviest I had ever been, on the weighing scale. In retrospect, it is still lighter than I am now, and also worth noting that I was much weaker. But, I started to panic, and I didn't want to get any heavier, despite the fact that I'd felt incredible being able to eat to fuel my workouts, and I had enjoyed getting stronger. Head bowed, I tucked my wings behind my back. I decided to watch what I ate. I told myself I wasn't going to lift above a certain weight, and told myself it was for the best.

CHAPTER FIVE

Strong Is Not a Size

A lot of this book is about reclaiming the joy around movement and being a liberated badass but, for some in larger bodies, the size of their bodies has been up for debate and scrutiny from a young age, which has had a much more profound, deep and damaging impact on their lives. Because the definition of strong is so narrow for girls, however, instead of being empowered to see what their bodies can do and how their size might be used to harness their strength, some were made to feel constantly shamed.

I wanted to dedicate this chapter to discussing those tough experiences, as well as looking at how our fatphobic society makes it harder for plus-size people to feel comfortable in the fitness space, and draw attention to some of the inspirational women who have reclaimed their bodies, because I don't know what it feels like to go through an experience of alienation that starts from a very young age.

I asked my sister Priya about her experiences because when we were kids, I remember it being a running joke that she didn't really like doing anything physical. I also seemed to remember her being put on a diet at a young age. The subject came up again recently when I featured her on the See My Strong Instagram page, and the photo she chose to use was of her in the middle of a hike we had just done together.

My parents, Priya, Leela and my brother-in-law Shabby, all went on a family holiday in 2019 to the Ligurian coastline and one of the attractions of the area was being able to hike and walk between a string of fishing villages. Being active was something that Dad and I had shared for a number of years, and it was also something I shared with Priya, but the three of us had never done it together.

One crisp morning, we three set out and walked from our village to the next and it was one of the best experiences of my life. Not just because we were outdoors and watching the sea stretch in front of us in a vast expanse of turquoise melting into a hazy line of searing white sunlight, but because we were doing it together. When we reached the next village, every bone in our bodies ached but I remember every moment of the exquisite breakfast we shared, from that first coffee, to the sweetness of the fresh orange juice and the smell of newly-baked bread.

In her caption for the See My Strong post, Priya wrote that she grew up as curvy and a 'bit squishy' and being told that she wasn't sporty. She mentioned that she was even called 'a lump' and said it wasn't with malice but that it wasn't great for her inner narrative, especially given that adverts and media aren't filled with strong brown women. When I read that, I cried. I looked back at that time and realised how different our experiences had been. Although there was only a four-year age gap between us, I was still just a kid when she was a teenager, so I didn't really understand why the nicknames people gave her weren't OK at the time, and how deeply that would have affected her self-esteem and confidence. But as an adult, I knew how much those experiences must have shaped her. When she hit her twenties, she started exercising and eating differently and lost a significant amount of weight but I had never really asked her about it.

Had her experiences with body image always been negative, I asked her?

'When I was really young in Mangalore,' she told me, 'I loved running around and felt very free. I loved my body until I was told not to, I was chunky – not chunky, chunky – and so on throughout childhood and teenage-hood, which is normal but I was always made to feel bad about it. There was nothing major I could change about how naturally toned or not I was but I was made to feel like it was my fault.'

At school, she said, she was a shy and easily embarrassed teen, and sports felt competitive. If you weren't good at it, she added, the message seemed to be well, why bother? 'I don't ever remember exercise being encouraged for the love of it. It was always a competition.' This reminded me of one of the blockers mentioned by Will Parry around schools over-emphasising that physical activity needs to be competitive.

Now, having a daughter makes the stakes higher for her around changing how we frame physical activity for girls. 'Leela is already aware that "fat" is used as derogatory term and she has also said she doesn't want to be fat,' Priya said. 'That horrifies me yet doesn't surprise me. That stuff is so pervasive that we absorb fatphobia as easily as breathing. I try to tell her that exercise is good for her body and will make her life better. And I try to frame negative impacts of eating huge amounts of chocolate, for example, in its literal effects – such as having a sugar crash that makes you feel shit or your teeth rotting – rather than a worry about getting fat, which is a lot of people's first go-to. It's harder work to do this but it's worth it. I can't bear the thought that she would look at her perfect little body and ever feel it's not right.'

Modern-day society's attitude towards larger bodies is mostly negative, judgemental, berating, shaming and worse, it is considered socially acceptable to be vocal and rude about it, without considering there are human beings at the heart of these comments.

Reframing what I thought I knew about body size and fitness is something that only happened after I started powerlifting, and was able to see that strength came in many different shapes and sizes. It occurs to me how much better society would be if we viewed it this way, rather than the current way we look at plus-size bodies or bodies that are deemed to be overweight or obese.

In 2020, the UK government declared a 'war' on obesity after it was shown that when it came to Covid-19, obese people had worse outcomes. It prompted a campaign and a flurry of fatphobic comments towards visible, plus-size influencers by people who now felt they had justification to comment on people's bodies and choices. When I then posted on social media about how the government's obesity campaign was shaming and wrong, I had received DMs from people very keen to let me know how obesity was a major problem, sermonising about how people needed to make 'better choices'. These are often the same people who won't look at their own choices and consider that they might be risky, such as how much they drink per week.

There are people better qualified than me to talk about obesity and the higher health risks that might be associated with it but what I am going to talk about is the stigma surrounding it and how people feel emboldened to 'advise' or comment on another person's body because it is larger. Jade Seabrook, a plus-size model and activist, put up a great Instagram post that sums this up: 'Not one person was concerned for my "health" when I was thin with an eating disorder.'

Even the word 'obese' has such a negative set of connotations. Someone who has a body mass index of more than 30 might be more at risk of certain conditions but so is someone who is old, a man, or Black or Asian. People won't comment on my Instagram posts saying, 'Woah, better stop eating sweets because, being Asian, you're at a higher risk of type 2 diabetes' but they will feel perfectly valid going on Bryony Gordon's Instagram account and writing hideous comments about her weight because she hovers between a size 18 to 20.

There are people classed as obese who are healthy but the problem is, because of how we talk about obesity, we cannot fathom that this is the case. And, BMI – body mass index – continues to be the main measure by which we class someone as overweight, wagging the finger that they need to lose weight, despite the many reasons as to why it's an incorrect method of assessment. BMI was invented by a mathematician, not a doctor, and is notorious for wrongly classing weightlifters, rugby players and other athletes as unhealthy because it only takes weight, not muscle mass, into account.

The government's 2020 obesity campaign drew justified criticism because it put so much emphasis on personal responsibility (the old chestnut of blaming people for their choices) and not enough on other factors such as income and class inequality. It also completely ignored the strong link between obesity and sexual trauma, particularly in women. In 2012, a study titled 'Obesity as a Defense Mechanism' found that sexual assault and abuse survivors were much more likely to become obese than non-abused people.[1] This study, as well as a 2015 study from the University of North Carolina, also showed that standard weight control programmes didn't work on this specific group of people, indicating that experts and programmes ignoring or not factoring in the trauma that leads to obesity are the problem – not the individual.[2] Not only did the government's campaign leave this out of their strategy, it also used aggressive language such as the aforementioned 'war' on obesity, forgetting that this 'war' they are raging is against people's bodies, which further feeds into the cycle of shame.

Shame-based tactics don't work in the long term, and obesity is not the only health condition that illustrates this. Since dealing with Rob's issues, I've learned a lot about addiction and noticed how close parallels can be drawn to the language used around addiction. Consider, for instance, the 'war on drugs' which can be interpreted as the war on the drug trade but almost always places the onus on drug users, many of whom are vulnerable and/or dealing with a dual diagnosis such as a mental health condition. Like the strategy on obesity, a lot of responsibility is placed on the individual and says that in order to be accepted into society, they must be clean. If they fail to do so, then it means that they don't deserve love, help or acceptance. While drug addicts are unified by their damaging substance abuse even in the face of serious consequences, they may become one for a number of reasons. Treating the issue behind whatever prompts that drug use is what needs to be addressed and treated rather than holding the threat of social ostracisation and shame over them. Consider the parallel with obesity. When so much of the obesity strategy is focused on dieting – with not enough emphasis or support around the other factors that caused that obesity in the first place, the mindset around it gets reduced down to something they are bringing on themselves. If the goal is to get people to be healthier – whether that's physically, mentally or both – the approach has to be more nuanced.

Stringent dieting also doesn't always work in the long term, regardless of whether you are obese. The *British Medical Journal* published a big study in 2020 which looked at 22,000 people across 121 clinical trials and found that the effects of diets wore off after 12 months.[3] Another fascinating study called FinnTwin16 looked at over 4,000 twins in 2012, and showed people who dieted were actually more likely to gain weight than their non-dieting twin.[4] Women who had gone on two or more diets during the study were five times as likely to become overweight.

Why don't they work? Because dieting is actually really stressful. Any form of restriction is mentally and physically taxing, and when you're stressed, your stress hormone – cortisol – behaves in certain ways. Increased levels of cortisol might increase your fat and carbohydrate metabolism, which makes your appetite spike, and it might also affect where you put this weight on – for instance, if you're pre-disposed to collecting fat around your tummy or hips.

I don't mean to downplay amendments to eating habits – after all, there are those who may have to undertake weight-loss programmes for specific medical reasons. But there is a significant number of us who have tried lots of diets, and found they don't work. It doesn't mean that you can't attempt weight loss but trying gentler things such as intuitive or mindful eating to connect to what your body and mind really want, and a slow reduction of calories rather than restrictive diets, will put your body under a lot less stress.

To offer a glimpse of what body acceptance looks like, there are a growing number of women who inhabit the body positive and fat acceptance space, who demonstrate how much stronger and confident they are when they accept and empower their bodies versus shrinking them. It also doesn't mean that physical activity isn't a part of that – it absolutely is for many people. The difference being that they are working out for themselves, their own body standards and mental wellbeing – not for some arbitrary body image standard.

A lot of the leading activists who I interviewed in the body positive/fat acceptance space had a strong relationship with physical activity before diet culture and fatphobia told them otherwise. Stephanie Yeboah, for instance, loved sport. She still loves it, especially the competitiveness in football and badminton. When she was a girl, she was on the boys' football team, did gymnastics and went to a breakdancing class after school. In secondary school, however, she started putting on weight, and began to equate working out with what she describes as 'light trauma'.

'I joined the rounders team at school,' she says, 'however, I would be laughed at, jeered and beaten up any time I would run or be out of breath. It became the case that bullying in the classroom flowed into the sports ground and, because of that, I stopped taking P.E. and would instead make up an excuse every week and do an alternative class. It took a long time for me to be able to exercise in public, as that feeling of being constantly watched never goes away, especially when you reside in a hyper-visible body. However, I realised that I wasn't working out for others' approval or policing, I was working out for me and my opinions were the only thing that mattered.'

While some sports brands are getting better at using plus-size fitness models, it is still far from the norm and because they don't do much to change the actual fatphobic culture and mindset of the fitness industry, the nasty comments these photos generate when posted on social media are eye-watering.

The morning TV show *Loose Women* ran a segment in 2020 to give airtime to fat acceptance activists and actually added a disclaimer reminding people to 'stay healthy' as well – basically reinforcing old tropes that being plus-size means you are automatically unhealthy.

An old defence the fitness and entertainment industry clings to around promoting larger bodies is 'Well, we don't want to encourage obesity' – but it is baseless and without merit. Where is the scientific evidence to show that this is what happens when you advertise plus-size bodies working out and being active? On the other hand, consider the evidence that is there. Worldwide obesity has tripled since 1975 according to WHO and, interestingly, what they say about reducing obesity levels is that 'supportive environments and communities are fundamental in shaping people's choices, by making the choice of healthier foods and regular physical activity the easiest choice (the choice that is the most accessible, available and affordable).'[5]

Is society supportive and encouraging of plus-size people making fitness choices or does it shame them, and continue to shame them even after they've made the societally 'acceptable' choice?

Author and life coach Michelle Elman, who is one of my favourite body positive activists on Instagram, has a lot to say about it: 'I've personally had a number of experiences of comments that imply that I'm lazy due to my weight or assume that I'm inexperienced and "new to the gym" because my body doesn't reflect the results of someone who has been working out regularly for the last nine years.'

Michelle, like Stephanie, was active as a child and says her standard week would include tennis, swimming, roller hockey, ice skating and horse-riding. But, since then, she's had 15 surgeries for different things, ranging from a brain tumour to a punctured intestine. The surgeries got in the way of her engagement with physical activity and in secondary school she couldn't keep up with the class in sports such as cross-country running and took it as a personal failure. She began to hate her body.

At university, she has memories of refusing to join her friends in a Zumba class because she 'didn't want to be the fat girl in dance class'. But when she started recovering, Michelle was haunted by all she had missed out on and made a promise that she would try everything even if it scared her. She started running and horse-riding again because she realised that being bedridden for so long was way worse than letting her insecurities get in the way.

'One of the main shifts post-hospital,' she says, 'was that exercise wasn't about what my body looked like anymore but what it could do. I had spent years moaning about how big my thighs were or my stomach and the scars on them but my body worked and I refused to take that for granted anymore.'

And here's the thing. Slim or skinny people do not have the monopoly on joy around physical movement. And when we teach people that they do, we do untold damage to girls and women of every size that may takes years, if ever, to undo. The fact is that all people – regardless of body size – benefit from being active, whether that's going for a 20-minute walk a day or working out at home. There are countless studies that show the benefit to things like longevity when it comes to just moving your body a bit more. But when physical activity becomes a weapon used against plus-size people to try and get them to lose weight, it is a big problem.

It's a problem partly because it's shoddy science – exercise is not the main way people lose weight; it is well documented that, first and foremost, it comes down to what we eat and exercise only accounts for about 20 per cent of total weight loss. But mainly because weight loss is framed as the *only* incentive for plus-size people to do physical activity – nothing is said about how it helps you reclaim confidence in your body or the joy it brings. More dangerously, it can also be a trigger for eating disorders.

One example of how popular culture can embed such damaging ideas around food, weight loss and exercise was *The Restaurant That Burns Off Calories* TV programme which aired in early 2020. The premise was that 20 diners were invited to a restaurant to eat whatever they wanted, but unknown to them, a team of people in a secret room filled with gym equipment had to burn off whatever they ate. It was based on a scientific study that showed that when people saw how much effort it took to burn off the calories they'd eaten, it resulted in them eating 20 per cent less.

The show drew huge criticism, in particular from survivors of eating disorders and the eating disorder charity BEAT. One of the biggest issues is that for many people who are struggling with eating disorders or are in recovery, exercise to burn off what they've eaten is a huge aspect of their illness.

When I sent out my survey, I knew I'd probably get data to confirm how being self-conscious about one's body acted as a blocker to being physically active. But I was shocked at how hidden yet common eating disorders seemed to be among the respondents judging by the comments submitted. Some women also got in touch via social media, telling me about their experiences. It was clear there was an overlap between diet culture, negative comments about their body, bad experiences at school in P.E. and the constant pressure to be thin, no matter the cost.

Megan Crabbe, the brilliant body positive advocate known on Instagram as @bodyposipanda, is known for her down-to-earth messaging and gorgeous, colourful hair and style. When she was younger, Megan was an active child and captain of the football team. But she got more entrenched in diet culture, which she says was due to a collection of different things but magazines were a big trigger. 'I was around 12 or 13 when movement changed for me and it stopped being about joy or social connection, and it started being about changing my body and burning off calories,' she told me.

Megan was diagnosed with anorexia nervosa at the age of 14 and had an exercise addiction. When she went into recovery she had to stop all kinds of exercise and teach herself to be OK with being still. She had to focus on her surroundings and examine how movement made her body feel, rather than connecting it to numbers. 'To this day I avoid the kind of rigorous exercise where the point is to make up for something I've eaten or to change my shape,' she says.

Another incredible bo-po activist influencer who also talks about her battles with eating disorders (or ED) is journalist and chef Latoya Shauntay Snell. She is an ultrarunner and has over 100 finisher medals. I came across a video of her working battle ropes and skipping and I remember thinking how she looked like poetry and strength in motion.

In 2013, Latoya embarked on a weight-loss journey because she weighed over 120kg, due to a few different things including depression. Facing long-term disability after a herniated disc, she thought losing weight would solve all of her problems. Although she lost a lot of weight initially and it improved her mood and health, she developed anorexia nervosa and orthorexia. (Orthorexia is the obsession with eating foods that are considered 'proper' and 'healthy'; it was particularly rife when people were peddling kale, bone broth and courgetti around 2014 to 2016.)

'Stereotypes of people who go through eating disorders are depicted as skinny white women who want to look like a model,' Latoya told me. 'My reasons for doing what I did stemmed from wanting to be what I thought an athlete was supposed to look like.' A so-called friend told her that she was too fat to be a runner and advised that she go on a super-restrictive diet of 1,200 calories while training for a marathon. She ended up collapsing at work and that was the wake-up call she needed. She gained the weight back and says: 'As far as vitals go, I'm still in the same position but I feel powerful. I have a lot of stamina and sure, I do feel the weight, but it doesn't limit the way I move nor affect how my reflection makes me feel.'

Although she's in recovery, doing her first marathon after being diagnosed with an eating disorder was terrifying. 'What I think caloric restriction taught me,' she says, 'is that it reduces you down to feeling like a rabid animal. It impacts your fitness level. Depriving yourself of recovery days or not getting adequate sleep means that you will probably not perform to the best of your ability when it really counts.'

For Latoya, there is a lot she has accomplished through running that has taught her about the beauty and brilliance of her own body. And, although she wasn't entirely comfortable with the idea of being an inspiration for others at first, she knows it's important. 'At the time, I had no idea what "body positive" meant but I knew that I could run for miles as long as my mind didn't clock out on me,' she said. 'I knew that I didn't imagine doing my first 18-mile run on the hottest day of the year back in 2014 and jumping on my mountain bike to ride 100 miles the next day. If I could do that, I know I'm not alone.

'When I went to road events, I did see people like me on the course but they weren't the ones who got the cool profiles in magazines. Why? Because people love perpetuating and selling what seems unattainable or a select few can maintain.'

If you're still not convinced, consider these fundamental truths and then draw your own conclusions. Diet culture – the culture you've grown up in your whole life – has convinced each and every one of us that slimness will make us happy and fulfilled. It sells you products, tells you to do certain types of workouts, puts certain people on the cover of magazines, celebrates weight loss, pays celebrities and influencers to encourage you to want their abs or their bums. But, if it really was sustainable and made you happy – if they really had your best interests at heart – you wouldn't need them for very long. Never lose sight of the fact that your happiness and health are not good for their profit margin, but your dissatisfaction and misery are.

While I wish I hadn't experienced trauma, it led me to powerlifting. And powerlifting allowed me to finally see the matrix for what it was.

In a powerlifting competition, you compete within federations – mine is called the Amateur British Powerlifting Union (ABPU) and was founded by Emma Ylitalo-James, who is a formidable lifter and has always championed women and gender equality in the sport. You're then organised in terms of weight category and age. That then determines your competitor set and you can win medals depending on your categories.

The idea of weight categories can be triggering to some, however, I've known people with a history of eating disorders who have taken it up and who have found it hasn't impacted them in the way they feared it might. Partly because, although it's a competition, it's a well-worn phrase that in powerlifting the person you're competing with is yourself. It differs from other sports where you fight a specific opponent, say martial arts, because on a powerlifting competition day, you have no idea who will be in the same group as you. The aim is to lift well, lift consistently and beat your own personal records. If you happen to win your category or the competition, it's an incredible bonus.

The first competition I attended was a humble, life-changing lesson in realising that what we think a 'healthy' person looks like is so wrong. I saw women of every shape and size compete and it was impossible to guess how much they could lift just by looking at them. What you did know, however, was that they were extremely strong. This taught me that we cannot make assumptions about a person's capabilities by their appearance, so when we carve up our flesh and starve ourselves in the name of aesthetics, it is a false idol, and not worthy of worship.

In particular, the category which drew my interest the most was the super heavyweights, or the SHWs, which is a category for women who are over 90kg. In this arena, size is celebrated because it equates to strength and they are an absolute force to be reckoned with. I had never before seen plus-size female bodies walking around in singlets, lifting weights, exuding such confidence. It was refreshing, it was necessary in overturning old beliefs, it was powerful and I wanted to see more.

When I called up Emma to ask her about the whole process of hosting competitions and how she has seen the sport change, she told me that in the last six years, she has noticed about a 50 per cent increase in female competitors. For her, the SHWs are the sexiest of all the women. 'They come out there and they've got that "*raar*" or that "I'm just sexy" look, walking onto the platform,' she says. 'That is how women are supposed to be and this is a platform – excuse the pun – outside of social stereotyping, where women can be super sexy and fearsome and be themselves 100 per cent and be appreciated.'

Leighanne, who is 38 and a super heavyweight lifter in my federation, started lifting around the same time as me. She trains in a gym in Eastbourne and joined a group called Misfits Barbell, started by a guy named Adrian who is dedicated to increasing the profile of female lifters. She holds European and world records – her most recent was a squat of 160kg – and, like the rest of us amateur lifters, does this as a hobby. Adrian also encouraged Leighanne's daughter Chardonnay to get involved and now they both compete.

'I've had to deal with being big throughout my life,' says Leighanne, 'and always just laughed it off whenever anyone used to make a comment, but deep down it ate away at me. But now I know who I am. For years, women have been looked down on in sports but with new generations of us coming through, it's empowering to be able to prove that women are able to compete no matter their age or size.'

The more I got into lifting, I saw how the things that I'd heard women rebuke themselves for actually made them well suited to the sport. For instance, strong thighs and larger glutes make for amazing squatters. Shorter arms make you amazing at bench press. This made me think about my own community. I had seen how South Asian women, especially those growing up in the West, spent most of their lives feeling bad about their own bodies because they didn't look like the Western ideal. I mean, most of us just aren't shaped that way – take a look at any carving on a temple for boob and booty evidence. On social media I was able to connect with my community in a way that I wasn't able to in real life, and came across other South Asian women – especially plus-size – who'd gravitated towards weightlifting because they were just fed up of being told to work out to lose weight.

An amazing body positive and fat acceptance activist who talks a lot about intersectionality is Artika Gunathasan, who came to my attention with her lifting posts on Instagram. I then saw her in Tally Rye's book *Train Happy* as one of the models demonstrating certain moves and I remember thinking how proud I was to see a plus-size brown woman in the fitness space. Artika has a lot going on in her life – she used to be a science teacher and is now a carer for her sister who has learning disabilities. She has also battled with mental illness. There isn't much time left in the day to focus on herself, but lifting offers a reprieve from all of that and has been part of her recovery from disordered eating, which was triggered when she was seven and was taken to the doctor because she was having trouble breathing. In hindsight, Artika says it was most likely a symptom of anxiety, but the GP told her mother to put her on a restrictive diet and strict exercise regime, and she hated it.

'I have spent most of my life resenting my body for not conforming to society's ideals,' she told me, 'for never being thin, for always quickly regaining any lost weight through dieting. My body has always been a source of shame: bodies that look like mine are often the butt of jokes or the worst-case scenario for what can happen to a body.'

It was only through spending time on social media and watching other plus-size womxn (the term used to be inclusive of anyone who identifies as a woman as well as non-binary people) – and in particular, plus-size Black and brown womxn – that she began to view her body differently. Though, ironically, Artika's journey with lifting actually began when she was looking for YouTube workouts to 'tone and trim' while 'maintaining her curves'.

'I know,' she says, 'cue eye-rolling.'

Artika had previously thought weightlifting was just for professional bodybuilders but when she started lifting, it gave her confidence. Now, watching herself get stronger and more competent at the lifts reminds her that she can do anything she puts her mind to. She explains, 'That strength has also improved my body image as I can now view my physical form as being more than its appearance.'

In the search for other women lifters from my own community, I came across the inspiring Indian-born lifter Suhani Gandhi, who is known as 'India's strongest woman' and comes from the same city as my family – Bangalore. She started winning state-level medals in 2016 and, in 2019, came third in the Strongest Woman competition in the UAE and won the Arnold Classic novice strongwoman competition, which for her was a milestone. It meant she was then the first Indian woman to be invited to take part in the prestigious Arnold Classic in the States.

Despite her incredible strength, Suhani has always received comments about her weight and had previously been on a cycle of losing weight and then putting it back on. She played tennis but it led to bullying about her size and it spiralled her into depression for three years. When she saw a doctor about it, he advised her to lose weight. At this point, Suhani was fed up. She knew she liked to move her body but she wanted to do it in a sport where she didn't feel like she was constantly being judged about her weight. She tried weightlifting and described it as a 'cloud lifting'. 'My whole life,' she said, 'I was struggling to lose weight and be like other girls. But the truth is I neglected myself. Weightlifting has been a tremendous change for me and has made me believe in myself.' Her achievements also mean she gets respect from people because she's going overseas and representing her country.

Of course, it doesn't mean that weight training is a silver bullet. Many women find reclamation and healing within their own bodies across a number of other activities, such as yoga or running. If any of this has inspired you to take up some form of fitness but you're feeling unsure where to start, Tally Rye suggests asking yourself how you'd like to move your body if you didn't have to think about weight or appearance. That might be trying lots of different activities, whether it's a YouTube dance video or a boxing class, and noting how they make you feel. She also advises curating your social media feed so that you follow people of all different shapes and sizes, as well as people with a similar body size, colour, age or ability to you. And if you use fitness trackers of any kind, instead of focusing on how fast or far you can go, listen and check in with your body.

'The problem with focusing on weight-loss goals,' says Michelle Elman, 'is that you never give yourself the opportunity to enjoy the actual movement because you just see it as a means to an end. As humans, we are designed to want to move our body and if we think back to when we were children, we naturally wanted to run around and move our body. The thing that ruined it was diet culture and the capitalisation on exercise that has led to the idea that movement should be gruelling, punishing and hard work. But there was a time you liked to ride your bike before you called it spinning and there was a time that you liked to dance in your kitchen before you called it Zumba.'

Aside from reclaiming the joy of movement, what also seems to be a no-brainer is to have different bodies represented at all levels of sport and fitness. Bianca, who took my survey, said that, as a size 18, she has found huge inspiration in the body positive accounts she follows on social media. But she also says that she would have loved to have seen more inclusivity 15 years ago, as it would have given her more confidence in the gym.

We can't change the experiences we had at school or as young women. But we can change how that past affects us, and how it has been holding us back. We are raised in a world designed to keep you obedient and small, to make you doubt yourself long after the mean comments are uttered. And diet culture needs all of that, because if it wasn't there, if you removed those shackles, if you let yourself stand tall, if you said *that's enough*, you would generate an internal power so vast, so filled with light and dignity and strength, that you wouldn't need the rubbish they are trying to sell you.

I will never know what it's like to inhabit a body that is relentlessly commented on, attacked and judged by society, but I know something about breaking through to a different place, free from the limitations of others, and myself.

I know this, because eventually, finally, I changed my story.

CHAPTER SIX

Becoming My Strongest Self

If you looked at my life at the beginning of 2017, you would have thought that I was doing remarkably well, all things considered.

Eighteen months after my husband died, my first book was about to come out, I had a well-paid job and a career that was going onwards and upwards. With my newfound love of lifting weights, I was physically the strongest I had been. But mentally, I was starting to crumble again. I had returned to work three weeks after Rob died in June 2015 because I was scared that if I didn't have organisation, purpose and structure around me, I would literally die by falling into a void of grief. But since that first day back, I had never really stopped.

Initially, raw grief is described as a fog because it is impossible at times to find any clarity or focus while you are in it. I believe it's because we are never truly present in the current reality, that there is so much of our heart and mind that is locked in the past and in the future of what will never be, that the present seems pointless, and immaterial. But this fog eventually clears because, like all things in the world, you are a living creature who wants and needs to be healed. When this healing begins, emerging into this new state is often painful because your senses are new and everything is adjusting and recalibrating. You aren't given endless time to figure it out – you have to do this alongside your everyday life that includes paying bills, going to work and doing errands.

While I loved my job and I was grateful for the stability it afforded me, working in corporations is brutal. The landscape changes all the time, and the reason it pays well is because it demands a lot. I had reached the point where I just didn't have any more to give. So in the summer of 2017, I quit. I did the maths and, after finally paying off my credit card and loans, I had enough saved up to go on a seven-month trip. I wouldn't be left with much when I returned but it was a chance I was willing to take. If I stayed in my job any longer, I was risking burnout to the point of not being able to function and I knew that I might not survive that on top of already grieving for Rob.

During this trip, I got to spend the time I always wanted with my parents in India, as well as three months of it in New Zealand, with my in-laws, Prue and David. In and around that, I spent chunks of time on my own, travelling around. For a time, lifting weights was put on pause and instead I did the things I always loved doing on holiday. I kayaked in the sea and across little blue lakes, paddleboarded on rivers, hiked up mountains into valleys of emerald with snow caps dusted diamond white. It was the most intuitive way of moving my body and it felt good. I felt a sense of absolute purity in terms of how I felt about Rob, my grief, and where I felt his presence most, in the joining of natural elements like the land and sea.

But when I got settled in Auckland, although I was fairly active, I fell into more of a routine, and I ate and drank a lot. By the end of the seven months away, I felt as if I'd put on weight but I didn't realise how much until I stepped on the scale – and it was about six kilograms heavier than I had ever been. I'm embarrassed to recall this now because it just seems so fatphobic but I felt so much shame and disgust at my own body. I tried cutting down what I ate and working out but nothing seemed to work, and every time I had a glass of wine or a bit of cheese, I had this crushing sense of guilt. The best way I can describe it is that I felt as if I couldn't trust my body. As irrational as it sounds, I felt as if I'd put on weight if I even just looked at food. Given that it coincided with me turning 37, it just made me feel worse about getting older.

When I returned to England in late spring 2018, in a body I hated, I decided to do the 5:2 diet – this is intermittent fasting where for two days of the week you consume only 500 calories and I had heard from a friend of a similar age that it was very effective. When I did my research, there seemed to be some credible people supporting it from the health point of view. I have since retracted this opinion because, firstly, I consider myself to be mostly an intuitive and mindful eater, secondly, these same 'credible' people would go on to create highly problematic 'quick weight loss' programmes, and thirdly, my experience with it made me loathe doing any form of severe calorie-controlled eating.

In the first week, I thought it was a breeze, and in the second week I was extolling its virtues, but by week three and four, my body did not want to do it, and my brain rebelled. I was still committed but at about midday every day, my brain would send me a very clear, expletive-laden message that was hard to ignore: *This is stupid, we hate this, I hate you, stop doing this, you dickhead.*

Intermittent fasting started off as refreshing because, at first, on the days I fasted I didn't think about food and it freed up a lot of space and time for other things. However, as things progressed, I realised it then meant that I needed to work my social calendar around it and I was starting to feel irritable and fixated on food. Eventually I realised that whatever the supposed health benefits, anything that causes you to fixate on food is not a good thing. Moreover, the programme doesn't take into account the disparities between how intermittent fasting might affect women in a way it doesn't affect men, depending on where you are in your menstrual cycle (which I will cover later in the book).

At the same time, I remember feeling absolutely suffocated by social media. I didn't realise it at the time but the accounts I followed made me feel terrible. Most of the women had strong but slim physiques and it contributed to a sense of disgust towards my own body because I couldn't seem to wrestle control over it. Why could they do it and I couldn't? I internalised that loathing completely. Not once did I question that I was comparing myself to women around 10 to 15 years younger than me. Or whether what I was seeing on someone's feed was even a real picture. I got completely sucked into the vortex of 'fitspo' – the word coined to describe the trend of posting slim, athletic bodies with some kind of motivational spiel to get people to be active. Bikini Body Guide programmes were massive at the time and all it did was make me feel terrible about myself.

While I get that some people want to chart their progress, there's a section in Tally Rye's book *Train Happy* where she hits the nail on the head about why transformation photos are problematic. It's because it markets the idea that you can get this body in 12 weeks but, more than that, if you get this body, you'll be happy. 'What the photos fail to show,' she writes, 'is what usually happens after that 12 weeks. When biology kicks in and fights back at the intentional weight loss by making it harder to maintain and sustain the methods that got them there in the first place.'

At the time I didn't know this, but two things happened in my endless scrolling through social media, to change my negative thinking. The first was that I came across Ban Hass, a personal trainer and anti-fitspo activist, who was shining a light on some of the hidden aspects of fitspo and bringing people to account. We ended up becoming friends through Instagram and then in real life. We sat in a café the first time we met, she with her flowing black hair and glossy skin, and like a beautiful, wise mermaid, told me some serious truths.

'Following your favourite fitspo cookie-cutter workout plan or nutritional guide will NOT give you their body,' she said. 'Genetics play a massive role in body composition and often people forget this while they're scrolling or considering purchasing a workout plan. In addition, for all you know they might not even be following their own plans. They could be posting at-home body weight workouts but hitting the gym and lifting heavy weights five or six times a week. They could be posting delicious, rich food on the 'Gram and sticking to a calorie-controlled diet in real life. Or vice-versa. We just don't know. What we do know is that two people will never get the same results following the same programme because we're humans. Not robots.'

I remember her words blowing my mind. It hadn't even occurred to me the problem might not be me, but them. Or rather, the role social media plays in propping up the archetype of slim, toned white women as the image of fitness and because there is little accountability around transparency on social media, it allows people to manipulate the information behind the image. It was around the same time that I also came across

Laura Thomas, author of *Just Eat It*, and, because I was able to pitch an intuitive eating feature to an editor, used that as an excuse to seek the answers I desperately needed.

When she uttered the words: 'We trust our phones more than we trust our own body', I realised that I had completely lost faith in my body. I *did* trust my phone more than I did my own body. I had also broken a fundamental promise I had made to it after I had recovered from having surgery for the hole in my heart, which was that I would nurture and look after it. I didn't know where to start, only that the diet had to go. And I realised that I needed a trainer to help reset this pit I had dug myself into, mentally and physically. Although as a freelancer I was worried about money, I felt it was an investment I needed to make.

Tyrone had long since gone back to Australia and, in any case, I didn't work from central London anymore so I needed to find someone closer to home. My local gym didn't have anyone I wanted to train with but then a friend recommended a trainer in a different gym in Richmond, about a 15-minute drive from me. When I went to the gym, I discovered it was located at the top of so many stairs you end up a melted, wheezing mess before you get to reception. I had been told to ask for Jack Toczydlowski. But Jack wasn't in and I was already cranky from the stairs. I left my number and an abrupt message for him to give me a call.

On the way home, I kept thinking *What if Tyrone had been a one-off? What if I didn't like Jack? What if this whole lifting weights thing had been a phase?*

At the time, I had no idea how life-altering that journey up the stairs would be.

There are three men who have been pivotal to my life. The first is of course my father. The second was Rob. The third was Jack. I don't mean that in a creepy way, I mean he literally altered the course of my life. In the first few text messages, I told him that I wanted to be strong, lean and 'trim some fat'. When I turned up for the first session, I wasn't quite prepared for Jack, who is actually Jacek.

For a start, he was huge – like imagine a mountain of muscle, with tattoos, and a beard. My monkey brain instantly squeaked because it couldn't quite make the leap that someone who looked so strong and muscly could teach ole noodle-arms here about weights. But from that first meeting, he defied the stereotype of what I'd come to expect from guys with his physique. He was polite, super respectful, knowledgeable, listened and wasn't patronising.

Jack, it turned out, was one of three business partners who owned the gym. Originally from Poland, he was an ex-professional cage fighter and now the gym's head strength coach. Half of the place was covered in mats as it was a martial arts gym and primarily taught Brazilian jiu-jitsu, while the rest was sectioned off into a weights section – Jack's domain. As we trained, I noticed Jack commanded a certain type of presence in the gym. I noticed how people would invariably ask him for advice or check they were doing something OK. The vibe I got was that they respected him and what was refreshing about it was that this respect didn't seem to just be accorded to him because of his size, but seemed to be about something much deeper.

When I started training with Tyrone, I was a wisp of a person battered by grief – weight training had helped me to form reason and structure out of the remnants. When I started training with Jack, although I felt more corporeal in terms of belonging to the world, I was newly returned to England after being away and trying to construct a new identity that wasn't tied to a corporate job that had defined me for so many years.

Jack and I would talk as I trained but, at the beginning, I

don't think we shared a huge amount of personal information. I knew he was married to his childhood sweetheart, Aga, and I knew vaguely that he had retired from fighting and did something competitively called powerlifting. He was a guy with muscles, of course it made sense for him to do something like that – even though I didn't really even know what powerlifting was. Nor did I ask. At the time, I was working seven days a week trying to get my freelance business set up and I had to finish writing my second book, *In Search of Silence*, so everything felt consumed by work.

The set-up at the time was that I'd train in my local gym which was a commercial gym about a five-minute walk away, and then every fortnight I'd catch the bus to Richmond and have a session with Jack. Three months into this came a pivotal moment. I'd now been lifting weights intermittently for about 18 months by that point, including my time off for my trip. I wasn't lifting too heavy but I was still working hard in the squat rack and doing deadlifts, which I still didn't see many women doing in commercial gyms.

Commercial gym is the term used to describe gym chains like Fitness First, David Lloyd, Virgin Active and they tend to have a bit of everything, from treadmills to weight sections. (They are also where you are likely to find your gym bros and posters advertising weight-loss programmes and cosmetic surgery – but more on this later.) Jack's gym, which was called Elevate, was the opposite of that – a community gym, which may not have the bells and whistles of a commercial gym but was likely much more welcoming and friendly.

When I'm in a commercial gym, I know that I have to be prepared for the gym bro atmosphere in the weights section. Nowadays I don't even register guys who behave like that, but previously when I was new to weightlifting I was hyper-aware and survived it by trying make myself as unapproachable as possible from putting headphones on to looking stern. In a gym that has a weightlifting community like Jack's, however, there is a certain etiquette around sharing equipment – you don't leave your weights lying around for others to tidy up for you and you give people the same amount of respect no matter what they lift.

One day, I was training at my local commercial gym and a South Asian personal trainer I had seen around (and scowled at) came over. I took off my headphones ready to bite his head off – fully expecting him to give me some unwanted advice. He introduced himself as Aleem. I could tell that he had a very light stammer when he spoke and I immediately softened. My dad had a bad stammer when he was younger and although it has gotten much better, it still sometimes flashes into his speech. My sister and I adore our dad, and know how much it affected him and how hard he worked to overcome it, so anyone who has a stammer instantly gets a free pass from us.

As a result, I paid attention to Aleem in a way I probably wouldn't have done for anyone else. He told me that the gym was running an unofficial powerlifting competition and did I want to enter? I barked a laugh. 'Er, no,' I replied. For a start, I didn't do competitive stuff in gyms – I saw the leaderboards of various rowing times and HIIT workouts and it wasn't remotely appealing. Powerlifting sounded shit scary, plus wouldn't lifting heavier mean I was much more likely to injure myself? I thought of the men I knew who had lifted, from my dad to Niaz – they'd all had bad back injuries.

'Just think about it,' Aleem continued, 'you don't have to sign up right now.' I nodded, already thinking *no way, not a chance*. But then he uttered the final line that sank into my brain and refused to leave: 'If you did do it, it would be a really good way of encouraging more women into the weights section.'

Wasn't that what I had desperately wanted? Wouldn't it be amazing to come to the weights section and see different people in there, other than bros doing chest and arms?

A few days later, Jack and I were having a session in his gym and I mentioned my conversation with Aleem, fully expecting him to laugh it off. But Jack didn't laugh and said: 'I think it sounds like a great idea.'

'Really?' I replied. 'But it seems so, I don't know . . . ' I gestured with my hands, '. . . out there.'

I have to give Jack credit for how he handled it. He wasn't over the top and he didn't put on any pressure. 'Well look at it this way,' he said, 'I can put together a programme for you that will help get you ready for the competition. If you do the competition and you don't like it then all that will have happened is you've done a programme to get you strong and you don't have to do it again. But competitions are really fun, and I have a feeling you are going to end up having a lot of fun on the day.'

At that point, I couldn't quite see what was fun about it – I mean, fun was getting wangoed on wine and hanging out by a swimming pool, not lugging weights around – but I agreed to try it. I had ten weeks to train for the competition and, in that time, I saw my strength go up exponentially. I also finally hit that 100kg mark – the number I had laughed at when Tyrone first suggested it. But more than that, I saw what happened when I took off that dampener around my potential, stopped worrying about food and really went for it. If I could give that potential form, I would describe it like lightning crackling over a limitless sky, as if a part of myself which had been imprisoned for so long was finally released.

As it was a mock competition taking place in my local gym,

Jack wasn't with me on the day but had prepared me as best he could. 'They'll start with squat first, then bench press, then deadlift,' he said.

Aleem and his partner Maariyah – who is also a badass South Asian powerlifter – were running the logistics of the day, so after getting weighed in, we were told how the day would go. As I waited to start, I could see people chatting to one another and I felt as if it was my first day of school – stuck in a bog of awkwardness. But that feeling of being left out quickly dissipated when one of the female competitors, Elaine, started chatting to me and told me how nervous *she* was. She was so friendly and warm, and that then got us chatting to other people there. Men competed in one group and women competed in the other and we both cheered each other on just the same. I had never seen anything like this, in a room full of total strangers.

When it came time to do my first squat, I was very aware of being watched by people and, although I felt so exposed, when I sank downwards and pushed the weight back up, I heard the applause and felt something deep inside starting to knit together a layer of resilience. The price of transformation, it seemed, was being willing to be vulnerable and to do something scary in order to realise a truth about yourself. For me, this was that I am strong, I am capable and I can display this strength even with a room full of random people watching me. As I chatted to people competing and cheered them on, I realised Jack was right – this was such a pure form of fun. But more than that, was the sense of achievement.

When you train for a powerlifting competition, you have a sense of what you want to lift for your three attempts, for each three lifts – squat, bench press and deadlift. You never hit the numbers for your third and heaviest attempt in training because you don't want to peak too soon and burn yourself out. Instead, you hit your first and possibly second attempts. So when you hit your third attempt on the platform and it's a number you haven't hit before, it is unlike any other feeling. The adrenaline and elation that courses through makes you draw on your mental strength and physical strength in equal amounts to create a singular point, and that point feels like serenity. When you first experience it, it is so powerful it almost seems to rewrite your emotional and mental DNA. That's why I think it is so healing for people who have experienced trauma, or who have struggled mentally.

Stacy Bama is one of the most prominent personalities in powerlifting and ranked number one in the world for having a weight total of 650kg, while lifting at a body weight of 67kg. A weight total is the sum total of the heaviest amount you can lift in squat, bench and deadlift. My weight total, for instance, is 292.5kg lifting at a body weight of 65kg. She says that most of us gravitate towards the idea of fighting against resistance because it is familiar. As someone who is in her late twenties, is gay and from South Carolina, and has recovered from a broken back, she knows something of this. 'If you have faced hardship and the weight of the world on your shoulders but continued to stand up against it – it sounds much like a squat,' she told me. 'It is almost like the hardships and traumas you have endured before powerlifting have served as training. When you have proven to yourself that you are already mentally strong and resilient through life's struggles it creates an underlying sense of confidence that no weight on a barbell can ever compare to.'

After I did that first unofficial competition in the gym, for the first time, I finally understood that the only thing stopping me feeling limitless was myself. That day forward, I exploded into my full power.

The very next morning, I knew I was completely different when I stepped outside my flat to walk to the supermarket. On my street, I saw a group of men walking towards me. Normally I would have kept my head down and moved out of their way. But I held their gaze, my shoulders were back and down, my head high. They looked at me, there was no weirdness, and they flowed around me.

That energy – of moving neutrally but with power – is something that I have taken with me and it radiates from me. It especially kicks into gear in places I would normally have felt intimidated, such as when I am the only woman or person of colour. It doesn't just apply to the gym but to every aspect of my life, from walking down the street to entering a meeting or delivering a speech in front of hundreds of people.

'Standing in my power' is a phrase that I'd heard women use before – which refers to the intersecting point between every corridor of power within you, whether that's physical, mental, spiritual, emotional. Now I finally felt like I understood what they meant. It's the ultimate ascension of ownership within yourself; your blood, your bones, your very self, flows with something much stronger and more resilient that cannot be undone by the words of others because it is all yours.

Power for women is not the same as power for men. If we behave like men, we don't become as powerful as men because we live in a world of gender bias. Women and men can display the same attributes, but where they are praised in men, they are denounced in women. Where men are helpful, we are abrasive. Where men are passionate, we are hysterical. Where men are focused, we are selfish. Societally, women are raised in a world designed to reduce their power at every level, whether that's issues around maternity leave, pay, representation on boards, laws that censor basic civil rights around abortion and freedom of movement.

We live in a gender unequal world, but we also have different intersections within our own gender, across race, culture, religion, gender identity, sexual orientation, disability, body size and age, which means that we experience the world differently. Most of us hold privilege that we don't often realise and the differences of this privilege between certain intersections can be vast. A cisgender heterosexual white woman, for instance, is much closer to the privilege of a white male, compared to, say, a cisgender, heterosexual Black woman. Because the structure of power is multi-layered, there is no single solution that will fix it, but that doesn't mean there isn't room for change or evolution.

Women trying to exist in a structurally sexist and racist society may find the corridors of power tricky to navigate, but two things can help. The first is actually working towards dismantling these structures by normalising women in power. A great example of this is British Cycling and how they radically changed the structure of their organisation top down.

Cycling was growing in popularity among women and British Cycling wanted to get as many women as possible to ride a bike. Through a series of very different measures – which ranged from hiring a female chief executive to improving female representation on their board; from introducing equal prize money to increasing the number of female coaches – the increase in women taking up the sport is whopping. They've hit their target of getting one million women on bikes and membership has grown from 9,500 to 29,000. In a survey they ran, over half of women who said they had increased the frequency of their cycling from once a year to once a month said it was because they've been influenced by British Cycling, so change can happen when organisations are willing to think in a comprehensive and bold way.

But admittedly that kind of change is rare, and we have a long way to go before we get to a place of equality because people in power rarely like relinquishing that power. The second thing that has been proven to help women succeed in their careers is actually doing sport or physical activity as a child.

One of the best-known studies to back this up is the EY Women Athletes Business Network and espnW research from 2014, which was a global survey of 400 women, 49 per cent of whom were at C-suite level – which refers to the top-level positions held by company executives. Interestingly, 74 per cent of women said that a background in sport positively helped career progression and realising their potential, while 61 per cent said it had a positive experience on their career. Other attributes credited to a background in sport included responding well to failure, taking the initiative and making them better leaders.[1] The strong connection between sport and having better leadership skills in adult life is why it is included in successful sports or physical fitness programmes for young girls. Conversely, in 2018, when a report from the Office of National Statistics showed that boys spend almost twice as much time doing sport as girls, Chris Wright, the director of wellbeing for the Youth Sport Trust charity, said that he believed there was a direct link between the future prospects of girls and the amount of sport they did. He referenced how often successful businesswomen talked about being active in sport when they were younger, and how at the opposite end, a lack of physical activity was known to contribute to poorer mental wellbeing in children and teenagers.

The School of Hard Knocks is a social inclusion charity for children and adults. Based all over the UK, they have a three-year programme which includes rugby coaching for kids who are facing challenges inside and outside school and also teach women rugby and boxing, particularly women who are living in deprivation with chaotic circumstances. Many of them, says Rosa Innes, Director of Programmes for Scotland, are stuck in a benefits trap, where getting a job will leave them financially worse off, while others have mental health problems, housing issues and challenges with childcare. Their programme has had an incredibly strong track record of getting people back into employment but also 88 per cent of participants, says Rosa, rate themselves as 'improved' in confidence, motivation, ability to face challenges, hopefulness and sense of belonging to a community.

Lisa O'Keefe from Sport England said about her own trans-ference of skills from being a rugby player to working as an executive: 'One overarching thing that rugby did for me was help me find my voice. It helped me put myself in leadership positions, whether that was on the pitch or in the club and I'm not the sort of person who naturally puts myself forward. However, when the chips are down, I do and that has definitely come from rugby and is something I genuinely would not have done before.'

My gym is also home to a lot of martial arts athletes, specif-ically Brazilian jiu-jitsu (BJJ), and whenever I see glimpses of a class, they tend to be rolling around on the floor grappling with each other, with the ultimate goal of trying to force their opponent into submission using a variety of chokes and holds. BJJ is relatively young for a martial art – it was developed as a singular martial art from Japanese ju-jitsu in the 1920s and then entered the mainstream after being incorporated into mixed martial arts (MMA) fights. In the last 15 years, there's been a massive surge in academies. I've definitely noticed a lot more people – especially women – popping up on my Instagram in gi, the cotton kimono sometimes used for rolling.

Jack's wife, Aga Toczydlowska, is one of these athletes. I got to know Aga a bit better when we spent more time together at powerlifting competitions and discovered that she is clever, sparky, considerate and funny. I really appreciated the support and the gesture when she came along to my first competition and then to my book launch and, from there, our friendship grew fast – a thick, bramble of love. My friendship with her was such a surprise because it reminded me of the friendships you form when you're a child – just filled with this intense purity. You are on the same wavelength, you just love each other and you protect each other. In other words, she's a ride or die, and one of the biggest loves of my life.

Like some of the other female BJJ students at the gym, Aga has a high-flying corporate job. I wanted to know more about her journey to the sport and how it impacted her positively, personally and at work. Also, seeing how symbiotic the relationship is between her career and her sport, and how the two complement and strengthen each other, actually made me want to try grappling – which says a lot given that I previously wasn't keen on doing martial arts myself.

She first started doing martial arts when she was 13 growing up in Poland, where a full contact karate style called Kyokushin was popular because there was not a huge range of choice for extra-curricular activities and because it didn't require expensive equipment. She ended up meeting Jack when they were teenagers at a martial arts camp. He was a professional athlete and introduced her to a variety of MMA which included BJJ.

'I took to BJJ the most,' she told me, 'finding my natural flexibility was a considerable advantage and my relatively small size for once not being a handicap. What gives you advantage in BJJ is not your gender but your agility, ability to outsmart your opponent and (to a certain extent) your flexibility/joint mobility.'

In terms of what it gives to her life, she says: 'It definitely helped me to build strong self-esteem. In BJJ, most of the time you are a part of a mixed-gender training group and there's no such thing as "good for a girl". It's a very equalising sport. And it requires you to respect and acknowledge superiority of those who have been honing their skills for much longer than you have, even if they are younger, or smaller, or a woman.

'In my professional life, it has helped me to manage my level of stress. Your entire mental energy goes into training and it puts other things into perspective.'

Martial arts in general can be an incredible way to enhance how you feel and present yourself at work. Adena Friedman, president of Nasdaq, famously said that having a black belt in taekwondo has helped her become more fearless in business and helped her deal with setbacks. If you're averse to taking risks because you're terrified of failure, martial arts seem like the perfect way to continuously practise failure and learning.

A very clear example of how women are treated very differently from men for pursuing exactly the same goals, is seen in the arena of physical strength. By that I mean women who are very visibly strong. I've found the majority of people – particularly men – don't really like it, they are suspicious of it and are afraid of it. While a man beginning a strength journey may feel it's his divine right to do so, be cheered on, handed a protein powder tub and a slap on the back, a woman beginning a strength journey will have to overcome her own internal doubts about getting bigger but also contend with various comments and unsolicited advice from her social circle or online. It is my experience that even if a woman breaks free from the conditioning that small is best, there is still a field of landmines waiting to smash her self-confidence to bits.

When I was lifting weights with Tyrone, I got a nice level of feedback from people, particularly men, because at that point, I hadn't yet reached my strength potential and I still looked small and feminine. But the minute I decided I wanted to commit to powerlifting and signed up for my first official competition with Jack as my coach, things changed. For a start, everyone and his uncle tried to scare me off with injury stories. A mate advised me to be careful. That I could severely injure my back. Family friends who didn't even weightlift decided that their own tenuous personal experience and YouTube qualified them to give me advice about it.

My mum and dad were worried and kept bringing up their worries about injuries, but to give them credit, when I sat down and explained it to them, they seemed to handle it well. For instance, I told Mum about why lifting weights is so good for your cardiovascular health; in fact, a 2018 study showed that it was better for you than running.[2] More importantly, I told her that it was the only activity proven to ward off osteoporosis and improve bone density – which is four times more common in women than it is in men.[3]

A family friend of ours had also very unhelpfully shown her an 'injury fail' video – which are horrible videos of weightlifting gone wrong, and are almost always exclusively men. I explained that a lot of those are a result of someone loading something way too heavy on the bar and attempting it – so they end up in a very bad position of not being able to handle the weight. In powerlifting, you are slowly and consistently working yourself up to a bigger weight, in a controlled way. It's also highly likely that the majority of average guys in the gym who lift and sustain an injury did not learn from a trainer. They most likely learned it off another mate, or their dad, or a cousin, who most likely didn't compete and learned it from someone else. So most people learn shitty form, which they then pass onto some other guy and that then inevitably leads to injury because they were doing it wrong the entire time – hence the narrative that weights cause injuries.

Women are not alone in receiving this kind of 'advice' – male lifters also get this – but for women, the burden is substantially bigger because we also have to deal with other irritating aspects such as being mansplained to in gyms, verbal abuse or people thinking it's OK to comment on our changing bodies or sexuality. While it might seem incomprehensible that a person could lift a crazy amount of weight and *not* injure themselves, here's the truth. People can injure themselves while doing a routine lift – I'm not denying that. But you can also do that lifting a bag out from the boot of your car or bending over to tie your shoelaces. It's not any *more* risky than going running, which is incredibly high impact – for instance, with each step, you land with a force of about two to three times your body weight. When you factor in that resistance training as a whole (not just heavy lifting, but anything that involves resistance against a weight) can help women health-wise in such a huge way, whether that's heart health or stronger bones, I think it's not just sexist to discourage women from strength training, I think it's downright irresponsible.

If you learn good form, you will lift in a safe way. Most women who come to weights learn through a trainer or a community. We are almost certainly more considered about safety because our identity isn't anchored to machoism or thinking we know best when we don't. We're not too proud to ask someone for help.

I spoke to Jack when these 'helpful' bits of advice came through and he was able to explain lifting, rest and recovery to me in a neutral, non-patronising way, and the two takeaways were that I had to allow myself enough time to recover and repair between sessions, but I also had to eat enough to fuel my workouts. One of the biggest causes of injuries, which stems from our 'no excuses' gym culture, is people over-training and not allowing their bodies enough time to rest.

The 'you'll injure yourself' comments were a bit annoying, but easily put to one side by speaking to people who knew what they were talking about. The most difficult to deal with, however, were comments around my physique. I get that they were well meaning but, at a time when I was figuring all of this stuff out, and it was so new and so wobbly, it almost stopped me from lifting. They were often only little things like, 'you're looking really strong, but don't get any bigger,' or 'men don't really like muscular women,' or 'wow, you look like a wrestler!' I get that it was an adjustment for people and all of us have been conditioned to think women should be small, and to think that is attractive. But it was unnecessarily hard to navigate at the time. The only reason I didn't quit was because of the self-belief powerlifting had given me. That, and a completely accidental meeting with the first professional female Asian powerlifter I had ever seen, which happened a week before my first gym competition.

I was in the area and popped into the gym to say hello to Jack. I then clocked a woman who had the most incredible legs I had ever seen. This was Neha Prasad-Ainsworth, who would go on to become one of my friends. Neha was training for her competition in a different federation called GPC and I didn't know it at the time, but she was the overall British female champion. I had never seen a physique like hers on a brown woman or seen anyone squat as much as she did – I think she was doing 160kg on the day I was in the gym. It made me think *oh my god she is amazing. Her legs alone deserve worship.* Something about seeing Neha made this more tangible.

The other important thing that changed something for me was the experience of being part of a team. Ever since his first powerlifting competition, Jack was amazed at the sense of community in the sport, and the feeling of goodwill and friendliness to other competitors – which was so different to his previous career as a pro fighter. He wanted to pass that on and was lit with the spark of creating a team to introduce more people to the sport. At the time, however, he couldn't get anyone else to commit to it apart from his training partner Lindsay. In part because it's not a well-known sport, but also because you can tell people it's fun and that the community is amazing, but it doesn't translate well on paper. You have to see it to believe it. When some of Jack's other clients saw Lindsay compete, and heard her confirm what Jack had been saying about competitions, it encouraged them to join and then it gained momentum. Around the same time that I signed up to my first official competition, Jack's team was finally coming together, and the name they gave it was Barfight.

The reason why I say Jack is the third man who changed my life is because none of my strength journey would have been possible without him. Unequivocally, this journey changed who I was on a fundamental level. He is the brother I always wanted – if my brother was white, muscled, with tattoos and a huge brain.

When Jack set up Barfight in January 2019, he invited me along to a training session and said they would get food afterwards. By this point, Jack and I were becoming friends. He knew about my story with Rob and what I was overcoming internally to powerlift. I think he knew that I could benefit from being around people, even if I didn't quite know it myself. But when he suggested coming to this session, I really didn't want to. I could not have thought of anything worse than working out with a bunch of complete strangers and then having to exchange small talk over dinner.

But there was something to be said for breaking the seal on my self-imposed isolation.

No one I knew lived remotely near me – even my best friend Mal was about 40 minutes away – and I had gotten used to being in my own little bubble, venturing out to see friends when it suited me. This way of living had helped me while I was grieving but, having just coming back from an incredibly fun holiday in Thailand with Mal where we went out loads, I felt ready to try new things. Maybe I was ready to let more people into my life.

So I went along hesitantly, even though most people in the gym were really friendly. My teammate and friend Lu was one of the first to come over and chat to me – we were a similar age and she'd just taken up powerlifting. Having my first official powerlifting competition coming up in March gave me something to talk about and ask for advice. I also met Lindsay for the first time, who is like a powerlifting whisperer meets Wednesday from the Addams Family. It's hard to describe what she does but she's someone who is a great mental coach and helps you overcome your doubts and talk you through your concerns around lifting. Jack and Lindsay said they would come with me on my competition day and I was so grateful. But I was baffled when some of the people from Barfight said they would come to support me too. I barely knew them – why would they do this?

We joke about it now, but I said Jack's attempts to get me to socialise was like rehousing a feral cat. He's also done this for a fair few other lost souls and that generosity of spirit is probably what made me first realise that he was a friend. One of the hardest parts, however, wasn't joining a team, but being vulnerable enough to ask for help. I realised I had a major problem around this because, again, I had built up such a huge wall around myself because of Rob's death. I never wanted to be in a position to ask for help – it was the whole reason I started training with Tyrone. But, it turned out, in a competition you have to if you want to do well. You need someone to take you to weigh-ins. In a competition you do three attempts of each lift, and after you finish your first attempt, say, of squat, you have to go straight to the head judge and tell them what your next attempt will be. In a competition, if you fail a lift, you can't lower the weight on it – you can only go up, so this part matters a lot, from selecting the right weight to remembering to put your attempt in. Being part of a team means someone can help you with that, and help you believe in yourself. You can try to do all of that alone but with a team, you are so much stronger.

I didn't like asking for help because I didn't want to be rejected. But when that rejection didn't come and instead people stepped up, it was such a critical part in changing what I thought I knew about relying on other people. It wasn't weakness, it was strength.

My ascension into feeling my strongest mentally and physically wasn't because Jack cheered me on or wrote me a good training programme. It's because at every single level, he understood that you need a supporting structure to hold onto, mentally and emotionally, to try weights and persevere, when you're then dealing with the rest of the world who is going to try and talk you out of it. He made me part of a team that represented a well of collective strength and I took that into every space I entered, no matter how intimidating.

One of the most common responses on my survey was that accountability around physical fitness or having a buddy to train with would help people to try or stick with physical fitness. Barfight provided that for me. They were the structure I needed to encourage me and help me grow when everything in my life was trying to scare me away from it.

The bottom line is that since starting powerlifting, I have come across overwhelming evidence of how strength sports better your life if you're a woman. For older women, it is like an extra life on a video game. It allows you to get stronger without injuring your body in a high impact way and it gives you power, presence and visibility in a world that wants to throw an invisibility cloak over you. For women recovering from trauma, it can be part of the healing process, whether that's ownership of your own body, or serenity in your mind. For girls and young women, it can give you a critical realisation that you are much stronger than you think you are. Above all, it is achievement that only you can build for yourself – meaning no one can take it away from you.

I asked the youngest team member in Barfight, Emily, who is 17, what powerlifting meant to her. Our nickname for her is 'Duckling', and I saw how hard she worked at training as well as juggling school work. She has had to deal with juvenile idiopathic arthritis since primary school, yet at her first competition got four British records.

'Long story short,' she said, 'powerlifting has made me feel like I could do anything. Especially when my younger years were filled with "you can't do this", "you can't do that" due to having arthritis. Nothing was simple, movement-wise. If you told me back then that I would now be able to pick up a 90kg deadlift, 67.5kg squat and a 35kg bench I would have thought you were mental. But powerlifting gave me the chance to show what I could do, mostly to myself.'

The good news is that communities have sprung up to encourage women who want to get strong, and that these are continually challenging the stereotypes of women's strength. CrossFit, strongwoman, powerlifting, olympic weightlifting – the number of women competing and just doing the classes for fun is growing. Though it isn't lost on me that you have to really seek out these communities and come to it already with a certain amount of 'fuck you' energy to the status quo.

Lifting weights is not the only way to get strong, or to feel strong either. Feeling strong is first and foremost a mindset and it's something that everyone has a right to because it is powerful, transformative stuff. And it's never too late.

CHAPTER SEVEN

No One Has the Monopoly on Strength

It's a general belief that men know more about strength just because their bodies produce more testosterone, enabling them to build muscle more easily. Some men do, some men don't. But these binary ideas of what each gender should or shouldn't do, what they have more claim to, isn't based on anything substantial and worse, it doesn't benefit anyone. It certainly doesn't benefit men, many of whom I have no doubt feel intimidated and weirded out by the expectation to have big arms and a six-pack. And as we have seen, it doesn't benefit women, who are conversely ridiculed or put off from gaining muscle. It doesn't benefit non-binary or trans people who are excluded from the conversation entirely and prevented from being physically active and accessing something that might make them feel mentally great. It doesn't create good, positive spaces for physical activity where people are included, made to feel accepted for who they are rather than excluded for who they aren't.

For me, overcoming my social conditioning and taking up strength training depended on several things:

1. Having a good, knowledgeable trainer with a gender neutral approach.
2. Having a safe space to get strong and train.
3. Being part of a community that over-rode the current narrative of women's strength.
4. Online communities and the women's strength movement.

What I had to overcome was a lifetime of:

1. Mansplaining in gyms.
2. Bad experiences and feeling self-conscious in gyms.
3. Belief that women with muscle looked like men.
4. Thinking that looking 'like a man' was bad.
5. Lacking role models.
6. Rigid, binary views on gender.

The good news is that when I started researching and looking for like-minded women, I found a growing movement of collectives, gyms and clothing brands that embodied this all-encompassing sense of women's strength. It was vital during a time when I felt very unsure and uncertain about things such as my body changing and getting bigger.

The bad news, however, was that it was evident – both from my survey and chatting to women online – that not only was there still a massive prejudice towards women with muscle (and we're talking about the vaguest sense of muscle, not even body-builder physiques) but also that there was something rotten at the core of fitness, particularly looking at how commercial gyms ran and operated, as well as attitudes among some personal trainers.

There are some amazing personal trainers out there but it

kept cropping up in my survey that, when it came to poor experiences with fitness, a significant portion of personal trainers were not factoring in things like the menstrual cycle and menopause, offering up unsolicited nutritional advice and eating plans or just being patronising and gendered in their approach to fitness – e.g. HIIT is for women, weights are for men.

(A big caveat here: I know not everyone can afford a trainer and while I advocate having one at the beginning stages of learning technique particularly around technical weightlifting moves, if you can't afford it, then that's OK. There are plenty of people who fill the gaps by learning what they can online and then connecting to a fitness/strength training community in real life so they can learn without paying for it, or if they can afford it, doing group PTs. There are also low-cost gyms such as the non-profit gym Projekt42 in Edinburgh, Easy Gym, PureGym, Xercise4Less, as well as local community groups based around strength training.)

If you've found fitness intimidating, had a terrible experience with a personal trainer, if you don't like gyms because they make you feel bad about yourself, if you feel unsafe in fitness spaces, if you feel like you have to constantly be alert that some dude is going to come up and mansplain to you, or hit on you, it's not something you dreamed up or imagined. This stuff is very real. This is mainstream fitness, and currently it does not value or promote women's strength as equal to men.

I sort of got into a disagreement with a prominent male Instagram fitness influencer who is known for his no nonsense style. I say 'sort of' because we didn't have this conversation directly with each other. I'll explain. I actually used to like this guy's content – he was one of the very few who'd focus on the differences in men and women's physiology and hormones and how women shouldn't feel bad about having different levels of progression than men.

So I sent his agent some questions I wanted him to answer for this book. I couldn't use the answers, but more worryingly was his dismissal of a question I'd posed about body expectations for women, and how they originate from the patriarchy. To paraphrase, he said that women subject ourselves to images we see on social media and we're responsible for the comparisons we draw. And that the pressure to look a certain way doesn't come from men, but from other women.

In other words, it's our fault.

Now I know the 'p' word (patriarchy) often makes men react as if they've smelled a fart but I was shocked, then dismayed, that someone with such huge reach and influence – also over women – just basically dismissed structural gender inequality, gender bias and basically blamed women for the fact that they may feel unhappy with themselves by comparing themselves to others. When I fed back to the agent that this was a problematic answer, the agent must have fed this back to the influencer, who didn't respond directly to me but instead published a post on Instagram – not naming me however – about how I had called him a misogynist (I didn't) and then defended what he said, saying it was based on his own personal experience.

Now, some things to say here. Which is, firstly, if something is based on your personal experience, you say it's based on your personal experience (which he didn't in his written response back to me). You don't just ignore historical and scientific evidence and then assert your own view as fact. This is something I've seen happen time and again on social media and the reason it's so dangerous is because the person saying it is leveraging their own expertise in a totally different area, to talk about something they aren't knowledgeable about, in this case, gender constructs.

The second thing is that there's an overwhelming sense of privilege here and a failure to look at the power imbalances within gender, within diet culture, and to *blame it on women who are the most marginalised* makes me wonder how anyone can be an advocate for women within fitness if they don't even get this basic fact.

When women police other women, or even when girls are mean to each other at school, people love to write this off as something that is just in our nature. The truth is that so much of this can be linked to the issue of scarcity – which is caused by the lack of opportunities and by beauty standards set by being in a patriarchal system.

Mérida Miller runs Project Fearless for girls aged 9–14 in Amsterdam, which uses a mixture of physical activity, practical tasks and community work to teach girls core life skills. She says tackling 'scarcity' in girlhood is the biggest part of their eight-week programme. 'The scarcity mindset is that there isn't enough water, food, money and success, and your actions stem from that fear. It gives a reason as to why women are stereo-typically mean or catty towards each other,' she says. 'It's self-protection, e.g. there's only room for one female leader at the top so I'll do what I can to get there. But we get the girls to question if that's in line with our moral values or who we want to be. There is space for all of us to be leaders, to be a teammate and support each other at the same time. There isn't just one leader and there isn't just one way to lead.'

I happened to be chatting to body positive advocate Megan Crabbe the next day and I told her about this exchange with the influencer. She said: 'The tendency to just point the finger at the people who are suffering the most in the hands of this power imbalance is a classic tactic. It's very clever because, from the outside, you might think it's about women putting down other women but we have internalised this the same way that we internalise all kinds of misogyny and we uphold this because we've been taught that this is the only way to exist.'

It also overlooks all the crap women receive from men when they attempt to build muscle. If I'm thinking about my own experience, while other women have made me feel self-conscious about my body fat, I've only ever been made to feel bad about my muscle by men.

Shortly after competing at the Euros in 2019 – my first ever international powerlifting competition, where I deadlifted 120kg and squatted 90kg – I was hanging out with some friends by a swimming pool. Although I was well into the empowerment aspect of powerlifting and proud that my body had done some amazing things, that old internal monologue came back when one of our male friends said to me completely unsolicited: 'You look great, but don't build any more muscle.' Why do men feel they have the right to comment on women's bodies in this way? Is it because they view muscle and physical strength as their domain? Is it because they are scared of physically strong women?

Kelechi Okafor told me a story that I think highlights this perfectly. A few years ago, she was really into her training, was super lean and thinking about entering a fitness competition. She was waiting for a package and when she met the delivery guy, she saw it was a West African guy. This is how she described the exchange:

'He goes: "I'm sorry to say this but I have to ask, you're so pretty – your face is like a woman but your body is like a man. I wouldn't let my wife be doing this thing that you're doing. So you know I just wanted to check – are you a man or a woman?"'

Kelechi said she was consumed with rage. 'If he had really

believed that I was a man he would not have asked that question, but it's because he knew I was not a man, but wanted to assert something about his preference and my desirability. I think that that is where the conflict is for a lot of women. Do you want to sacrifice desirability in a mainstream sense in order to achieve your goals?'

And that's what I felt I was battling for a while. I didn't want to lose desirability but I noticed how all the compliments I got were from women who admired my strength and never from men. I also saw how visibly uncomfortable men got when I went on a date and mentioned I did powerlifting.

'Ultimately,' said Kelechi, 'ask what is that desirability about, and it's about appeasing men. It's "don't worry I'm not on your turf, I won't be stronger than you". I find all of that so interesting. That is why they don't want women to be strong – because they're scared of them having power.'

I realised that trying to get the people in my life who did not do powerlifting to accept or understand it was a futile exercise. But to be fair to them, if someone had tried to explain all of this to me several years ago, I wouldn't have understood it either. It's not just about unravelling what you think you know about your own body, societal expectations and strength, it's also about having visible role models in mainstream media or movements pushing back against sexist ideals or calling out mansplaining in gyms.

One person who did this by turning her own experiences with weightlifting, social conditioning and sexism into a comedy show was Jessica Fostekew. Her relationship with fitness was moving her body mainly in ways she didn't enjoy, barring a bit of outdoor swimming, until around 2014, when a male bodybuilder friend introduced her to some weights and she loved it. But then she fell pregnant and she stopped doing exercise altogether – which is actually a fairly common thing according to the women who took my survey because there isn't a huge amount out there about how to re-engage with fitness in a joyous way after your body has been through a huge transformation like creating a baby. Most of it tends to be weight-loss related.

Two years ago, however, she got a trainer and started doing deadlifts, squats and chest press, moving to heavier weights. 'In terms of my body,' she said, 'it's taken years of rewiring but I love seeing the muscles grow. I don't calorie cut ever because that leads down a dark road to disordered eating for me. On the plus side, when people say to me things as a supposed compliment (rudely and ignorantly) like 'you don't look like you weightlift' I think 'well fuck off because I do weightlift' – and I WANT to look like I weightlift. I LOVE what it looks like when I flex my lovely massive guns in the mirror and what the muscles look like on my back and shoulders. It's the sexiest I've ever felt about my body. I wish more women were able to reframe their self-perception on that front.'

A superb account I came across on Instagram was You Look Like a Man, which has a huge following and takes sexist things men have said about women and puts them in cutesy affirmations. It's hilarious but also depressing, when you realise that these are things said to actual human beings. It was started by Jessica Fithen who is based in Indiana in the United States, who had struggled with body image for most of her life. 'I never fit what I believed society told me a woman was supposed to look like,' she told me. As an army veteran, she had always been active and did running, Zumba and spinning, but she fell in love with strongman, which, she says, was the first time she was told not to be smaller.

Strongman is a type of functional strength training where

the goal is to be as strong as possible and uses a lot of compound movements. A compound movement is an exercise that involves several different muscle groups at the same time, such as a deadlift or a squat. I've done a few classes and loved it – you do things like pull sleds, whack tyres with hammers and carry Atlas balls. CrossFit incorporates more high intensity training but can include elements of Olympic weightlifting, gymnastics and other types of strength that overlap with strongman. While CrossFit is not quite my thing (too much cardio), it has been a huge gateway to strength for many women above and beyond any other type of training and in the arena, there is no distinction between male and female strength. You're just strong and that's it. The female athletes, particularly people such as Annie Thorisdottir who was the first woman to win the gruelling CrossFit games two years in a row, are insanely good.

Through strongman, Jessica connected with a great community of women but after posting her first video of her doing an Atlas stone load, she started to get trolled. 'A stranger commented, "You look like a transgendered creature." All because my arms dared to show any visible muscle mass – and I was doing a "male" activity. The misogyny and transphobia became more and more evident the further I progressed into my career, almost always by strangers, and almost always by men.'

The more she talked to other women who took part in strength sports, the more she found that it was common and expected that women received comments like this. 'One day I took a comment I had received, "You look like a man," and wrote it on a picturesque background like a corny motivational quote, and shared it on Facebook, as a way to make fun of their absurdity. The floodgates opened, and women from all over the world began sharing my post and adding their own comments they had received.

"Go home and raise a family."

"No real man will ever want you."

"I want a woman, not someone to wrestle."

"You powerlift because you have nothing else."

"Do you really want to look that way in a wedding dress?"

"Stay in the kitchen.'"

Jessica isn't saying that men don't receive comments or criticism on their videos but that these tend to be about form. A woman, however, can receive a range of comments around her appearance, her femininity and suspected drug use, told she might become infertile and asked if she's growing a penis.

To echo Kelechi's experience, Jessica says that women don't seek validation from men, but men feel they need to make it known that her body doesn't fit their view of what they find sexually appetising. Also, she says, 'Never underestimate the power of pure old-fashioned jealousy. Strength sports are seen as something only men can be good at or should participate in. Instead of simply being impressed that she has worked so hard to achieve such a monumental number, he spends his time cutting her down, and "putting her back in her place" in an effort to re-establish his perceived need to be dominant over her.'

While I don't engage with trolls online, I will challenge people in front of me to get them to confront their own thinking. For instance, when men say things like 'you're strong for a woman', in the past I would have said thank you. But I've realised I don't want to thank them because the subtext of what they are saying is: 'you're strong for a woman and women are usually weak.' Now what I say is: 'I'm strong, full stop.' And more often than not, they usually apologise because they hadn't realised that what they thought was a compliment is actually backhanded.

An incredible role model in this space is the US bodybuilder and BJJ champion Kortney Olson, who is the founder of a revolutionary fitness brand, Grrrl. Instead of standard numbered sizing, Grrrl uses the template of different women for clothing (so you might be an Ali or a Heather). The brand is super inclusive and the strong, bold messaging is centred around women being free to be whatever they want.

Kortney is the embodiment of that. 'I believe strength and muscle have given me the ability to be on a man's level without feeling intimidated. Along with martial arts,' she told me. 'Our beliefs control everything. This societal belief that women are the weaker sex is a crock. Once we can collectively realise that it's a scam and that we are strong AF, not just physically but also mentally, this is how we change the game.'

CHAPTER EIGHT

Gyms, R U OK, Hun?

It's a running joke that Jack's gym is like the alternative dimension in a sci-fi film. You know the kind – where you go through a wormhole and you think only ten minutes has passed but then you emerge back into the outside world and everyone you love is now 90 years old or dead. OK, not exactly, but the point is it's a place we spend hours in without realising how much time has passed. But that's not always how I felt about gyms. Previously, they were places where I felt as if all my failings were magnified.

In my survey, over 40 per cent of women said the environment of gyms made them want to get in and out as quickly as possible. Thirty-six per cent said it was a place where they compared themselves negatively but I'd venture to say many of us have felt like that at some point in a gym, and not just women.

There are several points to make about that. Comparing yourself to someone else can happen anywhere – in the supermarket, waiting for a bus and so on. But the reason it's an issue in gyms is because the messaging we're surrounded by is already making us feel inadequate. 'The majority of insecurities women experience in the gym are around their appearance, from sweating to having a red face and yet this is never shown in commercials,' wrote Polly, who took the survey. 'It's usually people working out with their blow-dried hair and a face full of makeup and then we wonder why women feel insecure in comparison.'

I always feel like the images and posters you see around gyms are outdated, from the problematic messaging around 'summer bodies' to losing weight in January post-Christmas; cosmetic surgery ads to only ever using slim fitness models. Everything is signposting you to what you are not rather than celebrating what you are.

'Being in a space that doesn't feel inclusive, and is male-orientated, features only small women, and offers no help,' were some of the reasons why Erika, who took the survey, felt that gyms were problematic. 'There is no diversity in the sizes of instructors for personal training/classes so you feel they don't understand your issues. There is a lack of mental health aware-ness and the constant social media (from my gym at least) of "look at Katrina killing it" and Katrina happens to be a 20-year-old blonde, slim girl with no back rolls. This doesn't reflect what is meant to be a social gym for the community.'

This is such a huge missed opportunity because part of the fun of working out is socialising and being part of a community. CrossFit is teased mercilessly for being a cult (because everyone who does it basically talks about it a lot) but it is a sport that is responsible for encouraging a lot of women into trying out and sticking with strength training *because* it has a strong community and socialising aspect to it. By contrast, in my experience, there is a lack of community associated with main-stream and commercial gyms. (CrossFit doesn't have this issue partly because, like powerlifting, it usually takes place in special venues geared to it as a sport.) Mainstream gyms are part of the fitness establishment and, unfortunately, the fitness establishment is still overwhelmingly banging the weight-loss drum. Rather than pivoting their services as a place for people to have fun with fitness, they remain a place where you end up feeling bad about yourself, and intimidated by other people. We then internalise the fact that we don't like gyms as if it's some personal failure, without considering that they just aren't set up very well to be inclusive or enjoyable.

Several women who took the survey said that they felt unwelcome and self-conscious at gyms because of their size. Michaela wrote: 'As a woman of size, gyms can be a terrifying place. When I have previously gone to gyms and classes I have experienced across the board negative comments and barely-disguised disgust. It was the reason I was so attracted to the PT option, but it is so expensive.'

It's something I hear over and over again. And it's important to be aware of the underlying issues because there is a narrative around plus-size people being too lazy to stick to fitness. No one is properly considering whether the environment staff and members create has anything to do with it. Yvonne wrote in her survey answer: 'At a lot of gyms and fitness centres, it's very apparent that too often the staff have an issue with and are very judgemental about fat people which is an immediate discouragement. I've also had experience of other gym users openly mocking/shaming fat people. This seems to be a very common experience. I would be far more encouraged and comfortable attending places that have a more inclusive, less judgemental environment.'

Like practically every other aspect of fitness, most gyms are too scared to deviate from the 'slim is fit' narrative for fear it may 'encourage' people who are overweight. But it strikes me that, unlike the diet industry who have literally millions of pounds to lose if everyone woke up and realised that it is crock of shit – gyms could actually make so much more money if they were more inclusive. For a start, they'd have more clients. It would also create a long-term approach to being fit and healthy, rather than the classic January rush at gyms that inevitably tapers off in February because people lose the enthusiasm to remain in a place that makes them feel terrible.

'Health is not an appearance,' says Michelle Elman, 'and it looks different on everybody but when we only include people who look a certain way, we unintentionally create a body standard where personal trainers are judged on what they look like and not their qualifications. Their body becomes their qualification because we have not shown that you can't tell someone's fitness by looking at them. When you don't feel represented in the fitness ads, you don't believe you are welcome in those spaces so in order to change this we need inclusivity.'

Becky Scott, for instance, actually became a plus-size fitness instructor because she was fed up of going to classes and people assuming she was just there for weight loss. She wanted to create a space for people like herself who wanted to move and feel good and were fed up with diet culture. 'It is absolutely essential that bigger bodies become more visible in all spaces including fitness spaces to challenge perceptions of fat,' she told me. 'My clients often tell me that the thing that got them through the door was knowing I was fat. It removes the fear of judgement and makes them feel less self-conscious or worried about getting sweaty or wearing the right clothes.'

In the same way that women may choose a female PT because of perceived commonalities, it's important to have plus-size PTs because slim PTs may not know what it is like to deal with fatphobia, or understand what the mental blockers might be. And Becky finds that it isn't just women in bigger bodies who gravitate towards her classes, it can be anyone who feels overwhelmed in fitness spaces or is fed up with diet culture. A common thing she hears is that people feel there is no 'pressure to perform' or push themselves beyond what is comfortable for them, so they can actually enjoy it.

Even though I am not someone who feels intimidated in the fitness space anymore, I almost always feel a spark of joy and ease when I see that my instructor isn't slim. I want to see as many different body types enjoying fitness because it feels more like a natural part of my world versus a weird bubble.

Feeling intimidated in a gym isn't exclusive to women, in fact one of the big surprises of my life was finding out that men feel the same in the gym too. I was having dinner with Niaz and Kumaran, talking to them about the exclusionary culture of fitness and they said: 'You know that almost every guy feels like that too, right?'

'What, intimidated in the gym?'

'Yeah,' they both replied, in unison.

I knew that Rob felt like that; it came out when we had an argument once about why he never used his gym membership and it blew my mind. But I'd known Niaz to be this muscle dude at university and loads of guys gave him respect for it, so it was really surprising that he felt like that in the gym at times. But I would still say it's more acute for women because it's not as socially acceptable for us to be visibly sweating or gain muscle as it is for men. Women are also less physically active than men and so when we look at factors that may be putting people off from exercising, there is an added component of gender. For instance, according to a *Runners World* poll in 2017, 40 per cent of women have been harassed while running outdoors (and it's even higher at 58 per cent if you're under 30)[1] while men don't get catcalled on a run.

Dr Stephanie Coen, who is an assistant professor at Nottingham University, ran a study which looked at just *how* gendered spaces were in gyms. She said that women were put off from going to certain spaces in gyms seen as overtly masculine, while some men avoided equipment that was perceived as feminine – so both genders stuck to particular areas.[2] When I asked her about it, Dr Coen told me that the gym perpetuates very narrow and rigid versions of masculinity and femininity. 'Tackling the problem of women feeling under scrutiny therefore requires us to go beyond thinking about only women or this issue as just a women's problem, but actually to think about how we can reconfigure these unhelpful gender relations,' she said. 'How can we foster more flexible and open formulations of masculinities and femininities in the gym that don't box people into feeling constrained to certain activities and spaces?'

For me, it's glaringly obvious, looking at the imagery – for instance muscly men standing next to slim and 'toned' women – which prop up the stereotype that men MUST have muscles and women MUST be slim (which damages both sides, I feel). But it's also about asking who actually benefits from spaces being so gendered – I'm hard pushed to see how it is good for anyone. If we are being so rigid about gender roles, we are also completely ignoring and writing off people who, for instance, identify as non-binary, as well as cisgender, trans or other people who aren't comfortable with being hyper feminine or hyper masculine.

A brilliant non-binary influencer, editor and model I follow on Instagram is Jamie Windust, who describes themselves as a gender non-confirming person (GNC). Jamie's Instagram feed is a beautiful collection of makeup-related posts and an insight into their life, but one stuck out in particular: a video of Jamie punching a boxing bag while wearing glossy red lipstick. The caption was about how Jamie realised working out was also about mental health, not just the body, and that people had scoffed at them even being in this space.

'When I was younger,' Jamie said, 'I would enjoy physical activity such as dancing but this wasn't necessarily approved by my peers as it was deemed as a "feminine" activity. It became harder during school as gender-segregated spaces meant that I felt uncomfortable as a queer person aged 13/14. It meant that although I enjoyed the physical activity that we would do in school, e.g. hockey, football, I never was able to enjoy it fully due to the gender-segregated space, and the intense homophobia from the people I was with.'

Jamie felt uncomfortable in gyms because they are such gendered spaces but then came across a gender neutral space in which to get changed and work out, and it changed everything. 'It's completely transformed my relationship with exercise. Actively pursuing it for mental health reasons was empowering as I am not focused on the changes in my body but more the release in my mind. It allows me to expel anger, frustration and sadness from my day that I would have previously dealt with in other, less helpful ways.'

Jamie's advice for other people in a similar situation is to remain composed and calm. 'Know that you are never doing anything wrong by being in the space you have a right to be in. Trans women pose no threat in female changing rooms, and non-binary people don't either. We are just trying to get on with our lives and head to the gym. It's always great if you don't feel comfortable using gendered spaces, to ask if the facility has gender neutral spaces, or a mixed changing area.'

I asked Farrah Herbert, who identifies as a trans woman

and posts about fitness on Instagram and featured in the This Girl Can 2020 campaign, about how she feels in the fitness world. A 47-year-old, full-time lorry driver, she was always active, and got into triathlons through trying open-water swimming, cycling and running. At the start of her transition, she found it hard because she tried writing to her triathlon club about the changing room situation and was ignored. 'Swimming was such a big part of life,' she said, 'and something I really enjoyed but I could not face presenting as male in order to access these facilities and I was so scared of situations in changing rooms if I went to the pool as myself. Swimming costumes are pretty unforgiving at hiding any unsightly bulges for pre-op trans women, so I just gave it up.'

After she had surgery, Farrah was still scared of facing abuse in changing rooms or being called out in women's yoga classes. But, as she has grown more confident, she says that confidence is like a muscle, and for it to become stronger, you have to use it more. The example she gives is around climbing, something she started doing just before her transition. She enjoyed the exercise but also the mental workout required when navigating footholds and overcoming the fear of falling. While she lost some of her strength after her transition because of the switch from testosterone to oestrogen, she kept going and found a trans woman to partner with. She was worried about being stared at during busy times at the climbing centre but she persevered with it and said it became easier.

'Rock climbing is about you challenging and pushing yourself,' she says, 'so it makes you stop thinking about competing and getting approval from others. It pushes you and makes you want to achieve more and that's a skill that's useful not only on the climbing wall, but in every aspect of your life.'

Gender is a tricky area not just in gyms but in fitness as a whole because it is often a place where the idea of gender is so stark and rigid. For instance, despite being a cisgender, heterosexual woman, I'm not comfortable in women's only gyms because something about the energy in them makes me personally feel strange, perhaps because it reminds me of being back in school, but also I don't think it helps or prepares me for when I then have to go into a mixed gender space. I can't control how someone else might behave but I can control *me*, and me refuses to be intimidated or cowed in a space that I have the right to be in. As Farrah says, confidence is a muscle that needs exercise too. My mantra is: *I have ownership of this space.* That ethos has flowed through the rest of my life by osmosis. Now, it could be an airport lounge, a supermarket or a bar, and maybe I'm the only woman there. But I don't feel intimidated. My head is high, my shoulders back and *I have ownership of this space.*

However, I do appreciate that some people will not work out in a mixed gender space and some of us may be recovering from particular types of trauma, especially sexual trauma, that may make being around men difficult. In London, there are increasingly LGBTQ+ friendly spaces and gyms but it is not evenly spread across the country. However, in Birmingham, Sport England funded a project called Activate designed to encourage the LGBTQ+ community into physical fitness and in Edinburgh, Projekt 42 funded free classes for trans people. Pride Sports, an organisation that works to challenge prejudice and make sport more accessible for the LGBTQ+ community, runs a UK sports club finder on their website and promotes networking and community events.

In London, there are a ton of community groups, such as Knockout Boxing, a non-profit friendly boxing club, as well as specific, permanent spaces such as Grl Gym, which is a 'safe space for queer, trans, POC, QTPOC, non-binary, genderqueer, big bodied, thin bodied, differently-abled, the shy, lonely, recovering and all allies (men included).'

I also came across The Underdog Gym in Walthamstow and fell in love with their motto, which is a 'boutique gym with empathy.' I spoke to Fabien Strawbridge who owns the gym. He is in his mid forties, and is British, Chinese and French. Fabien has had his own health issues – he has a triple fused spine with a titanium rod and metal scaffolding due to degenerative disc disorder which started as a teenager and he's had to navigate a tough road between addiction to painkillers, movement restriction and his own mental health. He understands that everyone starts at a different level of fitness and doesn't shame people for it.

Fabien worked for over 20 years in luxury retail but one summer, he took some dumbbells and kettlebells on a holiday with friends and when he started working out by the pool, he did little impromptu training sessions with them. He loved it so much, he got his PT qualification and quit his job.

'The Underdog Gym's ethos formed after a period of time when I was going to a particular testosterone-fuelled gym in the City that was near my work,' he said. 'I signed up for an intensive fitness programme. By week four, I was the only one coming back. The PT said he had underestimated me and thought I wouldn't last the course. I'm guessing this had *nothing* to do with me being the skinniest and the only gay one there. More importantly, it made me evaluate that if a fitness programme is so tough and people are consistently dropping out, what is there to be gained here, apart from the PT proving he's the top dog?

'I looked around the gym floor and realised that everyone was trying to be someone else in order to "fit in" with a specific "tribe". This made me think about how I wanted to celebrate those who felt invisible, the underdog, the ones we underestimate and take joy from when they come out winning. My approach is to celebrate what our individual bodies *can* do, as opposed to what we expect our body *should* be able to do.'

Underdog is sustainable – it uses solar power – and it's affordable, with prices starting from £22.50 for shared PT sessions. It also goes without saying that it is super inclusive.

'No one owns the oxygen in the weight training area,' says Fabien, 'and we celebrate people of colour, women, plus-sizes, LGB, trans, non-binary and many clients who just don't relate to the fitness industry's dominant social construct. I was also pleasantly surprised by how many cis male clients I have who also reject the toxic hyper-bro culture in commercial gyms.'

Commercial gyms have a long, long way to go, and there is a lot that needs to change about the very culture itself. I'm still haunted by a story a woman told me about when she was being shown around for her induction. The male PT breezed past the weights section and said: 'Oh, you won't be interested in that!'

Then of course, there is mansplaining, which is something that can happen anywhere, but, as Dr Coen says, the specific problem with mansplaining in the gym is that it 'naturalises men as the more legitimate users of the space'. In other words, it is a force that works to shrink women's use of space in the gym. 'For example, some women avoid certain spaces or activities precisely to avoid potential scrutiny and unsolicited "help" from men,' she says.

In the survey, mansplaining was shown to be a real blocker for women. Writing in the comments box, Sinead said: 'Almost every time I go to the gym I get mansplained by PTs and non-PTs, men trying to have conversations, when I just want to be left alone to lift weights like the men are. That level of hyper-vigilance takes up so much mental energy.' The male gaze in general was a turn-off. 'No matter how old and fat I get,' Naomi wrote in the survey, 'there are still guys who will stare. It's gross and off-putting when I just want to get on with my workout. It's tiring and annoying to always have to maintain a level of vigilance, for instance bending over to pick up a weight and wondering if someone is watching from behind. It hasn't stopped me working out but it has ruined my workout on occasion.'

Although I step into a gym to get physically strong, I have found that drawing on my inner strength is absolutely necessary to navigate those spaces, whether that's blasting my music really loudly on my headphones to hype myself up, or not letting myself be worried about whether someone is staring. Dr Coen thinks it's tricky to change this culture we have in gyms, but it's not impossible. 'I think some of the gendered dynamics that are so embedded in the gym are actually hard for people to see – they are so taken for granted as just part and parcel of how we understand the gym,' she says. 'But the reality is that these are systemic issues, and so changing them really has to be a multi-layered approach – from how gym staff are trained, to who is in positions of leadership in fitness, to how we talk about physical activity more widely.'

Much in the same way that P.E. in school is such a missed opportunity for creating good associations with physical fitness, so are gyms. The potential for creating positive experiences is huge. 'Fitness advertising in gyms is mainly towards people who want a "holiday body",' wrote Yuki in the survey, 'and I feel it could be aimed more towards people who use fitness to help their mental health, those who are recovering from injury or surgery – basically people who use fitness for different reasons, not just for weight loss.'

Language is also important, and a lot of what we hear in fitness classes or read on posters doesn't take into account people recovering from illness, people with visible and hidden disabilities, or people recovering from eating disorders. People with ED, for instance, have to contend with listening to vocabulary used over and over again that makes recovery hard, such as fitness professionals telling people they need to track their calories to lose weight. For people recovering from ED, tracking calories may have been actually a part of their illness.

'I am in recovery from an ED,' wrote Ash in the survey, 'and I used to compulsively exercise to the detriment of my health yet get nothing but praise for being so disciplined and "healthy". Being in recovery at the gym is hard. Instructors praising us for burning calories shouldn't be happening in 2020 but it's rife.'

Hope Virgo is an activist and campaigner around eating disorders, and her illness, which was anorexia nervosa, was initially triggered by sexual abuse. 'We live in a society,' she says, 'where disordered eating is normalised, where people are constantly being told to work out more, where people are often made to feel guilty for not going to the gym. Instead we need to be educating the whole of society on healthy living. Gyms need to be equipped to support those with eating disorders, making sure they are getting the support they need, being able to approach people they have concerns about and not pushing people into unhealthy ways of exercising. Too often fitness instructors still talk about exercising to earn food.'

Many PTs, I would venture to say, do not know how to train someone with a previous history of ED. Given that over-exercise and calorie restriction can be such prominent aspects of having an eating disorder, and how these two things both overlap heavily with fitness, I'm stumped as to why knowing about it isn't something that is made a mandatory part of either training to become a PT or running a gym.

'I have really struggled to find a PT who understands my relationship with exercise,' wrote Alex in the survey. 'In commercial gyms, the language around exercise classes still feels incredibly short-sighted – things like "let's work off all the sins of the weekend, etc" which for anyone with an ED past, is mega inflammatory. I have several friends who have complicated relationships with eating and exercise, who have completely stopped exercising because they cannot find a place that doesn't exacerbate their behaviours – which in big metropolitan cities and in a space with so much innovation, feels like madness. To provide safe spaces for those with ED pasts, the fitness industry needs to employ a diverse range of instructors and role models who don't necessarily fit the "fit/skinny" stereotypes and address language around exercising and why we do it.'

The statistics around how many girls and women suffer with and are in recovery from eating disorders are tricky, because it's currently based on people who are in treatment. And as Dump the Scales, Hope's campaign to change the guidelines around how people with ED access treatment, highlights, not everyone is treated because of the view that you need to be below a certain weight to have an eating disorder.

Men and boys also suffer from eating disorders but the numbers are still much higher in girls and women, and that increases across certain minorities, for instance South Asian women are most at risk. BEAT, the eating disorder charity, estimates 1.25 million people in the UK have one and 25 per cent of those are male.[3] Trans people have the highest rate of any group, according to a survey of 300,000 US college students published in the *Journal of Adolescent Health*,[4] which is thought to be brought on by the stress of transition and also the pressure of conforming to a specific gendered ideal. So eating disorders affect a significant portion of the population in some way, yet there is almost zero visibility or awareness of it in mainstream fitness. Another area in which this becomes problematic is the practice of PTs, gyms or fitness brands straying into the nutritional lane, when they don't have the right or knowledge to do so. A massive bugbear of mine, for instance, is when PTs offer up nutritional plans when they aren't trained around ED and aren't registered nutritionists – I've heard from several people how these restrictive plans have damaged their relationship with food.

When I asked in my survey about gyms, the other area that was brought to my attention was disability – whether visible or hidden – and how gyms either didn't cater to people with disabilities or didn't know what to do when someone asked for help.

Shannon Murray, who is an actress and disability rights activist, shared her story with me around her experience. When she was 14, Shannon broke her neck while diving into the sea while on holiday. She injured her spinal cord and was paralysed from the chest down. Until that point, she'd been pretty sporty – she'd been on the netball and swimming team, had weekly dance classes and occasionally went horse-riding with cousins. She grew up on a council estate and would spend a lot of time outdoors, running around and riding her bike.

After her accident, she had to relearn everything and, because her paralysis starts from her chest, balance was a big issue. I cannot imagine the strength of will, the resilience and Shannon's determination, but she got control over her body and started participating in adapted sports. At the hospital where she stayed for 10 months, she loved the rough and tumble of wheelchair rugby, did fencing and took part in the Inter Spinal Unit games, winning in the swimming.

'The problem was when I returned home and there were no accessible facilities for me to use. I wanted to feel equal in the gym but instructors didn't know what to do with me. I couldn't use the machines, so they just gave me dumbbells and really boring repetitive exercises. About seven years later, an accessible gym was built out in Stanmore which did have specialist equipment, but it was still an hour's drive away and it wasn't practical when I worked full-time. I also have to admit I'm not a fan of gyms. As soon as I go in, I feel like I'm being judged; that bro culture does my head in. Also, people tend to stare a lot at the gym and that's off-putting. I understand that people are curious to see how I'm going to adapt certain things to suit me but it makes me self-conscious and tense and consequently more likely to injure myself.'

This experience with gyms created a disconnect for Shannon and acted as a blocker for her around physical activity and feeling strong – something that was such an enormous part of her life before the accident. It wasn't until she reconnected with a friend who owned a spin studio two years ago that she had a revelation about exercise.

'She gave me a personal training session. It was incredible and made me realise I was someone who exercised; I had just been in denial for a really long time. It was like I had an epiphany. I enjoy physical exercise but for years I'd been denying that part of me because the existing environment makes it so hard for me to do. That made me really sad and a little angry. I have always said my disability doesn't stop me doing the things I want to do but I looked back and realised that in order to make peace with the lack of accessible routes to exercise, I have seriously suppressed an enormous part of who I am for nearly

30 years. If I'm brutally honest with myself, it has led to a degree of resentment.'

Several other women reached out to me through the survey to talk about their own experiences with disability and accessing fitness training. Adina said: 'When I've tried to participate and ask instructors for adaptations, I've felt ignored, and if I've tried to just sit out the bits I can't do, I've felt like I'm wasting people's time because my disability is not immediately visible. I find this incredibly frustrating and it exacerbates the resentment I have of my own body letting me down. I've given up because of this.'

Autism too is hugely overlooked by gyms, wrote Toni in the survey. 'I don't think there is a lot of recognition around autism and related conditions that can affect co-ordination, ability to follow instructions and sensory issues. Gyms and leisure centres are so loud, bright and busy and class sizes are sometimes huge so people can't get individual attention if they're struggling, which could lead to injury. But equally, they might not want the terrifying one-to-one interaction of a personal trainer. I can imagine gyms feel really inaccessible for a lot of people.'

And yet, being able to access a gym or fitness space and be physical, helps enormously. 'I did yoga before I lost my ability to walk,' writes Hollie-Anne, 'and when I discovered wheelchair yoga, it felt like reconnecting with part of my old life.'

The following account from Valerie summed up how fitness could be such a good source for generating personal power and therefore how important it is to also make gyms financially accessible for people. 'I have a chronic pain condition called fibromyalgia,' she wrote, 'which meant by the time I was 21, I used a walking stick and was on an assortment of painkillers. A few years in, I found out that I could get free gym access in my council gyms because I was disabled. I joined the gym and began to very slowly try to build up my strength. It was gradual but it began to work and I began to feel the mental benefits of it. Feeling physically stronger was huge and helped a lot. Exercise is so important for my mental health and helps me manage a chronic anxiety condition. I want to continue to get stronger and fitter. But it wouldn't have happened the way it did if I hadn't been able to access that gym for free at the very beginning.'

Several people suggested having PTs who were 'disability aware' would help, or at least being open to finding out more if they don't know. A good PT can literally change someone's life. 'I was incredibly fearful that I wouldn't be listened to,' wrote Sonya, 'when I said I couldn't do something. I'm all for breaking through limitations and positive thinking but I have real concerns to address too. I've since worked with two brilliant PTs, one male and one female. I very clearly set out my boundaries with them and we've worked well together. I started off lifting 4kgs and a year later I now lift 25kgs. But to get to that point I needed to feel safe, and that was achieved with PTs listening to me. Not screaming at me for being a loser.'

While there are some incredible organisations that cater specifically to the disability community, a lot of members of the community just want to be able to go to their local gym, have a good experience and feel every bit as empowered and strong as the next person. Shannon says emphatically that it doesn't have to be about separate classes if trainers could just think about adaptability.

Time and again, we've heard about how members of the disability community struggle with the line of thinking from non-disabled people around Paralympians, which is that if they can do it, anybody with a disability can. In the same way that you wouldn't just assume every non-disabled person wants to compete in the Olympics, why put that expectation on someone with a disability? As Shannon says: 'It's like we have two options: slow and gentle or competing for the Games. Please can we have a middle ground like everyone else?'

Boutique gyms exist because of the need for a more personalised experience, while commercial gyms exist because they can expand and multiply, making them more accessible in terms of location and cost. Both are necessary but what is clear is that the culture within mainstream fitness, and gyms in particular, is not working for the very population it is supposed to help or inspire. I understand that the staff at mainstream gyms (which focus on being affordable) may not have loads of time to spend with clients. But a lot of these gyms' shortcomings are actually things that can be fixed at a relatively low cost – such as the type of culture they foster, how PTs are trained, which PTs they hire and even the posters on the walls.

Although, in my survey, gyms were not remotely at the top of the list of favoured places to work out, one thing that emerged during the coronavirus pandemic was how important they were to people's lives in terms of maintaining their mental wellbeing. In other words, a gym is not just a place for the body, but also the mind. There are a lot of studies that prove the link between exercise and good mental wellbeing, and the most recent by *Nature* showed that resistance training helped to lower symptoms of anxiety and worry.[5] While it isn't a replacement for mental health treatment, if gym culture could change to become more inclusive, fun and less intimidating, imagine the possibilities it could open up in terms of helping even more people access it to improve their mental wellbeing. When you think about it that way, how gyms shape that fitness experience for people does matter. It matters a lot.

CHAPTER NINE

An Ode to Bodies, in Sickness and in Health

In my lifetime so far, I have lost my physical strength completely, twice. I'm not talking about a gradual degeneration, I'm talking about overnight depletion, as if someone turned off a light switch. One minute I was living my best life and the next, I had the strength of a rag doll.

The first time it happened was in 2012. I was 31 and was squeaking away on a cross-trainer in the gym after work. But, try as I might, I couldn't quite catch my breath. When it happened the next day and the day after that, my dad insisted I go to A&E.

I genuinely thought I would go in, the doctors would be irritated that I'd wasted their time, and I'd be on my way home within an hour. So it was to my utter shock that, after several tests, and several hours, they told me I had a hole in the heart, that I'd had it since birth and that it was an inch across. My heart had managed as best it could but had reached the point where it could no longer function properly. The fix was simple enough: block the hole with a metal device done with keyhole surgery.

Until that point, I'd never been in hospital, and the most

I'd ever been ill with was the flu. It seemed inconceivable. I had played tennis as a child. Sure, I wasn't exactly Martina Navratilova but I'd been OK at it. I ran around with my little neighbourhood pals. As an adult I went to the gym, I'd even done a walking holiday in the Himalayas, and kayaked on the sea.

I was asked to stay the night in hospital for observation. I remember the light drawing back through the windows as night fell and, in the soft darkness, hearing the sound of other people's bodies dying and healing. I was one of the youngest people on the cardiac ward and I lay there, feeling my mortality for the first time.

Apart from the fleeting moments of injury and illness, a cut finger, a bruised knee, the rattling cough of a viral infection, I'd never really thought about how my body functioned, because until that point, it just . . . had. But here it was. Slowed, hurting. Unable to go on as it always had. Saying: *I've taken us this far, but I can't do this anymore.*

In the two months that I waited for keyhole surgery, my body became symptomatic. It couldn't go backwards, or forwards. It was stuck at one point until it could be fixed. I couldn't run or do anything in the gym beyond walking. Energy had to be conserved and saved. If I overdid it, my heart would let me know with palpitations or filling my body with the sensation of ice.

It was fucking awful but it was also the most consistent and honest dialogue I had ever had with my body. The gym felt like a prison, a reminder of everything my body couldn't do. So I changed how I moved it. I started swimming for the first time. Slow, languorous breaststroke up and down the pool.

When I first started, I worried that people would wonder why I was going so slow and letting the septuagenarians overtake me. Then I realised. All the times I'd silently judged someone else for their progress, I'd had no idea what they might be going through, whether their body was OK. As my head dipped in and out of the water, and I felt that calm, regular, reassuring sound of my breath flow through me, I realised what a privilege it was to move, how much my body had done so far. But also, I realised worrying about what other people thought in the gym was irrelevant.

It is true for fitness as it is for anything else in life. Only one person has full access to your thoughts, your capabilities, your hopes, your dreams, what you want to achieve – and that is you. Why then do we allow the looks and comments of others to shape or form the journey we want for ourselves? What right do they have, when they do not, and will never know, the full size, shape and potential of our bodies and minds?

Just before my surgery took place, moments before I was wheeled into that bright, shiny operating theatre with dazzling lights and efficiency, the doctor told me that my body would be able to do so much more than it could before. I didn't believe him. Until, around four weeks after recovering, when I started to move my body again. The first time I went for a run after the surgery, which was about two months later, I felt it. It was as if an extra cylinder of fuel had been added and I felt my body surge with a power and capability I hadn't realised was missing before.

I will NEVER take you for granted ever again, I said to it, *nor will I judge anyone else for going at their own pace.*

The second time my strength failed me was during the coronavirus pandemic. I wasn't overly concerned about contracting the virus because, like many people before things escalated, I just assumed it would go away. The week before the UK went into lockdown in March, I went along to an unofficial squat competition that Jack and Lindsay had organised at the gym.

The idea of the competition was to try and 'max out', which is to play around with the amount of weight you could squat. I had squatted 102.5kg three months earlier and expected to maybe hit around 100kg. But Jack had other ideas and he somehow managed to get me to squat 110kg. My brain was in absolute shock that I had done it and not pooped my intestines out.

Given that the year before, I had done 90kg at my first powerlifting competition, a 20kg increase was unexpected and was utterly surreal.

But the next day, I felt like I was coming down with something. I didn't have any of what were then regarded as the symptoms of coronavirus but I felt completely drained of energy and I lost my sense of taste and smell for ten days. I recovered after two weeks and I had two weeks of getting back into exercise. I even bought a small amount of weightlifting equipment in case gyms weren't going to open up soon.

But two weeks into what I thought was recovery, it was again as if my body had been hit by a sledgehammer. My chest felt like someone was pressing down on it and it was hard to take full breaths. It wasn't serious enough that it required hospitalisation but I knew then that this was most probably Covid-19. I had never experienced anything like it before – just an energy-sapping state where if I exerted myself even slightly, I'd feel out of breath.

While the world carried on with home workouts and people Instagrammed their newfound love of walking, I could barely walk for more than ten minutes. As I felt my strength drain away and the weeks turned into months, I felt that I had lost a fundamental part of my physicality, my swagger, and I mentally felt the hole around that loss. It was such a sharp but necessary lesson in understanding the true weight of mental power that my pursuit of physical strength had given me. But it was also the beginning of a different mental journey; realising that I had to be defined by more than just my physical strength, because illness, wellness and ability are not fixed and predictable things, and they may change in an instant. While lifting weights had done a lot for my mental strength, there had to be more to it, if that physical strength was taken away for whatever reason.

In the first few months I didn't fully understand what was happening or why I seemed to feel OK one minute and the next utterly fatigued and struggling for breath, but as time went on, and with two tests confirming covid antibodies, it was revealed that I was one of many thousands dealing with 'long covid' – longer, recurring symptoms of having had the virus. It was one of the most mentally challenging experiences of my life, and the only reason I didn't completely unravel mentally was because of the immense amount of labour I put into recovering from the grief of losing Rob. When I was six months into still recovering from covid, I knew what I had to do to keep myself sane and that included keeping myself busy, resting when I needed to and understanding that I was working to a much bigger goal of healing. Unquestionably, it made me realise how important that mental work was in terms of my physical recovery. I saw a sports psychologist who helped me with this, and it was the final piece in the puzzle around being ill, healing and physical activity, and how all of these things are so interconnected.

For instance, a common but lesser known aspect of physical illness is the toll that it takes mentally and how, so often, there is so much focus on the physical recovery, especially in serious illnesses such as cancer, that the recovery of mental health is an afterthought. The reverse is also true: we can overlook the role physical activity plays in the general maintenance of good mental health.

While there is a very damaging idea that a way of treating mental illness is to be more physically active, if we look at mental health as a spectrum, and we look at how certain experiences – such as physical illness – may affect our overall mental wellbeing negatively, there is a case to be made for how we use physical movement as a way to work out some of the mental catharsis, create a feeling of internal strength and offer a measure of routine in an otherwise chaotic time.

All of which goes to show that, when we are talking about recovery as a whole from anything, including physical illness, mental illness, trauma, addiction, whatever it might be, working from a place that makes us feel internally strong is critical to the healing process. Physical strength and power isn't the simple fix, but rather a powerful weapon in our armoury. If it is the blade, mental strength is the hilt. That is why it has to be something you have forged yourself, not based on what someone else has told you.

When you are suffering from a physical illness, you will hopefully receive a treatment that will then heal you and make you well. But once you have returned to physical wellness, you are still dealing with an undetected attack that has taken place, and that attack is the sundering of control between your mind and your body.

On my Instagram platform, See My Strong, a significant proportion of experiences submitted are from women who have recovered from illness or are ill. When they talk about physical fitness, the emphasis is not around how it physically made them better but it's about the reparation of the relationship between their body and mind. It's about restoring trust, faith and love in a body that drew a short straw but has nonetheless survived and continues to survive for however long it can.

One of the most astonishing stories I featured was Sarah Thomas who, in 2019, at the age of 37, became the first woman to swim the Channel four times. It took her 54 hours and, due to tides, what was supposed to be 84 miles ended up being 130 miles. She even got stung in the face by a jellyfish and didn't give up. The year before, Sarah was treated for breast cancer and credited swimming as a way of mentally coping with treatment.

While some cancer survivors, like Sarah, have chosen to take on huge physical challenges and have found peace in doing so, others have told me they are fed up with the trope of being viewed as warriors and that they are expected to do superhuman things just because they have survived cancer. For many, simply being physically active and having routine and structure has been helpful. Also, getting out there and joining classes for example means that you might come across like-minded people who know what you're going through. As with any major event and transition in life, community is so important to not feeling so alone in your experience. For instance, Team Phoenix Foundation is a charity that offers a six-month social and training programme for survivors of breast cancer. The end goal is to do a triathlon but the real magic comes from making friends and socialising with other women who know exactly what you're going through.

One of the most prominent cancer awareness activists in the UK is Kris Hallenga, who has been living with stage four breast cancer since she was diagnosed in 2009, at the age of 23. Kris is extraordinary; I think of her as the offspring of a sunbeam and a human.

Along with her twin sister Maren, she founded CoppaFeel, the charity that raises awareness of breast cancer in young people, after finding a lump and visiting her doctor three times but not being taken seriously because of her age. Now 34, Kris made the move to quit London for Cornwall and found it was a powerful way of connecting with the outdoors, especially open-water swimming.

Back when she was first diagnosed, however, she was really worried about moving her body full stop. 'I had gone from believing I was a healthy 23-year-old,' she said, 'to someone with a very serious terminal illness and suddenly I didn't know my body anymore AT ALL. I had lost all confidence in exercising for fear of hurting myself or damaging myself somehow. It wasn't until I visited Marie Curie that I learned that movement would really help me physically and mentally.'

She was chatting to the consultant who was surprised she hadn't been exercising but, up to that point, no one had talked to Kris about exercise and how it could complement her treatment and mental wellbeing. She started moving more and did a 10k run. Eventually she did a half marathon. She also walks, and does pilates, and HIIT because she can do them at home.

'Moving my body more made me appreciate it. I went from being disappointed in my body for developing cancer to having a whole new level of appreciation for it. I have seen it change so much over 11 years but when I exercise, I can see strength build.'

Kris has some advice for other people who are struggling mentally with a cancer diagnosis and how they feel about their body, which actually I think could apply to so many other illnesses. 'Just know your body isn't constantly letting you down,' she says. 'Finding a re-appreciation is so important when you have cancer. When you start to move and gain strength you can get a sense of control back. They sadly don't tell you this when you're first diagnosed.'

Roberta, who took the survey, wrote about how she had

cervical cancer and two brain tumours and exercise helped with coping with the diagnosis. She describes it as the best form of mindfulness and says that it has helped her mental health and dealing with the side effects of treatment. She wrote about how the visibility of people who have cancer and are physically active is important because after her diagnosis, she says, she was 'ghosted' by a lot of friends who assumed she wasn't interested in exercise anymore.

People who have survived cancer contact me frequently through See My Strong in search of a community to connect with, but also because they want to tell their story and reach out to people who may be feeling lost and isolated. One person who got in touch was Nav Johal, who is 39 and was diagnosed with bowel cancer in February 2019. She'd had seven operations.

Nav had played football since she was a child with her twin Preeti, and played in the Greater London League and Surrey League. Being fit was such a massive part of her identity that, when she was first diagnosed, it was hard to wrap her head around.

'After I got over the "am I going to die" part,' she told me, 'I was told that I would be having a stoma. I told my consultant I did not want a stoma and did not think that I would be able to do my job, play football, go running, go to the gym with one. I'm sure some of the negativity in my mind was also how it would look, what I could and could not wear, how other people saw me. I was super fit Nav – I felt like all that would change.'

At her first appointment with her stoma nurse, she was shown a photograph of a guy who was in amazing shape. Then she was shown a fuller length photo and the guy had a stoma. She came away thinking 'OK, I can do this.'

The first major surgery would determine whether or not she would have a temporary or permanent stoma. When she woke up from the operation, she was relieved to find out it was the former. 'Being back running and playing football was pretty emotional for me,' she said. 'I didn't think it would happen, I doubted that I would run in 2019 because I felt a lot of pain and discomfort for a long time. My relationship with my body now is that I am kind to it. I realise now how vulnerable we are physically, and I think I have taken my body for granted and put it through a lot physically because I wanted to run faster, or run for longer distances, I wanted to lift more, I wanted to look a certain way.'

'Despite having no right arm below the elbow and a condition that causes her joints to dislocate spontaneously has not kept her off the climbing wall.' This was the slightly patronising, clumsy sub-head of an article about Anoushé Husain, who does paraclimbing when she isn't working as a civil servant.

Anoushé is an incredible role model, not just for South Asian and Muslim women, but for the disability communities and cancer communities. But that one sentence reinforces the biases and stereotypes we have about particular groups of people – which is, they don't exercise, aren't interested in it, can't do it. When we then praise people who make it 'despite the odds', it creates exceptionalism, which means that rather than being inspired by a person from their community, it seems like an achievement that is out of reach.

Anoushé was born without her right arm and has Ehlers-Danlos Syndrome (EDS) and has always been physically active from a young age because she comes from a sporty family who encouraged her to be active. She started swimming at the age of five and took up karate when she was around eight or nine. She struggled in P.E. classes and being picked for teams – not because of a lack of passion or ability but because people always wrote her off without finding out if she was good or not. For the last four years of school, she had an awful teacher who she says refused to adapt any of the classes for her.

When she was in her teens, a surgeon told Anoushé she had to stop doing karate and, as a result, she felt the loss of the focus and structure that sport had given her very deeply. Then she was diagnosed with cancer in 2011 and it broke her mentally and physically.

Cancer took a lot from her but what got her to try climbing and then keep going, was the process of just taking one day at a time. She was 23 when a friend suggested they try it. 'My friend's theory,' she told me, 'was climbing was going to force me to use my left hand above my head and so make gains in strength and mobility. The first session was awful but there were a few seconds where I was so focused on the climb that I forgot I had health issues and, while my climbing sucked, those few seconds of escape were more than enough to get me motivated to try to get fit again.'

She didn't take up climbing as a regular hobby until four years later, and then started competing. 'Part of the reason it took me so long,' she says, 'was I didn't have anyone to climb with and was intimidated about going on my own and how I was going to learn to manage holding ropes, etc. I was really self-conscious about being short, I thought you had to be tall to climb but actually being short has some serious advantages because it forces you to think outside the box and really develop your technical skills.'

Climbing is about more than just being physically active for Anoushé. It has made her physically stronger so she can do more, such as carrying her shopping and, after getting a prosthetic arm fitted, she does weight training too. But it's also about how it has helped her so much mentally. The minute her hands touch the climbing wall, her anxiety disappears to a separate, unreachable place. The mental release and inner strength that come with being physically active are especially valuable if she has a scan coming up and is feeling worried. It occurs to me how much more powerful a motivator that is than shame or guilt.

CHAPTER TEN

Let's Talk about Mental Health

I'm going to sound like an ungrateful scrag, but whenever I write about powerlifting for a national newspaper or magazine, especially in relation to mental health and coping with grief, they love to distil it into the headline: WEIGHTLIFTING SAVED THIS WOMAN AFTER HER HUSBAND DIED.

It's a partial truth of course. Lifting weights did help me after Rob passed away but it wasn't as if I did some deadlifts and then, puff! my grief disappeared. It's not something I'd suggest to people grieving deeply: 'I'm so sorry to hear about this pain that has carved a stairway of unimaginable torment inside you, and you probably question whether you will make it to the next day, let alone month, but you know what might help? A good back squat.'

It helped me because it provided a steady and safe environment within which I could better myself, grow and become strong when everything else around me was a whistling vortex of sadness. I never held anger towards Rob for ending his own life because that is always a moment in which I hold the purest form of empathy and softness, where I both recognise the pain he was in and wish I could have lessened it. But his decision blew apart the many lives wrapped around his, mine included. At the same time as experiencing a deep grief at losing him, I also experienced a relentless terror at knowing that my reality wasn't my choice and feeling the lack of control that came with that.

To then say weightlifting saved my life – it didn't. Everything and nothing saved my life. Therapy, my loved ones, my own desire to live, CBT, grief forums, the 12-step programme, travel, crying, music – all of these things collectively saved me, but no single thing did it alone.

What strength training did was give me a framework within which I could build my own mental health back up. It helped me to form a bedrock of serenity which had been eroded long before Rob died, when the rollercoaster of his addiction had smashed me to bits. It didn't fix things but it gave me something to hold onto deep down, when the hurricanes of grief, anger, sadness and bitterness spiralled across the surface. It created a space inside me, filled with white noise and calm, which I could access mentally when the going got tough.

Since being active in the mental health space, it is a story I have heard in some shape or form over and over again. Charlotte, who took the survey, told me about her dad who died suddenly from an overdose. When he died, she said, all she wanted to do was punch things. She worked with a trainer who showed her how to do it properly and the routine helped. 'I felt like if I could just focus on this one thing, I wouldn't spiral out of control,' she wrote.

It's undeniable that we are in an unprecedented time when it comes to the discussion around mental health and exercise. There are an increasing number of grassroots organisations and community projects springing up to meet this need. Even during the time of coronavirus, the Conservative government kept mentioning it as part of why they wanted parks to stay open – exercise is so vitally important to mental health, they said. (Some might say that if they really gave a shit about mental health they might consider actually funding services properly, but that's another conversation altogether.)

While it has become more socially acceptable to talk about mental health than ever before, it seems to me that we are still more comfortable talking about exercise within the context of weight loss, rather than how it benefits us mentally. You're far more likely to hear someone mention a run they went on to work off 'being naughty' around something they ate than you are to hear someone talking about exercise in everyday conversation in context of their mental health. We're more likely to set goals around the amount of weight we want to lose, or distance we want to run than to set ourselves the goal of going for a daily walk for our mental wellbeing to reduce stress levels, for instance. However, there is a compelling case for making mental health the main motivator over weight loss.

In the survey I ran, mental health and wellbeing came out consistently at the top of reasons why women exercise. Nearly 80 per cent said it had helped them when they were struggling mentally, while 67 per cent said it was very important for their mental health. Over 80 per cent of people said the emotion they most strongly associated with doing physical fitness was better mental wellbeing.

Performance-based fitness in particular – so either sport you do with a team, or fitness goals that are centred around performance (whether that's doing a head-stand, running or swimming a certain distance, or lifting weights) – featured as being helpful for mental health. Isabella wrote in the survey that, while being competitive can have its downsides, if you manage to strike the right balance, it can be life-changing. 'It empties your mind and frees it up from your daily worries and it also builds confidence and shows you that you are more capable than you think. Small wins, small increments to get to where you want to be. Somehow, as you start training on a regular basis, you will draw parallels with events in your life. You will be able to view them from your perspective but at a different angle. And the more you know yourself, the better you will feel with yourself.'

I related to this a lot. Lifting weights wasn't about forgetting my grief, it was about making peace with it. It was about giving myself a reservoir of worth or purpose on the days when I felt like I didn't have any.

One of the most moving stories I've heard around grief, exercise and mental health came from Stephanie Nimmo, a 51-year-old writer who charts her journey with grief on her blog 'Was This In the Plan'?

Stephanie lost both her daughter Daisy, and her husband Andy within 13 months of each other. Daisy was born with a rare genetic condition, Costello syndrome, and her health was deteriorating, when Andy was diagnosed with incurable bowel cancer. I don't know how Stephanie survived her grief but I suspect she had no other choice, and she needed to keep going for herself and her three other children. While Daisy was in and out of hospital, Stephanie ran laps nearby to keep herself sane and, when Andy passed away in December 2015, she took up open-water swimming. After Daisy died, she started cycling as well to manage her grief. The shock and stress of losing them both also triggered the menopause and exercise helped with that too.

'Running, swimming, cycling – just generally moving my body – were things I had control over in a world that for me was spinning out of control,' she told me. 'When you are a carer you lose your identity. I was Daisy's mum, Andy's wife – now

I'm a widow, a bereaved parent. But when I run or do exercise, I'm me. Grief is physical, it's debilitating, and the mental health benefits of movement were huge.'

I know what Stephanie means when she says grief is physical. The body remembers pain, and I remember it acutely. It's different for everyone but for me it was fire and sharpness, heaviness, oppressiveness, claustrophobia, madness, cloying. Anything that offered respite from that was cool, calm relief.

For Stephanie, swimming was incredible for that after Andy died. 'Just letting my body be held by the water, swimming continuously without stopping, feeling the icy water and trusting my body that it would adjust (even though it hurts). It was quite a metaphor and so healing. When Daisy then died, I started riding my road bike more, and would find myself on deserted lanes and I would shout all my anger out.

'As for now, well, grief, as you know, never goes, it just changes and waxes and wanes. I just try and make sure I keep my exercise routines going. I don't run with a watch or apps anymore, and I just run for the joy of it, to appreciate being outside after all the time spent in hospitals.'

I think about her words for a long time. How vital it is to bring joy to your body, when your mind is in turmoil and the world is painted in black.

In 2018, there was a huge study in *The Lancet* of 1.2 million people in the US, which found that people who exercised had fewer bad mental health days per month than those who didn't exercise at all.[1] Crucially, *more* exercise wasn't always better – in fact, over-exercise was associated with poor mental health – but on average, 45 minutes, five days a week helped. That didn't have to mean going to the gym but could include walking, housework, childcare and mowing the lawn.

One of the most interesting findings was that the reduction in poor mental health days was more evident in people who'd previously been diagnosed with depression. Someone without a history with depression might report 1.5 days of better mental health than someone who didn't exercise, whereas someone with a history of depression might report 3.75 days.

That still doesn't mean that if someone has depression, for instance, exercise is the fix. Or that they'd just feel better if they went for a walk. Serious depression, for example, as Rob had, is not going to be alleviated or fixed with a visit to the gym. People love to condense the mental health conversation into short, snappy tips and tricks but it depends where you sit on the spectrum. At one end, you have mental health which every single person is required to maintain. Somewhere in the middle you have mental distress which also can affect anyone and might be caused by life events such as divorce, grief or redundancy, or circumstances such as income, class or where you live. At the other end is severe mental illness which requires medicalised treatment and a range of other interventions.

When it comes to exercise, the over-simplification of how it supports good mental wellbeing can be a big problem. For instance, when the gyms were forced to shut in the second UK coronavirus lockdown, a lot of people complained in a well-meaning way that they should stay open because they were vital for our mental health. But a big pushback came from the mental health community who rightly said that while gyms could aid mental wellbeing, when it came to mental health the main thing that was needed was adequate mental health services. The nuance matters because otherwise it lets the current government off the hook for not providing proper care, which currently is the case. And also, there is still a huge legacy of the stigma that surrounds mental health in the belief that people could fix it if only they 'tried harder', and so the belief that gyms are where you go to 'fix' it doesn't help people who are ill.

When the nuance is removed, that gets distilled into telling people who are seriously ill that running or yoga might make them feel better. It really fucking doesn't. It might do at a later point when they are less ill but when someone is really ill, it's about as useful as a chocolate teapot.

One of the common misconceptions with mental illness is that it is only . . . mental. But every mental illness has a physical manifestation. In the case of depression, this is often feeling drained of energy and not being able to move or leave your bed. Anxiety can affect the digestive or urinary system, giving you a bad tummy or increasing the amount you urinate, or it may make you feel a fluttering in your chest.

Rob told me very early on in our relationship that he had depression but this was back in 2009, when the mental health conversation was non-existent. I didn't know much about depression and although he had chronic depression – the kind that would recur and be very bad for a few months at a time over the course of many years – I don't think even he knew the full scope of his illness. He also wasn't that ill at the start of our relationship so I had no idea how it might affect him and just assumed it wouldn't be 'that bad'. Due to the stigma around mental illness, he often was in complete denial of how far-reaching his depression was. To acknowledge it meant – in his words – that he wasn't 'normal'.

As I didn't know much about depression, I took my cues from him, around what he needed and wanted, but it didn't occur to me that he probably hid a lot of it because he didn't want to place the burden on me. At the same time, he was also self-medicating with heroin and addiction played a massive role in his depression spiralling out of control. The result was that I was running around trying to keep both our lives afloat and, because I was ignorant about it, there were days when I thought Rob might feel better if he went to the gym or went for a walk with me. I didn't nag him but there were occasional 'suggestions'.

The one time I had proper depression, which was for about three months in total after he died, I finally knew what it felt like. It was like walking through glue; every sense dulled and dampened, as if the fiery core of me had been taken out. I can't remember if I went running or to the gym in this time because trying to recall these memories is like trying to form solid shapes from vapour. I assume I did, but mainly because the only significant break I'd had from being physically active was during my heart troubles a few years previously.

In retrospect, I realised that when he was really ill, suggesting he come with me for a walk was laughable. And it spoke to my own ignorance and stigma that I thought if he just moved more, he'd feel better and if he didn't feel better that was because he didn't want to try.

I spoke to Anju Ambily, who got in touch with me to talk about her relationship with depression and yoga. In her childhood, domestic violence was an everyday occurrence and, although she went on to have a successful career, there was a bedrock of trauma. When she experienced corporate bullying, it triggered a deep depression.

She credits yoga with helping her to reconcile some of her previous trauma but also for lightening some of the heavier aspects of depression. It isn't an instant fix but part of a longer-term solution, she says. 'Yoga helps to stem the downward spiral that depression often is for me and helps me to re-emerge from a depressive episode much faster. I feel better almost immediately and it helps to keep me buoyant. It's given me a sense of control, allowing me to understand what I cannot control and should just let be.'

But there is no one size fits all. A few people messaged me through the survey to say that they would have found something like going for a run too daunting when they were ill. 'A lot of the "exercise is great for mental health" dialogue seems to be around running, which feels overwhelming when in the pit of depression,' wrote Hanna. 'More messaging about starting small and "every bit helps" would've helped me get started.'

This is just another reason why the 'no pain no gain' style of personal training and messaging that you're lazy if you don't push yourself is really problematic. Most people who are actively dealing with mental illness – not just depression, but bipolar, schizophrenia, anxiety, borderline personality disorder – almost certainly WANT to do things but their illness makes it much harder.

Starting small is a brilliant idea. Even if it's something like swimming or doing an online class with the video turned off. A lot of people with anxiety find that gyms exacerbate their anxiety and some people avoid them altogether or go at anti-social times.

But wouldn't it be incredible if gyms actually incorporated mental health into their offerings without making people feel self-conscious about it, given that one in four people will have a mental health problem at some point? It's also such a natural fit, seeing as many of us confide and tell our personal trainers things we would never tell anyone else. I remember recording a podcast episode for one of my favourite personal trainers and fitness influencers, Alice Liveing, and she said that sometimes being a PT was almost like being someone's therapist, given the things clients would feel able to talk about.

There are community groups that are working to promote fitness and mental health together. Good Gym, for instance, is an organisation that combines doing physically active things with doing good deeds for people, which is brilliant if you're shy around conversation because the task at hand will help conversation flow a bit more smoothly. Or there are running and walking groups such as Bryony Gordon's Mental Health Mates, or open-water swimming clubs that bring people together but mean you can still go off and do your own thing if you aren't feeling chatty.

Girls on Hills was started in Scotland by Keri Wallace and Nancy Kennedy ostensibly to get more women trail running but essentially the group teaches self-sufficiency because, on the whole, women are fine to run on flat surfaces but then doubt their abilities when it comes to navigating uphill terrain. Keri said she noticed that about 80 per cent of women who came to the group were actually going through a transition in their lives, whether that was illness, anxiety or divorce. Running in a group like that helped these women to open up and meet like-minded people.

One of the most prominent advocates for mental health and exercise is Fearne Cotton, who I ended up becoming friends with after she read my book *Chase the Rainbow*. She says running gives her a lot of clarity and she gets a massive boost from the serotonin after a run but also, when she pushes herself physically, she can gauge how much mental energy she has exerted.

'When I've done something physically taxing,' she told me, 'I know that really it's my mind that has done all of the work. I have had to stay focused to complete a big run or do a tough

HIIT session. At any point my mind could ditch out and tell me that I needn't bother, so knowing I have sustained focus feels good. It allows me to unlock my own inner mental strength. I have a much clearer mind after exercising. My demons are quieter and my worries a little smaller.'

When she was younger, her first love was dancing, then she moved on to running at 19 but, as she became older, she transitioned to the gym, which she said was 'never quite as fun.' She found yoga at 29 and fell in love with it immediately. And as a working mum, the flexibility of running and yoga meant she could fit it in easily. 'I wanted free exercise that felt easy to fit in to a busy schedule. I realised a few years in that it was doing wonders for my mental health without really being able to articulate it as mental health wasn't really discussed back then.'

Mental health also crops up time and again in powerlifting. In my experience, a lot of people come to the sport with some kind of personal story of mental health problems. It's something Jack and I have spoken about a lot, as he's had his own struggles and we both know a lot of other people who have, as well.

I'm aware that taking up a competitive sport may not be the best thing for everyone, depending on the history of your mental struggles. There is undeniably a strong correlation between competitive sport and mental health disorders – research shows that 35 per cent of elite athletes suffer from a mental health problem, particularly anxiety, eating disorders, depression and suicidal ideation.

But being part of the larger community creates a sense of connection which, when you are struggling mentally, is almost always the first thing to go.

As mentioned previously, those who have past histories of ED can find some fitness environments and the language used around exercise triggering. But while over-exercise is a concern, I've heard some people in recovery speak about how reconnecting with physical movement has been healing. The three activities that crop up the most in my opinion are yoga, dance and weight training. Yoga, I would imagine because it has such a huge spiritual aspect to it and, like dancing, is healing because of how it connects the body to the mind. Weight training is presumably because the focus is on getting strong, as opposed to looking at how many calories you've burned. (Although, just to clarify, I am speaking specifically here about weightlifting and powerlifting, not bodybuilding. Bodybuilding, while a strength sport that requires you to be super fit, involves restrictive eating and there are studies that show higher rates of disordered eating in both men and women bodybuilders.)

Lauren Woodhead, a 21-year-old student and journalist, told me that she was diagnosed with anorexia and secondary depression in 2016. As part of her treatment, for a few months she was banned from playing hockey or running and walking for more than 15 minutes a day. Eventually, she had gained enough weight to be given PT sessions as a Christmas present. Her story is an example of how having the right PT can be so instrumental and life-changing when it comes to mental health: 'From very early on, my PT has been focused on the mental rather than aesthetic benefits of weightlifting. She keeps an eye on my nutrition, especially while I am away at university, which is a huge help because it means I don't have to rely on my parents. If I'm struggling, my PT is usually the first person I tell.'

Lifting weights cropped up in the survey a considerable number of times in relation to people recovering from ED. Becca Caddy, who is a journalist working in the tech and science space, told me how it helped her. She was diagnosed with bulimia in 2018. While she is still feeling out the boundaries of her recovery, she said that goals that move away from cardio and calorie-burn help. She started doing boxing but a knee injury meant she couldn't do it anymore. Her trainer suggested trying some weights and they started with an empty barbell.

'Mental strength and resilience are things I've struggled with,' she said. 'Knowing I'm physically stronger now is extremely rewarding for me. It's much harder for me to restrict food and hate my body when I see all of the great things it has accomplished.'

One of the most maligned health conditions in society is addiction, and by that I mean we don't really understand it if we are not addicts. We moralise it and think that people are addicts by choice because they are selfish and weak. We conflate people who use drugs as a lifestyle choice with people who have had that choice taken away from them because of addiction. We don't look at the ruins of a person's life – the job they have lost, the family that has given up on them, the money they owe – and question what it is that compels them to destroy their lives in such a way.

I'm not excusing the pain caused by the behaviour of some addicts – I am fully aware of that. But I was massively judgemental about addiction before Rob and, after he confessed his drug use, I learned a lot – from understanding how the shame around addiction was a massive blocker to him acknowledging it and getting help, to sitting in my own support groups and learning about empathy.

When people find out about Rob's addiction I often see horror and shock in their eyes. They believe themselves to be so far removed from it, when the likelihood is, in some shape or form, they have known an addict, they are related to one, or are one themselves. I can say this with such confidence because of the most ubiquitous drug of them all: alcohol. We insulate ourselves from what we think addiction is by assuming the term only applies to hard drugs and yet alcohol is overwhelmingly the most harmful drug – it exceeds the dangers of heroin, crack cocaine and cocaine combined.

This was the conclusion of a team of over 20 top substance experts who in 2010 looked at and ranked over 20 different drugs and measured the harm they did across life expectancy, health risks, dependence, mental functioning, loss of relationships, crime, costs to society and family conflict.[2]

Professor David Nutt, who is currently the director of the neuropsychopharmacology unit at Imperial College London, was one of the experts involved in this study. On his blog, Professor Nutt wrote: 'Addiction is a major health problem that costs as much as all other mental illnesses combined (about £40 billion per year) and about as much as cancer and cardiovascular disorders also. At its core, addiction is a state of altered brain function that leads to fundamental changes in behaviour that are manifest by repeated use of alcohol or other drugs or engaging in activities such as gambling. These are usually resisted, albeit unsuccessfully, by the addict.

'The key features of addiction is therefore a state of habitual behaviour such as drug taking or gambling that is initially enjoyable but which eventually becomes self-sustaining or habitual. The urge to engage in the behaviour becomes so powerful that it interferes with normal life often to the point of overtaking work, personal relationships and family activities. At this point the person can be said to be addicted: the addict's every thought and action is directed to their addiction and everything else suffers.'

The reason I mention addiction is because while I've personally never been an addict and I don't use drugs or alcohol as a coping mechanism, I've seen how transformative physical activity can be for recovering addicts, especially those with dual diagnosis or co-morbidities like Rob, where addiction sits alongside mental illness. It's also something I've been contacted a lot about, from people who are in recovery who have testified to how internally strong it has made them feel.

In the last year of his life, Rob managed five months sober – the longest he had gone in 25 years of drug and alcohol use. During that time, being physically active, the routine of the gym, was something that gave him great joy. Yoga was also something he particularly adored because of the soothing, pink mist he felt during a class and he was surprisingly flexible given he was so new to the practice – far more than me. Going to the gym and doing yoga together was something that I didn't think was possible when he was in active addiction but I saw how, in recovery, it gave him an anchor, a feeling of being more than his addiction and a way of building something within himself.

One of the best voices in this space is Bryony Gordon. Running saved her life, she says, because running got her sober. Without it, she thinks she would have eventually either killed herself or died due to alcoholism. As well as dealing with addiction and having had long spells of depression, Bryony also has Pure O, a form of obsessive compulsive disorder (OCD) where a person can experience obsessive, unwanted thoughts but without the signs of compulsive rituals we usually associate with OCD.

When I asked her specifically around running and sobriety, Bryony told me that the reason she signed up for her first marathon was to try and get her drinking under control but it didn't quite work and, if anything, increased her drinking. But a few months after running the marathon, she went sober.

'I don't think that's a coincidence. The realisation that I didn't need to live like that and there was this other way. I'd had this belief most of my life, girls like me just didn't do things like that. We were party girls, smoking fags, and it didn't occur to me that it was possible to run a marathon. Running has helped since then to support that and when I feel anxious, upset, despairing, I know I can go out and all I have to do is give it a chance. If I feel exactly the same at the end of a run, at least I tried. But I don't usually. Even attempting the run is a little act of allowing me to believe I can do something that I often think I can't.'

I used to think sobriety was all about the first few days of being abstinent. I didn't realise that it is actually a process that takes months to stabilise and, even then, requires daily mental work. Having those anchors and a sense of structure is so important, then.

The reasons why someone might use are often incredibly complex and, as with other mental conditions, won't be fixed by being physically active, but what it can do is create a sense of achievement and self-worth, which has often been stripped clean from an addict. Physical activity doesn't just offer physical strength but consistency, progress and achievement that can be measured. A sense of wellbeing and feeling good that doesn't come via a substance but from yourself.

Georgie Okell, the broadcaster and mental health campaigner, wrote about her recovery from drug and alcohol use in relation to being an ultrarunner. Ultrarunning is long distance running above 26.2 miles (the distance of a marathon). She had always been sporty and was specifically good at individual sports like running track and skiing. But at the age of 16 it dropped off and at university everything became about drinking.

As she got older, she started running again but she'd get into a pattern around training for a race: 'I would go for eight-week training periods where I'd say I'm not smoking or doing drugs or drinking, and I'd bang on about it, and people would go "Georgie's doing so well." I don't think anyone was particularly concerned because I would manage it,' she told me. 'If I'm being honest, I look at those eight-week periods and there were always one or two weekends within that where I'd jump off the deep end and go to some parties. In my head, I had it under control.'

After years of trying not to drink and doing a sort of semi-sobriety, in the summer of 2017, she started training for the Loch Ness marathon but was also drinking herself into what she calls 'a dangerous state of depression'. She decided that what she needed was structured recovery and found the 12-step programme. Just five days into being sober, she got a tattoo that said RIP FUN and it hadn't yet healed on the day of the marathon.

'I could feel the tattoo while I was running and there was something about that that felt important. In Loch Ness, it was beautiful; I felt like I was at the start of something.' It is a race, she says, she will never forget. It taught her one of the most valuable lessons, which was that recovery meant she could still do the things she loved, and find joy in, like running.

For others who are struggling with their drug and alcohol use but might be in denial, she has some advice. 'If you are stuck in a pattern where you go out every weekend because that's what people around you do and it doesn't make you feel great, finding a hobby or exercise you love, finding a reason to get up early in the morning, can really help. It can show you, "Oh shit, I do have a deeper addiction problem because I have this thing I really enjoy but still I keep fucking it up and sleeping in when I've got a race on."'

It's clear when it comes to mental health, there are many layers that may contribute to the good or bad of someone's mental wellbeing. But some things come up time and again when someone finds that physical activity aids their mental health in a positive way: it is liberation, it is strength, and it is something they cherish and love for themselves alone, and find love for themselves within it, which is something many may not have felt for a very long time.

Before writing this book, I knew how important it was to chart the mental benefits of physical activity for girls and women but I also knew that it was important to discuss trauma.

Latoya Shauntay Snell told me about her mental break which was triggered by losing her twins. 'As a Black woman growing up in the 1980s and 90s in Brooklyn, New York, you are expected and conditioned to be strong,' she said. 'You don't wear your emotions because it's perceived to be weak, vulnerable and can be weaponised.'

She also found that running helped, connecting her to how she was feeling inside and allowing her to release her emotions. 'I hate that "running is my therapy" statement because therapy is therapy,' she says. 'But I can say running is certainly thera-peutic. Each time I went out for a run, I'd cry at some point. Even at the beginning of my fitness journey, I'd use it as an opportunity to grieve. Running helped me process the loss of my father after he battled stage four lung cancer, kidney and renal failure and our very complicated relationship. And running helped me acknowledge that I have broken layers in me that required help through a therapist.'

One in four women experience domestic violence at some point in their life,[3] 20 per cent of women have experienced sexual violence and trans people are the most likely to experi-ence sexual and physical violence, which increases massively across other intersections such as race; the most affected are Black trans women.[4]

For women who have experienced such trauma, going into heavily gendered parts of the gym, such as the weights section, might be very problematic. In some cases, going to women-only gyms, boutique gyms or LGBTQ+ friendly gyms may help but I also believe that gyms as a whole should be switched on to this given how prevalent sexual trauma is.

Through See My Strong and the survey, women messaged to tell me how physical activity helped them to reclaim the narrative around their own body, where they had experienced sexual trauma. A 24-year-old woman, Sara, got in touch, to say that she had survived sexual assault. She reported it but, like a lot of women, she'd had to wait a year for her trial to start – a time in which she was discouraged from having therapy. She had previously been a very confident woman, she says, but the assault changed that and she wanted to shrink and cover up. But during the Covid-19 lockdown, she couldn't be distracted from thinking about her body and tried yoga as a way of reconnecting with it. She said that it was like discovering a whole new love for her body. Her post on See My Strong was one of the most liked posts on my platform and it spoke to the truth most women know, which is that sexual assault is common and hidden.

In the survey, Alison shared her powerful story with me: 'I have been in two romantic long-term relationships where I was a victim of physical and emotional abuse. Coming out of those experiences, I realise that fitness is both a source of extreme anxiety for me but also the best way for me to feel grounded and connected to my body again. And I know I'm not alone in this.'

Eshe wrote about how she was attacked by a man with a knife and felt physically vulnerable. 'Training became my way of dealing with PTSD and helping myself to become the strongest version of me – physically and mentally.'

Harnessing movement and physical activity to help people with trauma reconnect mentally and physically with their bodies is a growing area. For many, that trauma may be buried deep down, so a light touch is necessary to still make it accessible for people who aren't ready to voice or identify what they've been through.

When I spoke to Kelechi Okafor, I asked her about trauma because it's something she covers in her fitness classes and she has spoken of her own sexual abuse. She was one of the first people with a high profile to focus on the healing connection between trauma and movement, and ran a 'twerking through trauma' class which was featured on the BBC.

'One woman who featured on it had gone through a lot of domestic violence with her partner,' she says. 'That really affected her confidence and so when she first started coming to classes, she was all covered up and very quiet. In coming to the classes she was reigniting her sacral energy using her body in that sensual way, in a safe environment, with other people that were on similar journeys. She started wearing less, showing up more, expressing herself. She said that she came to the class looking for somebody that could hold space for her while she explored her body and worked through that trauma in her own way.'

Pole dancing is also something Kelechi teaches and I always wondered how it was empowering for women and non-binary people, given that I strongly associated pole dancing with the male gaze. But I realised why, after watching some of the videos of her classes on Instagram. There is something incredibly joyous and freeing on everyone's faces while they're doing the class and it's a particularly good entry point if people have been away from fitness for a while.

'I think that the reason is sensuality,' Kelechi says. 'There is so much power in that. Especially as women and some non-binary folk, sometimes we disengage from our bodies because society places so much worth and value on how we look that you almost treat your body objectively in that way. Whereas pole dance is a way for you to re-engage and do something that is very sensual while building strength at the same time.'

Then Kelechi says something that hits deep, which should be written in the stars for everyone to see, process and live as a truth: 'People might think it's trivial that we do this through fitness and dance but movement is prayer. People throw around the concept that the body is a temple. But over time, I think especially as women, we've lost sight of worshipping our own bodies and choosing the ways that we practise that worship.'

Trauma, especially wrought at the hands of another, can make you believe that your body is no longer safe. It can make you question how strong you are, make you doubt yourself, make you blame yourself for not being strong enough. But remember that even the mightiest oak cannot sometimes withstand a storm that arrives on the darkest night. Whatever has happened, whatever the storm, however unfair, however painful, however sad, however violently it tried to wrench you from yourself, there is but one truth you need to remember: your trauma doesn't define you. It does not.

Remember that you are the land you arrived here with. Remember that though others may come and take without permission, that though they strip your cupboards bare and plant poison in your soil, you are glorious. You are the only one of your kind, and that alone makes you worth fighting for, and your spirit, your heart and your mind shine a light so powerful, it beams out your existence to the entire cosmos, even when things seem at their darkest.

CHAPTER ELEVEN

Women in Colour

I remember the first time I held my niece Leela on the day she was born. I hadn't slept much because we were in London and we knew Priya had gone into labour at a hospital in Brighton. We knew she'd had an emergency C-section and, the minute we were told we could see her, my parents, Rob and I made our way immediately to the hospital.

The moment I held Leela is imprinted on my mind because it was unlike anything I had ever felt before. *I would die for you, my life is yours,* I thought. The surrendering of your life in that way, to someone you have just met, who hasn't even had the chance to make choices and be a human being, speaks to the purity of life that a baby has. We forget this was once us.

A baby hasn't had time to accrue the messy collateral of life's decisions, and so the power of its potential is over-whelming. That's what I remember about her. I remember thinking how precious and fragile she was but also how she radiated with such power because she could literally be anything. She held limitless potential for good.

The tough truth of it, however, is that potential dims, depending on the circumstances of your birth. If you think of it as a light-filled room, there are a number of things that close the shutters of that room because we live in a biased world and we hold prejudiced views based on that bias, and we then build it into the structure of our society to keep those shutters closed.

There are hierarchies of how much your potential is encouraged and given room to grow, and how much harder life is dependent on race, gender, sexual orientation, disability, illness. These aspects of your identity then intersect with other things both within and outside your control, such as wealth, being a mother, being child-free, a carer and so on.

The most marginalised groups globally, however, are Black women and Black trans women.

The deaths of George Floyd and Breonna Taylor in 2020 reignited the global movement around Black Lives Matter, and that changed how we thought and talked about race, highlighting the gross and vast injustice at how Black people have been treated their entire lives, in comparison to white people. Racial injustice has been around a long time and nothing new was being said but what was fundamentally different was that, because of the coronavirus pandemic, white people didn't have the luxury of brushing it off or pretending like it didn't exist, as had happened time and again.

The biggest undertaking at the time was to get people to understand that it wasn't about whether they had been actively racist, like yelling slurs. Most people, I'd venture to say, are not. It was and still is getting people to understand that racism is structural, in the same way that sexism is structural. It wasn't just good enough to say you weren't racist – that's like patting someone on the back for not being sexist. What was required was for each person to commit to being anti-racist, and part of that work involved getting them to look at how diverse their lives really were. Many realised that, for instance, when it came to fitness, they hadn't noticed the lack of Black fitness people they followed on social media, on the cover of fitness magazines, how white their fitness studios were or even the lack of diversity in the sport they enjoyed watching.

The penny started to drop which was that collectively, a lack of diversity works to perpetuate a stereotype about fitness, which is young, white and lean, and that in turn influences not just the uptake of activity in certain communities, but how white people perceive Black and other people of colour in those spaces.

A good way of getting people to think about how diverse their lives were was by asking them to look at their social media feeds and asking how many Black fitness influencers they followed. The conversation then broadened out, and yoga in particular became a very interesting area to see people's attitudes to race and culture, because it has long since been a practice where brown people have been whitewashed out, and Black people are under-represented. When some white people said they didn't see what the problem was, it had to be pointed out that if the definition of cultural appropriation was one demographic which enjoys more privileges (the white community) taking a practice from another demographic which is subject to a higher level of oppression (in this case, the South Asian community) and at every level erasing the subordinate community, from the people who teach it to the people modelling clothes, then yes, there was a big problem. For many, it was a shock, and many were defensive.

We live in a society which, at present, places whiteness and Western features at the top of the attractiveness pyramid. Social media algorithms therefore are designed to promote whiteness because it prioritises content that is more popular and whiteness is the popular choice. That means when accounts are suggested for you or surfaced, they are more likely to be white influencer accounts. This is just one illustration of how making your world – whether that's social media, your friends circle, the organisations you work with – more diverse requires more effort. Instagram finally admitted the bias that existed in their algorithm due to pressure and a campaign after they kept taking down the photos of Black plus-size model and influencer Nyome Nicholas-Williams.

Representation matters at every level of life, especially when it comes to physical movement, girls and women. Just 17 per cent of the women who responded to my survey said they felt represented in the fitness industry, while 46 per cent said they didn't feel represented at all. Those are damning figures, especially given that 39 per cent said they'd have a better relationship with fitness if they were better represented and 41 per cent said that they would have had a better relationship with fitness when they were younger if they'd been better represented. Zainab, who took the survey, wrote: 'As a young Asian Muslim British girl, I use exercise to empower myself but find it hard to relate to many fitness bloggers because I don't look like them. If anything, it makes me want to be whiter and to match my lives up to people without a similar culture to me.'

When it comes to ethnicity and race, lack of representation can have serious consequences. The latest report from Sport England shows that Black, Asian and Chinese people are the least active groups in the UK.[1] However, it's not just about being healthy or moving more, it's about giving every girl the equal chance to access it when they are younger because of the parallels it has to success, empowerment and leadership. When we then look at under-representation of Black women at senior management and board level, for instance, it matters.

That representation also has to be intersectional because gender, like race, is not a monolith. It is redundant to celebrate more women in sport, if all or the vast majority of those women are young and white, because they do not represent women as a whole. This should be important to everyone because an industry that is not particularly inclusive around race will also not be very inclusive around other things, such as age or body size.

There are two women I credit with planting the seed that I could actually pick up a barbell and it wouldn't be a ludicrous thing.

The first was my friend Pariena, who is South Asian. We met years ago while working for the same magazine and had kept in touch through Facebook. About six months before I made that first step towards hiring Tyrone and telling him I wanted to get strong, I saw a video that Pariena posted on Facebook, of her doing a 60kg deadlift.

It blew my tiny mind. Pariena was a brown woman, I said. Pariena has kids, I said. Pariena is a similar age to me and . . . maybe this means I can do it too?

Thunderbolt moments are actually pretty rare but that was one of them. Pariena was the first regular woman who looked like me, who I had seen lifting weights and that made me want to try it too. Because now it seemed possible and the video proved that it was.

The second woman is the Indian actress, athlete and model Bani J, who I came across on Instagram and instantly fell in love with. Bani is absolutely covered in tattoos; I too have some big, visible tattoos, but it is pretty rare to come across South Asian women who looked like her. When I saw that she did proper lifting, I thought: 'Maybe I can actually do this?'

I began to become obsessed about that statistic, that out of every demographic in the UK, South Asian women were the least active. I started to think about what was making it harder to get physically active and made a list.

1. The lack of role models and mainstream fitness definitely didn't help. For instance, I don't ever remember there being a South Asian fitness model or personality on the cover of *Women's Health* and at fitness events, the number of South Asian personalities or influencers were few if any. The same was true for fitness models for activewear brands. This seemed really fucked up to me – I'd never seen fit, strong brown bodies used to represent fitness for most of my life.

2. In South Asian cultures specifically, we have considerations around modesty. For instance, that might be feeling uncomfortable wearing a swimsuit in front of men, or using a changing room with no cubicles to get undressed in.

3. Actually having fitness kit that wasn't form-hugging, but also at a reasonable price point.

4. We police women in our own community and the chief way of discouraging girls to be outdoors is colourism.

5. Constant conflict of ideologies which creates a torturous set of paradoxes. On the one hand, we have a culture centred around food and overfeeding, while on the other, we brutally comment on other people's weight. We are then told to lose weight by doing more exercise, and we are also told to stay out of the sun in case we get darker.

Not being represented properly in fitness is damaging. But it also shows that blockers for girls and women aren't as simple as just 'gender' and 'race' and that cultural layers make it pretty tough too. It's one thing to have the confidence to try something but being discouraged by your own community makes it even harder work.

To give a sense of how oppressive colourism is (because someone once asked me if it was the same as white people wanting to tan), it is something that, in my experience, every single South Asian person has experienced and is aware of from a very young age. (I can only speak for my own culture but others from African, Caribbean, East Asian and Middle Eastern cultures may likely feel similar.) The origins vary for different countries but for mine, it is rooted in the caste system and then perpetuated by the British who gave preferential treatment the fairer you were during colonialism.

So no, it is not like tanning, which is a two-way door of whiteness that allows you to enjoy the privilege of being white and tanned all at the same time. Colourism is a system based on your proximity to the door leading to whiteness and it determines your worth, your access to wealth, success, work, marriageability. None of it is something you have control over and you are NEVER actually allowed through the door.

My only reprieve from the full onslaught of colourism was my green eyes because they were seen as proximity to whiteness. When I played tennis as a child, my skin darkening in the sun was something that was frequently commented on, but while it made me self-conscious, I can't say it put me off playing tennis or made me so unhappy I tried a skin whitening cream. However, when I really got a sense of how insidious colourism was, and how it related to being a blocker for girls and women when it came to physical fitness, is when I started doing outdoor sports in my late twenties.

*

At the beginning of 2008, I was completely burnt out from my job at NewsCorp and took a short sabbatical to travel around India. At the time, I hero-worshipped the travel writer and novelist Paul Theroux, and one of his books I'd been reading at the time was *Fresh Air Fiend*, which featured some of his experiences kayaking. It seemed incredibly serene but, at the same time, daunting.

Due to being about as financially responsible as a cocaine-fuelled child actor, I blew all of my sabbatical money in the first month. I managed to grab about four weeks' work in Mumbai, on an international magazine that was launching in India. While I was there, a bookshop around the corner from my apartment advertised a public appearance by, guess who – Paul Theroux. I saw it as a sign from the universe and went along.

It was great, apart from when I asked him what advice he'd have for women travelling and how I could do it as fearlessly as he had. He gave me some answer about gazelles being hunted by lions and likened that to women travelling alone, because of some men being predators. I'm still mulling over the response ten years later and maybe it's telling that I've never read a Theroux book since.

After leaving Mumbai, I went to Bangalore, where my family are based. The Maldives are a fairly quick and inexpensive flight away from Bangalore and I had always dreamed of going there, so even though it sounded fancy, I managed to wangle a free stay in a hotel in exchange for an article.

Resorts on the Maldives are often set on their own tiny islands, and by day two, gorgeous though it was, I was going bananas with boredom. While walking on the beach, I passed a little hut which had kayaks, and Elaine, the lady running it, suggested I try it. 'I'm too scared,' I said. 'I've never done it before.' She gave me such a withering *harden the fuck up* look that, out of sheer shame, I decided to try it out. The water was crystal clear and calm and our little island was protected by a reef, so although I almost crapped myself with fear the entire time and had to figure out how to use the paddle by myself – Elaine did not concern herself with things like advice – retrospectively, it was the safest place to step into my first kayak.

From that point, I fell in love with kayaking. It didn't matter that no one I knew did it – it unravelled me to the point of serenity and was something that stayed with me long after I put the paddle down. One of my dream places to kayak was Kerala, home to the backwaters, one of the most beautiful areas in South India – calm, still water framed in coconut trees, wending in and around people's homes set by the edge of the lake.

But it was there that I realised how much colourism could put women off outdoor activities. I was stared at – possibly because I was a woman travelling alone – but also I knew I was going darker by the day. Other Indians thought I was mad for voluntarily choosing to do this as a holiday because most people in Kerala did it for fishing or transport. I went a rich, molten brown and almost every relative remarked on it when I returned back to Bangalore. 'Sunburn' they called it – when I'd refer to it as a tan.

From then on, every time I kayaked in India, I felt that same scrutiny and assessment of being out in the sun. It was even more tangible when I tried surfing in my ancestral home, Mangalore. I visited a surf club called Mantra Surf Club who ran three-day courses and was also home to several girls who'd taken up paddleboarding and surfing. One of them was an exceptional young woman named Tanvi Jagadish, who was India's first female stand-up paddleboard racer. In the hot, humid air, we sat in the veranda, with the river in front of us, a kingfisher standing watch on the washing line.

Tanvi had fallen in love with the ocean when her grandparents took her swimming. When she started surfing, her parents didn't know about it; it was because her skin got darker and her hair got lighter from being in the sea and under the sun all the time that her mother got suspicious. When she found out, she made Tanvi sit at home for a year. But eventually, her brother persuaded her mother to let her pursue it, and then when people started to make fun of Tanvi for wearing swimwear, her mother turned into her biggest champion and told her to prove them wrong. Now, she does something that gives her such joy, the comments don't matter.

I recognise that joy. The reason why I kept kayaking and paddleboarding despite the comments about sunburn is because of the happiness I felt at being surrounded by open water. To know that a board is all that stands between you and the deep blue ocean connects you to the heart of the earth. It is capability, self-sufficiency, the very same freedom that catches in the underside of a bird's wing as it soars into the big beyond. All of that outweighed the worry about getting darker and what people would think of me.

Priya ended up taking up kayaking as well and one of the happiest moments was on a family holiday in 2019 when my mother also expressed a wish to try it out. The three of us took to the water off the coast of the Cinque Terre and she absolutely loved it. There was something incredibly healing and nurturing about the three of us taking to the water, doing one of my favourite things in the entire world, in part because our experience was multi-generational – this was something Priya and I shared with our mother and would share with Leela when she was a bit older.

When I looked into success stories of South Asian women who had done well in sport or physical activity, the presence of a supportive family was critical to their success. The more I got into powerlifting, I was also drawn to stories of South Asian women because I knew that in addition to overcoming the conditioning of their gender, they were also overcoming cultural expectations for women that could be limiting. And, as much as I loved powerlifting, it was also very, very white.

One of the amazing young women I came across was chartered accountant Karenjeet Kaur Bains, who was the first British Sikh female representing Britain at the World and European powerlifting championships, where she placed ninth. Just in her early twenties, she went on to be the Commonwealth champion for 2019, and her father – a former bodybuilder and powerlifter – is her coach. Karenjeet no doubt will go on to influence and inspire the next generation of female lifters, but if you are reading this and have never done weights or are unsure of where to start, someone who I was inspired by and who I know will inspire women – regardless of whether or not they are South Asian – is Bhavna Tokekar, a stay-at-home mother.

Bhavna is a 48-year-old Indian woman who won four gold medals at the Open Asian Powerlifting Championships of AWPC/WPC in Russia in 2019, and three gold medals and a world record in bench press at the World Open Powerlifting Championships in December of that same year. What makes her all the more remarkable is that she only started going to the gym and experimenting with weights when she turned 40.

'I have been married for 22 years,' she said when I called her, 'and I used to work before marriage, but my husband is a fighter pilot and I wanted to be around and support my home and my family. For 16 to 17 years, everything was done for me and, because of that, I had lost confidence to the point where

I couldn't go to the bank. After powerlifting, my confidence came back. I could speak on a stage, I can speak to you right now and before, it was very difficult for me to talk to a stranger, or talk about how I feel. I had stopped interacting with the outside world. After I started powerlifting, it marked a change in my attitude and changed me totally.'

Bhavna first started going to the gym when she was 40 because she had a skin inflammation problem and the medication she was taking caused her to gain weight and have mood swings. While there, a male bodybuilder suggested she also try the weights section.

She explains, 'I'd heard so much about if you lift weights you'll look like a male and develop muscles. You'll be huge. And the other part was that I didn't want to hurt myself and break my bones. So initially I was quite scared of it. He said: "You don't have to lift heavy, why don't you just try it out."' The only sport Bhavna had ever played competitively was table tennis at school. But after overcoming her fear of lifting weights and watching a lot of YouTube videos and going on Instagram, she came across powerlifting, and decided that she wanted to try it. 'I thought I should at least compete once,' she said.

She says a lot of her relatives don't actually know what it is that she does. And she has had some unbelievably harsh comments from some friends and relatives. I could hear the emotion in her voice when she started speaking about it: 'I got a lot of negative feedback such as "it is not done generally by women", "why should anyone do it after 40?", "she has a good husband, what is the problem?" According to them, I wasn't huge so that I need to reduce weight. My husband and my kids were very supportive and are still supportive. But those comments hurt me, it continues to hurt me and there were times when I used to cry in the gym.'

But there are moments that make it worth it. Bhavna told me about the time a P.E. teacher used her story as an example in a class. One of the children went and told her own mother, that woman looked up Bhavna's story and as a result of it, started weight training.

Above all, Bhavna's story is an inspiring tale because even though social conditioning may have prevented you from reaching your full power until much later – as was the case with me too – it's never too late. 'I've seen ladies who have started at the age of 70,' she says. 'At 40, we do go through hormonal changes that don't affect men. To balance those things, weight training is the perfect thing to do.'

Strength training is an area I've noticed more and more South Asian women moving into but I've also seen increasing numbers of women move into martial arts. At Jack's gym, Elevate, there is a fair number of South Asian women who do Brazilian jiu-jitsu, and the manager of the gym, Ameesha Bhudia-Patel, who has also become a close friend of mine, is an ex MMA fighter and represented Team GB in judo when she was a teenager.

Someone who does a lot for women of colour in ju-jitsu (which is different to BJJ as it originates in Japan) is Mumtaz Khan, who is the founder of Bradford-based Onna Ju-Jitsu. She's been outspoken about how she thinks there is bias in how Black, Asian and non-white candidates are judged in ju-jitsu competitions and a lot of her coaches are from those backgrounds. P.E. was her least favourite lesson at school, she says, and she had low self-esteem. When she was 20, she had a disagreement with an African man over who had booked the hall she normally played badminton in. She swore at him and he disappeared only to re-emerge in a ju-jitsu gi and a black belt. To her surprise, he offered to teach her and she took him up on his offer.

'When I started ju-jitsu,' she said, 'I had to train with six men, which was really challenging for me due to cultural restrictions at the time. My dad had threatened to kick me out of the family home if I continued my training and my mother thought I was going to be kidnapped by my sensei. Times have changed. Attitudes have changed. As a female coach, I have been able to provide female-only sessions. I have been able to create an environment that respects the needs of the local community and provides solutions to meet these needs.'

Mumtaz decided that she wanted to go to university part-time and open her own ju-jitsu club. In her final year of university, unbelievably, she went on *Deal or No Deal* and won £24,000, which gave her the seed money to start Onna.

While there needs to be better representation and attitudes need to change culturally, the importance of grassroots communities and organisations like Onna are really important. In 2019, Onna received financial support to help train a wider group of people. The result? They have 77 per cent female coaches and 94 per cent of them are Black, Asian and from other ethnic minorities – because they recognise that it's important in order to get more women from those backgrounds interested as well. 'Having female coaches delivering female-only sessions has enabled many Muslim girls/women to engage in the sport and it is widely supported by the local community with most of its members joining through word of mouth referrals,' Mumtaz explains.

Cricket has also been a very successful way of connecting with communities who might be hard to reach. Shruti Saujani is the city programme manager for the England and Wales Cricket Board (ECB) and has done a lot of work to get South Asian women of all ages to pick up a bat and ball. Part of that has been about creating local groups and clubs for girls and women to try it out.

Being able to plant the seeds of fitness this way also means that certain people can make physical activity a part of their lives, rather than feel they need to keep their culture and their love of fitness separate.

Muslim women of every race have been heavily overlooked when it comes to representation in the fitness space but, in the last year, I have noticed a definitive shift both on social media and in the products sold by major sportswear brands such as Nike.

I attended a launch for Nike's Muslim swimwear line in early 2020. As I walked around the event, there were so many women excited about the launch as well as athletes who'd featured in the campaign. And yet, I realised, Muslim women are not given many opportunities when it comes to accessing physical fitness and sport. Aside from issues of low income – people from Pakistani and Bangladeshi heritage are the lowest hourly paid in the UK – there are cultural considerations, a lack of representation in the mainstream and, previously, a lack of actual sportswear to allow Muslim women to work out.[2] The burkini, created by Lebanese-Australian designer Aheda Zanetti in 2004, was a gamechanger but suitable headwear that allows girls to sweat and work out has only been a recent addition.

Nazira Bemath actually ended up creating her own line of headwear after chatting to her sporty daughter Malaika and discovering that a lack of proper kit was preventing Muslim girls from being active. Malaika is 13 and her school's sports ambassador. Although she doesn't wear the hijab, part of her role is to get more girls involved in sport. But, she told her mum, a lot of them didn't want to get involved because of their hijabs and getting hot and sweaty.

'It's a hygiene issue,' said Nazira, 'as the normal hijabs they wear during the day are not breathable or sweat-wicking. But also, their hijabs were just not fit for purpose – pinning and tucking means there is a health and safety issue.' Malaika said that she was convinced more girls would take part if they had a 'sports hijab'. Nazira worked with a fashion designer friend to then make her own.

I asked if I could talk to Malaika about it. Malaika is confident and she says a lot of that is because she feels strong and capable, and sport helps her cope with changes in her body, something she sees a lot of other girls struggling with.

'I think girls from BAME (Black, Asian and minority ethnic) backgrounds are encouraged to do better in academics than sports,' she said. 'Most of my friends go to tuition after school, while I go to the gym. It's not seen as important in our communities and, if you think about it, there are hardly any female role models in sport from BAME communities. I guess this is another reason why girls don't follow sport – maybe if we had more role models girls would get more interested and feel inspired.'

Some incredible Muslim role models that spring to my mind are the British rugby player Zainab Alema, who plays for Barnes RFC; the German boxer Zeina Nassar, who is their national featherweight champion; American Ibtihaj Muhammad, who is a champion fencer and a Nike athlete, and Nouf Alosaimi from Saudi Arabia, who founded Pink Bubbles, a female-only diving community.

Women like this are needed more than ever, given that the restrictions faced by Muslim women aren't just around a lack of kit but legislation that excludes them out of bigotry. I will never forget when France introduced the burkini ban in response to a terrorist attack, which is so bizarre and offensive given that the burkini was created to give women the chance to enjoy swimming just like anyone else, to empower them and allow them to be modest at the same time. Banning it seemed like the most ineffective measure, as it not only narrowed the options for women further but also seemed to me to be an aggressive counter-measure aimed at Islam as a whole, rather than targeting terrorists. While the UK hasn't done anything like that, it is hardly progressive – it wasn't until 2017 that the ban on wearing burkinis in amateur swimming competitions was lifted.

When women are shown the way and not held back, there is no telling what they might achieve. When Nike launched its Pro Hijab in 2017, figure skater Zahra Lahri said: 'It's a reminder to us Muslim women that we can achieve anything in the world. What Nike has done for Muslim athletes is a dream that we never thought would happen.'

A brilliant grassroots organisation that's a good example of supporting Muslim girls and women is Muslim Girls Fence, which is a collaboration between Maslaha, an organisation that challenges Islamophobia and inequalities facing Muslims, and British Fencing. There are two groups – one for secondary school girls and another for women over the age of 16. To me, fencing has always seemed pretty elitist and I was sure it was mainly taught in private schools but Shaheen Kasmani, who is the senior project manager, says that's what's actually great about the project: it creates a safe space, centring the needs of participants and making a sport that is normally tough to access because of cost more accessible.

'If you don't happen to live locally to a sports facility, you have to account for travel, and an area that may be unfamiliar and not at all diverse,' said Shaheen. 'Unfortunately, we are living in a time where right-wing hatred, racism and Islamophobia is on the rise, so it's also about safety and feeling welcome. There are reasons why Muslim women are less likely to participate in sports activities and some of these may seem obvious but a lot of the reasons boil down to structural issues of discrimination. If sports were more inclusive generally and honestly tackled these structural issues more widely, not just in terms of basics like representation or clothing, then participation might be more widespread. Communities are often described as "hard to reach" but what we've found is that it's the sports sector and sports facilities that are often hard to reach."

In the same way that all women don't experience things equally, women of colour aren't a single, homogenous group either. One of the most important things to emerge from the attention focused by the Black Lives Matter movement is how the experience for Black women is so much significantly worse than it is for other women of colour and that the level of aggression and inequality they experience deserves its own conversation and platform without the rest of the POC community diluting the conversation. The reason why this is so important is because of the differences in how we are treated.

For instance, if you're female and South Asian, you tend to be ruled out when it comes to strength. That's because, from a positive bias point of view, we're generally viewed as small, petite and feminine.

Black women, on the other hand, experience the opposite treatment, where they are assumed to be physically stronger just because of their race. As a result, I've heard of cases where girls and women aren't given as much assistance in exercise classes because instructors assume they're able to 'handle' it.

The reason it is so important to discuss strength in the context of race is because it highlights precisely why we need to have broader representations of women in fitness. If you're reading this thinking, 'Wow, I'd love people to assume I'm strong,' then that's probably because your life hasn't been affected by people assuming you might be more aggressive, resilient, even impervious just because of the colour of your skin. Black women endure this daily and it's a bias that can be damaging and exhausting because, as Kelechi Okafor says, that type of strong is 'void of vulnerabilities, void of emotion and is unfeeling in nature. Black women's bodies have never been attributed with humanity or with empathy,' she said. 'When people say you're strong, while there is strength in vulnerability, that is not the kind of strength that we're talking about. These terms are very loaded. We look at white femininity and how it's placed as delicate and almost fragile and then black as strong, hard and unfeeling. It's a false dichotomy and means that Black women are continually left out of conversations about femininity and womanhood and that isn't by accident.'

The reason why representation is important – and this is particularly significant if you are not Black – is that, unless your friendship circle is super diverse, you will only ever have these views reflected back at you. And, as we have seen, social media is not set up to educate you unless you deliberately seek it out. Following more Black influencer accounts helps to dismantle the stereotypes you have unconsciously absorbed and supports women who make a business of it. Also, research shows that when we see more diverse images we are happier because it's more reflective of the world we are in versus some artificial bubble.[3]

Black women in particular, to me, are under-represented in mainstream fitness, whether it's in adverts, experts consulted by the media or influencers. Even when Black women are used in adverts, it tends to be lighter-skinned women because they are deemed more attractive due to their proximity to whiteness.

A campaign by JD Sports that was meant to be all about diversity came under heavy criticism for not using any dark-skinned Black women. Journalist and co-author of *Slay in Your Lane*, Yomi Adegoke, wrote a feature about it and remarked that while dark-skinned Black men feature in sportswear campaigns, the same is not true of women. The disparity in how darker-skinned Black women are treated is something the supremely talented actor and director Michaela Coel has spoken about extensively following the huge success of her TV show *I May Destroy You*. She is well worth reading about and listening to on podcasts if you'd like to know more.

A festival that was created in response to the invisibility of Black women in the fitness space is NoireFitFest, created by yoga specialist and intuitive wellbeing coach Donna Noble and spin instructor and nutritionist Lorraine Russell. One of the things they highlighted was that while elite Black athletes are hugely famous, that hasn't translated into the everyday fitness industry. It's important, they say, because according to the Sport England report, only 56 per cent of Black people meet the guidelines of 150 minutes of physical activity per week. Some of this is down to representation, while another reason might be that Black people don't feel comfortable or safe in certain spaces. Grassroots groups are springing up to create that space, however.

Black Girls Hike, set up by Rhiane Fatinikun, is an example of this movement – it exists to create a safe space for Black women to enjoy the outdoors without worrying about discrimination. Hiking is not something associated with Black people, she wrote in a piece for *Women's Health*, and isn't marketed at them. Given the levels of suspicion and micro-aggressions that Black people face every day, she didn't feel comfortable joining hiking groups, which are almost always dominated by middle-class white men. Her group helps other Black women to explore their love of hiking in a safe, supportive environment. Some other amazing initiatives include Boarders Without Borders, founded in 2017 by Amna Akhtar, a community of women of colour who like boardsports such as longboarding, surfing and snowboarding. The rugby player Zainab Alema set up a grassroots initiative called Studs in the Mud to make it easier for girls and women to access rugby more easily after facing various hurdles such as feeling unsafe when going to rugby clubs which would often be in secluded areas, but also being stared at by other people when she was kitted up in a hijab.

One of my favourite success stories, of what can happen when sport is made more accessible, is Khadijah Mellah, who learned to ride at the Ebony Horse Club in Brixton, an organisation that believes riding and horse care can have a life-changing effect on young people growing up in disadvantaged communities. Khadijah's mother is from Kenya and her dad from Algeria and she is the first hijab-wearing jockey in a British competitive horse race. Not only this but, despite being so new to racing, she won the 2019 Magnolia Cup at Goodwood – a world famous, renowned charity event for women riders.

Another incredible organisation is Swim Dem Crew, also based in London, created by Nathaniel Cole and Peigh Asante with the goal of making swimming more inclusive and social and it's also for Black people who want to learn and feel joyous with swimming. But it's not just a question of exclusion. Black children, for instance, are three times more likely to drown and a disproportionate number of Black people don't know how to swim because of myths that circulate and the lack of safe spaces to learn.[4] There is only one Black swimmer on the British team, Alice Dearing, who is a marathon swimmer and on a mission to overturn the idea that Black people don't swim.

When you aren't even seen as a viable option in sport and

fitness because of what you look like, that is a huge problem when it comes to accessing and talking about strength. There is so much incentive for making our fitness spaces more inclusive, not least because there is great energy, power and creativity to be gained learning about different identities. It doesn't take much to shuffle over a little bit to create room for other people.

I will close this chapter with Kelechi's words on strength, and why it is critical to open our minds and change what we think strength is, both for ourselves and others: 'Redefining your idea of strength has been my focus. Helping other women to do it, but especially helping Black women to do it. My strong allows me to be vulnerable, my strong allows me to cry, my strong allows me to be joyful, and my strong also allows me to be physically powerful. And I want that for as many women as possible.'

CHAPTER TWELVE

The Power of Periods and Werewolf Mothers

'Magic comes at a price,' says the witch or wizard in practically every story where magical things happen, referring to the balance of all things – when something is created and called into being, something alters and disappears.

The shifting transformation from menstruation to menopause is of course biology and science, but how it moves between the stages of being able to give life and not, to me, is magic. It comes from the place of vastness of all things that change shape; I think of this like the home of werewolves, where we shift and stretch and roar, a place of blood and fire and life that we are all connected to, and there is incredible power to be had in that.

But many of us have not been made to feel like that. Going off the back of living on this planet for 40 years, I've noticed that many of us have held a kernel of shame ever since our first period and then, whatever our journeys were subsequently, our transformations were not handled peacefully, with care or love. Many of us were just left to figure it out ourselves. Whether the change was prompted by puberty, motherhood, menopause or something else such as illness, some of us have felt lost, untethered from our former selves, unclear of how to move forward with purpose and power. With each change, power is needed in vast quantities – to support you when the change happens, and then afterwards, when your body and mind is trying to adapt to the new landscape it now finds itself in. In an ideal world, you should only ever grow more powerful the more your body changes and moves through the cycles, but because women are expected to carry on as normal, or revert to what they used to be or made to compete and keep pace with cisgender men who do not undergo anything like this biologically, each transition breaks women down and disconnects them from themselves.

When we aren't connected to our strength – whether that's because of toxic ideas around weight loss, youth or 'normality' – it can create a dissonance that leaves us permanently disappointed in our own bodies and, yet again, beating ourselves up for what our body does or doesn't do, rather than admiring and respecting the transformation it has undergone.

I'm not a mother and I may never be in the biological sense, but I have seen time and again, the pattern that emerges around how power is stripped from mothers after they give birth. I have seen women who have questioned their sense of self when they come back into the workplace because of how their motherhood is weaponised against them. In the survey, pregnancy and motherhood came up repeatedly as reasons why women disengaged from exercise. Women feeling like they didn't have time for fitness was often mentioned but also self-consciousness at having a body changed by birth.

In this chapter, I'm going to cover periods, motherhood and menopause. Even if you're not a mother, like me, you might find it helpful in terms of challenging what we've come to associate with motherhood and consequently depictions of mothers. Whether you are child-free by choice or not, society still insists on defining us by that status, and pitting us against each other, in a way that men are not. We likely have friends who are mothers and knowing this stuff helps in terms of understanding them better.

For a number of years, while I liked the idea of having children, the prospect of motherhood itself scared the hell out of me. Mostly because, while it seemed fulfilling and overflowing with love, it seemed to change who you were, be incredibly tiring and make you a stranger in your own life. What I didn't realise was that some of this might be a self-fulfilling prophecy of believing that motherhood has to be back-breaking sacrifice because of what we'd seen in older generations. But there are women who do not want it to be all-consuming sacrifice, but perhaps don't know where to start or how to give themselves permission to be different. To help with that, this chapter will aim to cover the stories of inspiring women who are also mothers, and will be inspiring even if you aren't one.

But first, periods.

Confession time: I was a very late bloomer. I'm not just talking about my boobs, which were like plant bulbs that started to emerge halfway and then appeared to have given up. While other girls switched from Tammy Girl crop tops to bras, I required no supportive elements beyond an elasticated band. This was highlighted most starkly when changing for P.E., where it became increasingly evident who were the haves and have-nots of the boob world. I remember a friend who was teased for having a chest flatter than the art room table, almost overnight come into possession of a pair of bouncing D cups.

The topic of periods also started to surface and soon it seemed like everyone had started theirs but me. I remember waiting and praying so that I too could be part of the gang. What an idiot. I should have enjoyed the period-free years for as long as I could.

When I eventually got my period, I was 15. I realise that this is extremely late given that some girls started at nine. When mine began, I was at home and I told my mum, who just handed me a sanitary towel which she deemed explanation enough and I don't remember us having much of a chat about it. Asian mums don't really do period or sex chat, so this was definitely true to form.

I hated the sanitary towel; it felt like a nappy and constantly reminded me I was on my period when I just wanted to get on with my day. When the first day of my first period was over, I remember thinking: 'No fucking way. There is no way I am going to go through decades of this– there has to be an alternative.' And there was: tampons. I went to Boots, bought a packet for myself (bear in mind this was pre-internet days so there were no helpful YouTube videos saying: 'You've got this, girl!'). I then spent about 15 minutes in the toilet with the pamphlet figuring it out and I didn't look back.

Over the years, however, I've learned that this was unusual. A lot of South Asian girls aren't encouraged or are actively discouraged from using tampons because of the association between virginity and inserting something inside yourself. Yeah, because nothing says sexy time like being on your period and a wad of compressed cotton. I didn't feel the need to ask my mother for permission around something I put inside myself, and she was probably too squeamish to discuss it.

I'm also lucky because I have always had light periods, so with the help of tampons and a couple of ibuprofens, their impact was minimal. It wasn't until I spoke to Priya, who did have heavy periods, as well as other women, that I realised how debilitating it could be. That was even before I learned about women who had polycystic ovaries or endometriosis, which make periods an absolute hellscape every month where some women can't physically move because of the fatigue and pain.

Periods are a blocker to physical strength for girls and women because of the significant pain some experience – which was not taken seriously back in my day – but also because of the shame we have around periods – so worrying about leaking while working out. We live in a society that is completely inept in adapting to girls, women, trans and non-binary people who have periods, as well modelling everything in health and fitness around cisgender men who don't have periods. 'I used to do karate,' wrote Terry in the survey, 'and periods stopped me going once a month, because the suits are white.'

Tackling the taboo of periods in fitness is everyone's issue. Given that the tax on sanitary products in the UK was only removed in 2020, society's attitude so far has been that periods are a girl or woman's issue, that they have to suck up and deal with, rather than acknowledging the fact that the human race would literally die out if it wasn't for the menstruation process.

The taboo of periods isn't just centred around the danger of public embarrassment or jeering comments either. Girls and women aren't generally taught things about the menstrual cycle beyond how it biologically happens, even though it can have a massive effect on them when they are doing exercise or sport, not to mention if they are dieting. In athletes, for instance, it can result in higher levels of injuries – female football and basketball players are three times more likely than male players to suffer from anterior cruciate ligament injuries. Fluctuations in hormones may affect how tissues function and high oestrogen levels have been connected to how the hamstring muscles work, which may make women more prone to injuries depending on their periods.

Chelsea Football Club became the first football club in the world to tailor training to menstrual cycles for female football players to maximise performance and reduce injuries. But what does it mean for non-professional athletes and women who like to exercise?

Generally speaking, the menstrual phase, which is when you bleed, is when your progesterone, oestrogen and luteinizing hormone is at its lowest level, which basically means you're going to be at your most tired. Rather than pushing yourself, listen to what your body wants to do.

The follicular phase, which lasts up to 10 days, is when your oestrogen levels rise and this means you'll start to have much more energy, so if you want to train lots or try new classes, this is a great time.

The ovulation phase, which lasts up to five days is when your hormone levels are at their highest, and you're at your highest level of energy. Go bananas, basically.

The luteal phase then begins which can last up to 14 days and is when your hormone levels start to drop and you might feel sluggish. Your basal energy expenditure (so the energy you burn just by sitting and not doing anything) may be higher too, which is why you might start to feel hungrier than normal.

Did you know any of this stuff? I didn't know any of this until a few months ago. It matters because if you don't do exercise, and you end up starting a new activity at a stage in your menstrual cycle when you might have the least amount of energy, it may end up putting you off continuing with it, if the activity feels unpleasant and knackering. All that time when I beat myself up for being lazy in the gym, or when I thought I was being greedy because I was hungry, I had no idea that my hormones were pulling strings in the background. If I had known this, I would have been a lot kinder to myself.

The lack of information combined with a society that doesn't want to talk about periods, or manoeuvre around them in any way, means that we try to push through being on our period, even if it is so bad it is causing serious physical pain. Also, because historically periods are taboo, there's a lot we don't know about the fundamental biology of our bodies.

I think it would help if P.E. teachers factored in periods when teaching exercise, as well as PTs being more clued up. Being equipped with information about our own bodies gives us the best possible chance at creating a positive fitness life for ourselves. 'I wish more coaches and trainers had a better understanding of how the menstrual cycle affects the women they're training,' wrote Gisella in the survey. 'It's absurd to me that some coaches walk around with a 90 per cent female client base and have NO idea about periods.'

One thing that has helped hugely is sports stars being vocal about how periods affect their performance and training, as well as recognition by clubs and organisations such as Chelsea.

In the survey, over 30 per cent of respondents said that their periods always stopped them from working out, while 27 per cent said their period sometimes stopped them from working out, which is a big percentage.

Vivica, who has heavy periods, wrote that she finds it affects her ability to do intense exercise and she feels more emotional. She says: 'With periods, generally the attitude is to encourage women to be like men and just ignore it. I know this probably comes from a place of wanting to encourage equality but the reality is you can't just ignore massive physical and emotional changes every single month. And women have such different experiences with their periods that you can't generalise either.'

I now know that I may have to adjust the time frame when I might be aiming for a big lift. Or that I'll possibly need to eat a bit more that week because my energy levels might be a bit low due to my hormone levels. Understanding that allows me to read and respond to my body's needs, as opposed to always pushing it beyond the point of comfort because I think it's slacking off. That kind of relationship takes trust, but it also takes knowledge, and that knowledge is something that does need to be handed out by the people who educate and inform us about our bodies during our formative years – whether that's our teachers or our parents – and as adults, by our doctors or personal trainers.

Instead of supporting and recognising periods, our society makes us feel like we're somehow responsible for them, and the lack of information we are taught about our bodies creates feelings of isolation and disconnect when things go wrong, take longer to heal or don't function the way they are supposed to. There are some similar parallels with motherhood. Women are all too often expected to carry on or return to their lives as if they haven't created, housed and birthed an entire actual human.

As someone who doesn't have kids, I feel like I can say this in an unbiased way: what the fuck is up with that?

I have never been pregnant, and I don't know if I ever will have children. My body is still capable of having them (I think) but Rob is the only partner I have ever thought about having them with, and I'm currently single. Given the STATE of modern dating, that's unlikely to change anytime soon.

When you think about having children with someone, it's

different to getting married. Getting married is the initial flutter of the engagement ring, the type of wedding you'll have and whether your two families get on. You're not entirely sure what married life will look like, only that it will be the two of you, together.

Wanting children together is a dream pulled from a place that comes from both of you, but also comes from a place of longing and hope. Our child did not exist and never will. But there were moments when she was almost real enough, where she was given shape and thought and her soul name was briefly murmured into existence. When I understood Rob and I would never have her was not when he died, but several months before that. It was when I realised, and I think he did too, that his addiction was too volatile, too chaotic and unstable, for us to ever subject a creature we would love more than anything in the world to it.

While even writing this recalls a deep, tumbling well of sadness, it speaks to the part of our life that died forever, rather than me never becoming a mother – which is a different thing altogether. I think that if I, and my body, truly wanted it, we would have no qualms about becoming a mother alone.

I'm aware that writing about biological motherhood, and how it relates to strength, might seem odd given that I am not one, but perhaps what I can offer here is an unbiased observation, as well as the advice from experts and the lived-in accounts of mothers. The reason why I have included a section on motherhood in a book about strength is because pregnancy and giving birth is one of the major transitions a woman's body will ever go through, physically, mentally and spiritually, yet consistently, there are things that work to rob women of the strength and power that comes with knowing you've created a life.

Motherhood is still largely framed in terms of self-sacrifice and endurance. The mother must bear all, carry all, even at great cost to herself. Mothers are sacred: an all-creating, all-encompassing figure who is at the core of the family, who is the person that will always be there when the chips are down. This idea of motherhood, however, doesn't just create a bigger emotional and domestic burden for women to carry, but the endless cycle of guilt becomes part of how mothers are policed and are made to justify choices in other parts of their lives, in a way men are not.

'The myth of Mother' is how Kelechi referred to it in an IGTV video, off the back of a lot of little comments she gets from other mothers whenever she posts a video of herself working out or going for a run. 'You're so lucky to have the time,' they say to her. In the video, Kelechi confronts this head on. She says that it's not like she has lots of time sloshing around, rather she has all the same stuff other mums have to do but she prioritises going for a run because it's good for her mental health.

'How about a good mother is someone that also prioritises her needs because how can she prioritise other people when she can't give to herself?' said Kelechi.

I asked Priya about it because it was a revelation and she confirmed that she gets it all the time. Given that being physically active can help mothers in a number of ways, both in terms of reconnecting with their bodies as well as managing a better sense of mental wellbeing, it's essential those obstacles are removed.

In the survey, a mother named Jenny wrote about how exercise had helped her through the whole process of becoming a mum. 'I had always been a gym goer, but after my daughter was born I got really low and found myself a bit lost. Then I found a mum and baby spin class and it really improved my mood. I found women who shared my passion and had a purpose for each day, instead of moping about the house. Fitness saved me at my lowest ebb and now I appreciate it as more than just a chore. It's something I have for me, separate to my identity as a mum. It has really helped my mental health.'

Of course, mothers are not just expected to be flawless, nurturing beings, there is also the expectation and pressure that you need to 'bounce back' to your previous body shape before you had a baby. In other words, diet culture. It takes vast amounts of power to create a life and when that process is over, there is a pressure to go back to what it was like before it went through this enormous, life-changing thing.

This pressure can make the relationship with fitness an insurmountable mountain. It seems too hard, impossible to even get out and move your body, particularly when you consider that physically you're dealing with recovery from post-partum effects which for some can include significant injuries, as well as grappling with sleep deprivation, and some mothers will be dealing with post-natal depression or at least the emotional overload of being a mum. All of this is a huge challenge when trying to recalibrate your relationship with yourself.

When I asked Priya about this, she said: 'I'd also add that after motherhood, as well as all those issues, your body just feels different – sometimes it can feel like it belongs to a totally different person. It's like being teleported into another human body and that discombobulation is also what puts women off exercise – the fact that their bodies just almost aren't theirs anymore. That's exacerbated by having to run around after a baby who is feeding from you and pulling and pushing your body – there are no physical boundaries in the way there once were and that can be tough.'

Motherhood seems to me to be more of a realm, than an intersection, because it's not just who you are or what you identify as, your mind and body have consciously gone to a place of formation and change. In this place, boundaries are broken and they become intangible. And when you emerge, the lines that define you are different, less corporeal. Having a strong sense of self seems crucial if you are to thrive and live and be serene, because the physical exhaustion, and society's keenness to pigeonhole you, will try to undermine that. The mainstream conversation around post-partum women and their bodies will have you believe that it is a singular narrative around weight loss, when in actual fact, not only is there a huge emotional component to it, but physically the experiences can be very different. For mothers who have had significant physical injury, which may require a year or two to recover from, it can be an isolating experience especially if that was the first time they've had major surgery. A 2015 *Lancet* study suggested that almost all women experience some form of *diastasis recti*, which is when your abdominal muscles separate, and can make a woman's belly feel different but also, make certain exercises difficult or dangerous to do.

I asked my friend Ameesha, who became pregnant while she was training for an MMA fight about it. She was a formid-able fighter and thought she would be back to training three months after giving birth, but it took a lot longer due to complications with her episiotomy. 'After giving birth, I would look in the mirror and not recognise the person looking back at me,' she says. 'I still had a big belly for quite a while. I recall always being embarrassed about how much weight I had put on, and would constantly mention how "fat" I was. I was worried what people would think, and felt that everyone, including family and friends just expected me to bounce back into shape. After all I was the sporty one, the qualified PT, and competing in high-level sport.'

Jack is also Ameesha's coach, and suggested she try power-lifting as it involved fewer training days than MMA, and being able to lift heavy weights started to make her look at her body differently. 'I wouldn't say I'm fully body confident now,' she says, 'but I am working constantly on changing the way I see my body. I've grown a human. I've become stronger. It's highly unlikely I'll ever go back to what I was, but that's OK.'

Seeking the help of the right experts, whether that's women's physios or PTs with experience in training post-partum women, is critical to being able to connect to physical activity in a way that is safe and right for you. It also helps you to set expectations that support you in a time that is already challenging due to the physical exhaustion caused by other aspects of parenting.

Clare Bourne, who is a mum of two and pelvic floor physio-therapist who helps women recover after giving birth, says: 'I think it is always helpful to think about timescales and the fact the changes in your body occurred over a nine-month period, therefore any changes that occur the other side are likely to take a similar amount of time, and for some, longer. For a lot of women this takes that immediate pressure off, that in the first few months they should be returning to their pre-baby self. I find education and understanding of the changes that have occurred and focusing on function not aesthetics is really helpful and key. For example, aiming to run free of pain or incontinence, rather than using running as a weight loss tool.'

Clare says that pelvic floor dysfunction, which may include incontinence or prolapse, can be a barrier to exercise and there is a significant link between it and depression, so getting it checked out and having help for it can open up a lot more options for mothers around physical movement.

Motherhood came up consistently in the survey as a reason why women disengaged from fitness and physical movement, because the goals seem impossible and unattainable. 'Motivation is a huge hurdle that women struggle with,' says Charlie Barker, who is a personal trainer and founder of Bumps & Burpees, a resource for pre- and post-natal mums wanting to keep fit.

'Feeling exhausted, finding time between feeding the baby and getting them to sleep, navigating work and morning sickness . . . it can be hard to summon up the energy and do some exercise when all you want to do is lie on the sofa and nap. I encourage women to also do that but being active can come in all forms – it doesn't just have to mean in the gym. You can count walking, playing with your kids in the garden, swimming, yoga in your pyjamas, dancing around your living room.'

There are also some quantifiable health benefits. 'Staying active during pregnancy can help to prevent excess weight gain,' adds Charlie, 'which will in turn help you to stay active towards the end of your pregnancy and, importantly, prepare for birth and motherhood. Labour can be long and it is definitely hard work. It requires physical and mental strength that you can build in the lead up.'

Although physical barriers are real and immense, Charlie says that, after birth, she has noticed how, time and again, it is the psychological barriers that are bigger. 'I find training women after they've had their baby is actually harder, due to the pressures they put on themselves,' Charlie says. 'I have to do a lot of realistic goal setting and working on mindset. Try to set short-term goals as well as long-term, so you aren't just focusing on being on the beach in six months' time but maybe work on your strength so you get rid of your back pain caused from holding your baby all the time.'

In early motherhood, time can feel elastic, so it's worth checking in with yourself as to what you are capable of in those early months. For instance, you might not be up for running two months after giving birth but six months might be a more reasonable goal to set for yourself.

Throughout this book, I've talked about the importance of community, and motherhood is no different. Clare says that a lot of new mums struggle with isolation and loneliness and being part of a class can help a lot, when you feel physically capable. 'Exercise can be used to help your body heal and recover and function pain free as a mother, which is so much more beneficial for us all than purely losing weight,' she says.

It doesn't mean weight loss can't be a goal, rather it's going to be zero fun and punishing if that's your only goal. If you can add other goals to it, particularly around strength or ability, it's easy to see that it's something that will literally help you physically with being a mother, from carrying your own children to having the energy to run around doing different things. And who wouldn't want that?

I'm going to tell you the story of Wendy Searle, a 42-year-old mother of four, who became the seventh woman in history to ski solo from the coastline of Antarctica to the South Pole. It's a spectacular story for so many reasons, one being that she had never skied before.

But first, I want to hold space for the women who want to become mothers and are struggling, or who have become mothers and lost their babies. Something I have heard time and again is how much experiences of miscarriage and/or fertility issues can turn you against your own body.

Every grief process is different, so it's not for me to say what's right or wrong – your grief is a tether to that place in the cosmos that is only for you and what you have lost. But what I will say is that there is a time to rage and be angry, there is a time to put some of that anger down, there is a time to grieve and be lost in sadness, there is a time to take your loss and move forward with it. The one thing true of all grief is that it teaches you the hardest lesson of all: the things that are actually within the scope of your control are tiny in comparison to the number of things that are not.

One of the most valuable lessons I have learned and continue to learn with the 12-step programme is the letting go of what you can't control and following what fuels and protects your serenity. Serenity cannot be given to you by anyone else, it can only come from you. Asking yourself what gives you serenity has to be done at the right time, not when your heart is broken by grief. Your heart needs to start healing and things need to be set down. When things are clearer, less foggy from loss, it's possible to see what might give you back a sense of control, without being controlling.

Your body is absolutely something that falls within that.

'Exercise during fertility issues,' wrote Padma in the survey, 'has been really important for claiming something back for myself having had my body prodded and poked. And exercise after miscarriage has also been a very healing thing.'

It's not to say that exercise will be some magical cure. More that grief has a way of breaking down every door in your mind and fertility grief especially can drive a wedge between your mind and your body. When the time is right, a walk in the forest to feel that slow, green life growing around you, the cool embrace of the sea or the hard protective anchor of a barbell may give you something to hold onto when you feel like the smallest creature being blown about in the gale you wished had never arrived.

Wendy Searle describes herself as 'Miss Average' in school and yet she completed a solo journey in one of the most extreme landscapes on earth.

For 42 days, she skied every day for up to 12 hours a day, with no rest days, and covered 715 miles in temperatures that went down to -35°C. She cried in her tent many times; she wanted to give up many times. Also: *she had never skied before.* But she didn't give up; she just kept going.

Wendy works full-time as a civil servant in Salisbury. She has four children aged between 11 and 21, and a husband. She doesn't come from money nor is she rich. She didn't get time off for training from her work life or her personal life. She didn't have bags of time, or extra help. She is just an ordinary woman like you and me who decided one day that being extra-ordinary isn't something you're always born with, but rather it is formed and shaped by the choices we make for ourselves.

She embarked on her expedition for many reasons, she says, one of which is to inspire women and girls to think about long-term goals and take on expeditions. 'I did gymnastics after school,' she says, 'and my parents valued education above most things but we weren't a wealthy family. I was OK at things. Academically I was fine but never outstanding. I went to a normal university and got a normal degree.'

Wendy describes herself as someone who has always had to work hard for what she had. She wanted to join the army but when that didn't happen – life and kids got in the way – she became a journalist, and then switched to working in defence communications.

The world of expeditions and big adventures is one she

describes as belonging to those with privilege. 'You never know anyone's story,' she says, 'but to me it has often been people who've managed to rely on the bank of mum and dad, or they've had the time because they haven't had the pressure of paying the bills.'

Wendy isn't wrong. When I think of people who go off on expeditions, either those I've come across because they were seeking corporate sponsorship or reading about them in the news, they are almost always white and male, usually with a private school background. If you go deeper (because there are rich women who can afford it too but who don't), it also is rooted in the gendered messaging you get as a child, which is that girls can aspire to being pretty, while adventures are for boys. (Boden got in big trouble for their children's clothing catalogue, telling girls to 'fill your pockets with flowers' and boys to 'start every adventure with a bike'.)

Despite not coming from a privileged background, Wendy always had a yearning for a big adventure that she says got covered up with juggling pregnancy, breastfeeding and then her career and children. She started Race for Life after having her first child, despite not previously being a runner, and then moved onto marathons and then ultrarunning.

But then one day, she was working for a military charity and a team came in to talk about doing a crossing of Antarctica. 'I didn't know much about Antarctica but was doing the PR for their expedition and I just got more drawn in. I did the training weekend with them and someone presented this lesson on polar injuries – and flashed up all these slides of fingers and bits of noses falling off. My colleague turned to me and said, "This looks absolutely horrendous," and I said, "Oh my god, this looks absolutely incredible." After that, I wondered if it was possible for someone with no money, time or experience to go from a standing start to achieving something like that. That's when the seed was sown and that turned into an obsession, and then a plan.'

The first step was finding out what needed to be done and that involved talking to ALE, the logistics company that arranges permits to Antarctica, deals with paperwork and gets you in and out. They also come and get you if you get into trouble. You then need to put together what Wendy calls a 'polar CV', of proven experience in things like handling long-range expeditions.

'The first real step was a two-week training course in Norway,' she said. 'You spend the first week going through every detail of what you wear, how you prepare the food. The second week you actually go on an expedition and it was one of the hardest things I've done and a complete baptism of fire.'

Once Wendy knew what she needed to do, she then got her family involved. The children helped out a lot at home and her husband did a lot of the cooking. What with training, her job and parenting to balance, Wendy had to make sure her week was meticulously planned because if it wasn't, then it meant she'd miss a training slot and there was literally no extra time to catch up.

Then there was raising the money, which she said was one of the toughest parts, especially because she didn't have any credentials. Getting her first sponsor was a significant turning point, but she says she begged, borrowed and stole what she could in terms of kit. The expedition, she said, was physically hard, but also tough mentally and emotionally.

'I was thinking about why it was so difficult,' she said, 'apart from being so cold and pulling this heavy weight every day. It was because you're never ever off duty. It's not like you can take a day off, or have a lie-in. Everything was about making progress. If you make a mistake or let your guard down, the consequences can be catastrophic. You're never ever thinking, "Oh, I'll just chill for five minutes".'

There was a bad storm that she got through but there were also small things, like making sure her hands didn't go numb. 'If you can't feel your hands, you can't call for help, you can't put your tent up. I would ski like a woman possessed until the circulation came back. Eventually it did, but for those few minutes, you're just waiting and hoping.'

Her biggest daily achievement was getting into the tent at the end of each day. That alone taught her that success was accumulative and she could use that to get further the following day. 'I never thought "I've made it" until the morning of the last day when I was 9.7 nautical miles from the South Pole and I could see it, because manmade things stand out there so clearly. And all the sacrifice telescoped into that one single moment of, I'm alive, I'm going to be OK.'

Mentally, it gave her a sense of self-belief and has made her feel like she can take on anything. But she also acknowledges that she is no longer the same person. Out there, in that vast landscape of snow and ice, something has changed her forever. 'I left my life in one shape, as a person,' she says, 'and I've come back slightly different. I don't fit that shape and I need to figure that out.'

As for her family, she says: 'It was a real sacrifice in terms of time and money and my whole family had to take it on. I didn't go out for more than a year, partly because of money but partly because I didn't have time to take on anything else. You make sacrifices for what you consider to be important. We haven't had a big holiday and the house is in ruins but we've achieved this amazing thing. By the skin of my teeth.'

Those two small words, 'we've achieved', for me, say it all

about how important the empowerment of mothers is when it comes to physicality. Whether it's a huge endeavour like Wendy's or simply going for a run, a walk or 15 minutes of stretching a day, something that benefits the individual, whether that's a sense of confidence or good mental wellbeing, benefits the rest of the family.

Yes, some men have to step it up in terms of parenting and domestic responsibility, and some do a brilliant job, but if mothers are the heart and soul of a family, doesn't it benefit families and societies to have mothers who are happy, healthy, mentally well and fulfilled? Also, if we are talking about the narrative of strength for girls and looking at where that begins, what we do as mothers for ourselves matters an awful lot. 'I took up physical fitness because I wanted to be a role model to my daughter,' wrote Maya in the survey. 'Women in my family just didn't do it. I was never taught to respect my body and think of myself as strong. It was much more acceptable to be seen as weak and in need of a man.'

I may not have learned about lifting weights from my mother but I do know the qualities she instilled in me were: 1) don't worry about what people say and 2) be brave and be bold. Time and again, this helped me to overcome my fears and social conditioning in order to take a risk.

It's also not just about what we pass on to girls but demonstrating to boys what the strength of women can look like. Rhiann wrote in the survey that she started working out to improve her relationship with her teenage sons. 'They respect my strength and fitness because it's part of my strength as their mother. We run together and my eldest is now flourishing in his running confidence because I dragged him out and got him going.'

Wendy told me that her youngest son, who is 11, commented

that she'd spent half his life working on her expedition to Antarctica. Imagine the power of that story for a little boy, growing up in a world thinking that if a woman with kids, working a full-time job, wants to and puts her mind to it, she can trek to the South Pole. She doesn't have to, but she *can*.

While not everyone needs to go on a polar expedition like Wendy, her story is the lighthouse on the hill for anyone thinking that they need to wait until they have enough time or money to do what they truly want, whether that's a trek across Antarctica or a jog in the local park. Sometimes you just need to take what you need.

We need more of these stories to assuage the guilt mothers feel about taking time for themselves, and help them realise that they do have a right to that time. We also need to think about the stories we learned from our own mothers and what served us well and what didn't.

Sometimes, we get so caught up with teaching the right lessons that we forget children learn some of the most powerful lessons in what is unseen. So what is the more powerful lesson here? Do we want to teach our children about weight loss and food guilt and bikini body? Or do we want to teach our children about our bodies being instruments of power that can carry us long distances, overcome illness and be a source of joy? Your body is the land you arrived with, and look what you grew, mama.

A mother who takes time for herself teaches that it's OK to take time for yourself. A mother who prioritises her mental health teaches that mental health is an important, non-optional thing. A mother who can be kind to herself teaches kindness to others.

The problem isn't that you aren't strong enough or your body isn't what it used to be before. With every passing minute, biology and time dictate that the body moves further and further away from what it has been. That isn't what holds you back. What limits you is a societal narrative telling you that your body's destiny was giving birth and now that it has fulfilled that, it doesn't need love, worship or strength.

The world is run by men, who will never step into that place of divinity, of blood and creation, where you and your body dipped into briefly. They will never be able to tell you that you are divine or powerful because they cannot comprehend that a person can go through such a physical and mental transformation and emerge stronger than before. So don't look to the world of men to give you strength. Only you know what your body has been through. Only you know the true extent of the strength you possess. And only you can claim it.

CHAPTER THIRTEEN

Everyone Should Read This Chapter about the Menopause (I Mean Everyone)

The decision to become stronger requires power. Power has to be fuelled by confidence, self-belief and self-worth. And yet, over the course of a lifetime, power is stripped away from girls and women in a number of ways, and one of the most under-represented and maligned transitions women experience is the menopause.

The menopause is said to have taken place when a woman has not had a period for one year – in the UK, the average age is around 51. Dr Shahzadi Harper, a specialist menopause doctor who runs her own clinic in London, the Harper Clinic, explains: 'It's caused by a change in levels of oestrogen and progesterone and also testosterone, so when it comes to fitness, health and metabolism all of these hormones have a huge impact.'

Peri-menopause, which is less known, is also finally starting to get the recognition it deserves. This is the transition towards becoming menopausal and can sometimes last up to eight years. It can start from as early as your mid to late thirties. This is when the amount of oestrogen your body produces can start to fluctuate, your ovulation may be a bit erratic and this may cause a different range of symptoms such as depression, trouble sleeping and hot flushes.

Both of these transitions are challenging for women on three counts. First, there's a lack of information aimed at educating women about what is actually happening to them, especially mentally. (I wasn't even aware of peri-menopause until a year ago.) Second, it begins at a time where women are rendered invisible and are not represented in the majority of mainstream spaces, from entertainment to beauty to fitness. Ageism bias in the workplace for women begins at 40, for instance, as they are overlooked for promotions and not considered worth investing in. Third, agency is taken away from menopausal women as they are widely depicted as caricatures: flustered, out of control, hot flushes, quick-tempered. It means that anything she has to say is instantly invalidated because she is viewed as a creature of hormones – unstable and emotional. Of course, while there are very real symptoms that accompany these two stages, we see time and again how women are undermined, are not supported during a time when they need it most and are going through biological changes they didn't ask for.

Thankfully, however, we are in a time where women in their forties and fifties are pushing back, especially in the fitness world. That matters a lot; in the survey, 75 per cent of respondents said there needed to be more inclusivity around menopause – and physical activity is one of the ways women can wrest back a feeling of control, meet like-minded others going through the same thing and use their physical strength to counteract the story society tells us that they are past it. It's no coincidence that a lot of women I see in the powerlifting world are in this age range; they certainly reject the idea of being past their physical peak.

'Menopausal women seem to be a media "thing" at the moment,' wrote Elizabeth in the survey. 'I appreciate seeing strong women "of a certain age" just getting on with it. I just didn't appreciate how it would affect me until l was halfway through it.

I've taken up powerlifting as a direct result of menopause – and seeing my mum now nearly crippled through osteoporosis.'

Also, side note. If you're reading this thinking, 'Well, this isn't relevant for me, I've got a while to go yet for that,' then buckle up. Familiarising yourself with peri-menopause and the menopause means you can better support the women in your life who are there but also it means you will be prepared for changes down the line when they do happen. Bear in mind that not all women going through the menopause are older women. It can happen earlier if a woman is going through a certain type of cancer treatment or when a woman's ovaries stop making certain levels of hormones, particularly oestrogen.

As Tarrin says in the survey comments: 'I entered the menopause early at 37 and was told I had premature ovarian failure. My body hadn't recovered from having two kids either and it took me a long time to find the right hormone balance to give me more energy.'

Take it from someone who is on the cusp of 40: this stuff has a way of sneaking up on you.

It's also important to talk about this because women entering peri-menopause and then menopause can go through symptoms that are life-altering, and without the right treatment or awareness, the impact on quality of life can be immense. Author Jeanette Winterson described two years of having a mental breakdown, while Meg Matthews – who launched a website and an app for menopausal women after realising there was not enough information out there – said that she had been suffering from a range of symptoms including inflamed joints, loss of libido, mood swings and nausea.

And there is a misogyny that has been spoken and written about when it comes to the menopause around research and when women go to their doctors for help. A survey run on

Mumsnet and Gransnet showed one in four women have to visit their doctor at least three times before getting the right treatment, including hormone replacement therapy (HRT).[1] HRT is one of the most controversial treatments because of the bad press it has had around increased risks of cancer and heart disease, but the results of a big study in the United States showed that it doesn't shorten a person's life.[2] It may not be right for everyone, but it does offer relief to women who do find it works for them. Dr Max Pemberton, writing in the *Daily Mail*, referenced a report that ran in the newspaper, which revealed how many menopausal women were being 'fobbed off' or prescribed anti-depressants as a fix – which is what happened to Meg Matthews who found they didn't work, and instead went onto HRT.

The solutions and treatments for women going through the menopause need to be better and there does need to be more research, which is something Dr Amal Hassan, who works as a sport and exercise medical doctor, highlighted in terms of how little research has been done looking into how testosterone can help women in the pre- and post-menopausal years.

Annabel wrote a comment in the survey about why more information would be helpful: 'There is way too little information around the menopause, what to look out for and particularly how strength training and weight bearing exercise can help with both physical and mental symptoms. I started getting hip pains in my early fifties and was worried about possible arthritis. I realised I needed to work on strength and mobility. It turned out to be menopausal symptoms so weight training has helped massively.'

I interviewed Heather Smith, former Associate Head of Innovation at Women in Sport, the charity founded to address how to make sport and fitness more equal for women and girls. She said that, five years ago, women, menopause and fitness wasn't even really on the agenda. But in 2018, they ran two insight and research projects on the impact of puberty on girls and menopause on women and realised there was a huge opportunity they were missing. 'It's a time when your physical self is becoming front of mind and you're looking for interventions and solutions to manage that,' she said. 'The women we spoke to about menopause mentioned getting back control and while they saw sport and exercise as great ways of doing that, the chances of them successfully taking it up was based on experiences they've had before.'

Previous positive experiences of fitness before menopause, then, count for a lot. If you've had bad experiences in a gym, for instance, then it's unlikely that you'll want to engage with it during menopause – which is just one more reason why it's so important to make gyms positive, inclusive spaces.

But Heather also mentioned that women who had excelled in a particular sport before menopause sometimes found it harder continuing in that sport. 'If they were competitive or very fit before, then coming back after a big life change was very difficult to balance,' she said. 'Especially if the baseline for their fitness levels in that sport was set in their twenties or early thirties. They just weren't able to physically do what they could do before. Finding a different sport and coming from a different starting point might be better.'

This is why visibility of older women in sport and fitness is so important – not just to provide inspiration for women currently going through the menopause, but because we should normalise seeing a trainer or women's health physio who is equipped to deal with the different set of challenges presented by women going through menopause. There is also a lot to be said for making the process of change less daunting.

While researching for the book, and after talking to Priya, who is four years older than me, I was forced to confront my fears about menopause and wrote them down in a list.

1. Scared I will be viewed as 'past it'.
2. Worried that my body will completely collapse and give up on me.
3. I won't be able to do as much as before.
4. It's the beginning of the end; the end being death.

In that list, I can see how a lot of that fear stems from not knowing much about it, hearing horror stories about symptoms and believing in the stereotype that menopausal women are somehow silly and unstable – but it also shows me how rampant my ageism bias is. Ageism bias and a fear of ageing isn't just something we thought up ourselves, but is fuelled by a number of things including:

Impossible aspiration: the presentation of the perfect body or face in entertainment and social media that you can't attain – in this case, youth.

Lack of representation: there are a lot of badass role models but, due to ageism, these women are horribly under-represented in the fitness industry. Meanwhile men of the same age are regularly shown going off on lovely big adventures.

Staying small: because youth is lionised, the aspiration for body size is based on 20-year-olds, which is of course laughably unrealistic.

One of the overwhelming responses through the survey was women saying that if they had known more about peri-menopause and menopause, life would have been easier and they wouldn't have been so hard on themselves. They just weren't aware of how the menopause can affect energy levels, not to mention the impact your mental health has on energy and motivation.

Dr Harper explains that exercise has benefits beyond just energy levels and potentially improving your mood: 'Joint pains and aches are just as common as hot flushes and during this time women lose muscle mass. This is called sarcopenia, and also bone mineral density goes down so, actually, exercise is very important to maintain muscle mass, bone strength and to stay fit and healthy as cardiovascular disease risk goes up also around this time for women.'

But also conversely, Jane Dowling, who is a PT, clinical exercise specialist and menopause advocate, says that managing your expectations around what you can do with your joint pain is also important, and to remember that these symptoms will not last forever, even though it may feel like it does. 'The decrease in oestrogen has an effect on our collagen therefore our joints can feel very stiff and sore,' she says. 'Also the lack of testosterone means that our muscles lose power. So many changes in hormones really can affect a woman's "get up and go", along with lack of sleep and gut health declining, and this can have a massive impact on energy levels. But we are also told that this is the most important time to become more physically active to help disease prevention. Self-care around this is important and it's vital to remember that small things can have a positive impact on symptoms. Walking for 10 minutes outside can have a positive impact on mental health; gentle mobility and stretching has great benefits on joint and muscle pain.'

Being aware of how the hormonal changes around menopause and peri-menopause affect your mental health is also important, especially because this can affect your energy levels and motivation. That means you tailor your training around your symptoms rather than trying to push through in a particular way and feeling terrible because you haven't got the energy to keep going.

'Mental health suffers due to low oestrogen levels,' says Dr Harper. 'Women experience low self-esteem and confidence, flat mood and they can also suffer palpitations and anxiety.

Along with poor sleep due to insomnia and night sweats, it can limit a woman's activity levels.'

Jo Moseley – a woman I admire a lot – is dedicated to raising awareness of how the menopause can affect women and writes about it on her eponymous blog. Jo became the first woman to stand-up paddleboard 162 miles along canals, coast-to-coast across Great Britain.

Jo, who's 55, is a single mum and lives in Yorkshire. She only picked up a paddleboard in 2016. It was initially part of a challenge she had set herself around doing some form of activity every day for 30 minutes as part of her recovery from injuring a knee. Way before this, however, in 2013, Jo said that she was in her local supermarket and just burst into tears in the biscuit aisle. Her parents were both going through chemo-therapy and, as a busy working single mum, she was feeling incredibly stressed and anxious.

'I didn't realise it at the time,' she says, 'but aged 48, I was also going through the early stages of peri-menopause.' She described this as feeling like she was 'permanently under the weather for years'. She had insomnia, joint and muscle pain, headaches and cold flushes, which would make her shiver. Until she became post-menopausal in 2019, it heightened her sense of anxiety and made her short-tempered.

'Shortly after the supermarket incident,' she said, 'a friend asked how much regular exercise I was doing and when I said "not much" (and hadn't for the past 20 years), she lent me an old indoor rowing machine. I started rowing each evening after work in our kitchen.'

When her mother passed away in 2013, Jo wanted to raise money for Macmillan Cancer Support in her memory and raised £10,000 for rowing a million metres. While doing it, she realised that exercise had a huge impact on her physical, emotional and mental wellbeing. 'Having felt so completely broken I began to feel joy again,' she said.

She said that exercising was the last thing she felt like doing at the beginning and it didn't occur to her that it might help with symptoms. She says that movement – whether it's dancing, walking or even just walking up and down the stairs – helps with her anxiety as well as dealing with joint and muscle pain, while indoor rowing helped soften her grief and helped her sleep. 'Now I know these are menopausal symptoms, moving reminds me I don't have a dreadful debilitating disease, it is just part of my body undergoing this huge hormonal change and I will be OK.'

But perhaps the most profound effect is that movement has helped reconnect her with her body. 'The symptoms can take us by surprise and we feel startled by what's happening. Our periods become erratic, unpredictable and heavier and we might put on weight more easily, or our bodies can physically hurt for no reason. It makes our body feel alien. For me, exercise has been a way to tap back into a positive relationship with my body.'

Jo says that the menopause has had more coverage thanks to high-profile names like Louise Minchin, Davina McCall, Liz Earle, Meg Matthews, Mariella Frostrup, Lorraine Kelly and Carol Vorderman, who have spoken openly about how it has affected them.

This Girl Can included the menopause in their 2020 campaign and online groups have sprung up to provide more information. Meno and Me is one of these groups, run by Jane Dowling. When it comes to tackling symptoms, GPs are not always best placed to understand it, she says: 'I was shocked to find out I was menopausal at 46. I went to my GP because I was having migraines around my period but my bleed was minimal, also I was having severe night sweats, anxiety, painful joints and muscles and severe fatigue. My GP told me it was due to lifestyle stresses. It wasn't. I have worked with many women who feel that they have the early onset of dementia and very successful women who have taken a step down from their roles either for good or temporarily due to menopause symptoms. Many women do not know that what they are experiencing is due to menopausal symptoms. I regularly talk on menopause in the workplace to train line managers and so many women are relieved to find out that they are not "losing it" or "going mad".'

What Jane is referring to is one of the symptoms of menopause, brain fog, which is forgetting things or not being able to recall certain memories. This is temporary because cognition can be affected by hormone levels, and some have found HRT helps with this. Also, if you're being plagued by insomnia and hot flushes, these are also things that can make your energy levels dip, which in turn have an impact on brain function.

Unfortunately, because a lot of women aren't aware of the impact the menopause has on their brain, they just assume this is part of the decline of getting older, or even worry they have early onset dementia. They mostly don't, it's just that their symptoms aren't being diagnosed and managed correctly.

Factor in ageism bias in the workplace alongside menopause symptoms, and it has a very real, discernible impact on older women because, as Jo says, some have quit their jobs, believing themselves to not be capable any longer cognitively.

Nicola McPhun, who worked in the police force for 22 years, runs the Invisible to Invincible Beating Menopause Through Sport and Support Facebook page. She started going through the menopause at 44 and brain fog made her lose a lot of her confidence in her abilities because she felt she couldn't rely on her memory and had to keep asking colleagues or double-checking her work. She no longer felt competent in her role and, although she loved being a police officer, she retired.

Alongside this, she felt a lot of anger towards herself and self-harmed. 'If I had known that anxiety, depression, brain fog were all symptoms of the menopause,' she said, 'I would have felt that I could ask for help instead of just thinking it was me. I nearly reached out so many times, especially with the self-harming but thought it was just me being ridiculous.'

Before she retired, Nicola did triathlons but stopped because the mental health symptoms she experienced affected her motivation and made her gain weight, and as a consequence she became very self-conscious about how she looked when she was training. Someone actually said to her: 'You're too fat to run' – because people can be absolute dickheads.

Realising what her symptoms were and how they were affecting her made a huge difference and it's why she thinks there needs to be way more visibility around this. Jane adds: 'I have found that women, once they have realised that what they are feeling is actually down to menopause and not something more sinister; it is a massive relief.'

Something that Dr Harper highlights, which is also echoed by Jane, is how challenging peri-menopausal and menopausal women may find mainstream fitness spaces. 'A lot of women feel that when they go into some of these gyms and fitness spaces where there are young fit people or young mums, it can be a bit daunting,' says Dr Harper. 'It can take a woman a lot to pluck up the courage and motivation, especially as she may be feeling tired or she's not happy with her body shape. Menopause can cause many women to gain weight especially around the middle and heavier boobs, so when walking into a class, they can feel overwhelmed or walk out because they feel they've got to live up to a certain image.' She also comments on the phenomenon of the pivot to online classes caused by the pandemic, which has opened up exercise to people who would not be comfortable going to a class, as they can do a workout at their own pace and not feel self-conscious.

But also, back to the same issue of diversity in gyms, it's important to have instructors and PTs who are aware and know how to train women who are menopausal. Jane says that even personal trainers like herself struggle with their own menopause symptoms and, because there is so much focus on youth and such a lack of visibility around the menopause in mainstream fitness, feel as if they need to leave the fitness industry, when actually, it's even more important that they continue working to help women who are being completely overlooked.

This is especially critical, says Jane, because physical move-ment can be a positive thing if you're experiencing symptoms. But also, symptoms won't last forever, so setting yourself up with good habits will be great for the later decades of your life, as well as give relief during this transition.

It's good to know about all of this no matter what your age. I asked my mum about her experience with menopause and she said she didn't think she suffered with it as badly as some women did. She said she felt moody but was so busy with work that she didn't give it much thought and still kept going to the gym as normal. I do know, however, that we never had a conver-sation about it (and perhaps that is something that needs to change) but also it wasn't something ever mentioned in school or in gyms. When you then layer on certain cultures, like mine, that don't talk about anything gynaecological at all and have a poor relationship with exercise, we find some women are even more disconnected from what is happening to them.

Mita Mistry, a 47-year-old therapist and columnist, who cycles, has done triathlons and Ride London, is peri-menopausal. 'We need to shed more light on this subject in Asian cultures,' she says, 'because many of our mothers and aunties historically didn't exercise or talk about menopause and subservient traditional customs means many are busy putting everyone else ahead of their own needs. For many younger Asian women, it can be hard to see the clear connection between self-care, exercise and menopause if it hasn't been modelled to us and it remains a taboo subject. It is changing very slowly as exercise and information become more accessible but awareness still needs to be raised.'

Osteoporosis and heart disease are thought to escalate during the menopause due to the dip in oestrogen produced by the body and the impact it has on your bones, joints and heart. Even if you are in your twenties and thirties, it's good to take up physical activity in a way that helps your heart health and strengthen your bones. It's baffling to me why this isn't taught to us much earlier on, rather than when we're actually going through peri-menopause and flipping out because we don't know what's happening.

An interesting way to check just how negative the narrative is around menopause and older women, and how that subconsciously may have affected you, is to ask yourself how you feel about it. Do you feel it is the beginning of the end? Are there any positives you can think of? Even the phrase 'middle age' – does it make you recoil?

A newspaper interviewed me about weightlifting alongside some other people of similar age and in the headline referred to us as 'mid-lifers' and I was mortally offended. It's because the template that I have in my head of what the menopause means and what midlife means is so unappealing and feels in opposition to my own lifestyle and values. However, this is the thing about templates. Not only can we change them, we don't really need them. What purpose do they serve, really? We aren't shapes drawn out on tracing paper but real human beings with many different ways of thinking and existing.

If the prospect of mid-life seems unappealing then we can change that. When I think of the older women I admire, what I admire about them is the sense of belonging they have in their own mind and body. There isn't a cell they possess that doesn't crackle with the power of fully knowing what they do and don't want. Sometimes that power is hard won, and very often it has been carved out of loss or realising that the world has sharp edges and that blindly obeying its rules doesn't get you anywhere. But physical activity is an incredible conduit for unleashing and tapping into your potential and breaking free of the same old dusty narrative.

Not so long ago, my dad asked me how long I was going to do powerlifting for. I think because he thought it was a temporary phase. I thought of all the impressive 60, 70 and 80-year-olds I had seen at competitions, who had regular lives like the rest of us, and who were still doing something they loved. I thought of how much it had helped me navigate my grief, and how it still helps me to validate my sense of worth as a woman about to turn 40, when it feels everything else is trying to define me by my ability to have babies and has already decided that my sensuality and attractiveness are on the wane. I thought of how much more I will need this, the older I get.

I looked him straight in the eye and said: 'Until I injure myself or until I'm dead.' I think he was shocked by my bluntness but my answer remains the same.

'Sport allows us to step outside of the stereotypes of what it means to be a middle-aged woman,' says Jo Moseley, 'and explore other aspects of ourselves that may have been hidden or neglected for years. The fighter, the leader, the weightlifter, the teammate, the instructor, the adventurer, the record breaker, the endurance athlete, the wild woman who relies only her own power to travel across the sea or river.'

CHAPTER FOURTEEN

Strong Has No Age Limit

When it comes to female empowerment, the question every interviewer loves to ask is: what would you say to your younger self? A more interesting question, I think, is: what do I want my older self to be?

I want my older self to exist in a state of utter liberation. I want her to have as much serenity and joy as her heart can hold before her light winks out and she goes on in her journey to join Rob and all the loved ones I will have lost by that point. But above all, I want my older self to be strong and for that strength to cut across every plane of existence within me, so that when I walk down the street, in all my beautiful, wrinkly glory, the aura of it billows around me like a cape.

This chapter is a love letter to all the older women in my life, past and present, and to all the incredible women who have stood at the crossroads of fear, ageism and zero fucks and chose the latter.

My blood is as much fish and chips as it is fish and tamarind. My heart is as much listening for the wild cry of gulls across the Arabian Sea as it is drinking orange squash in the middle of an English common. My soul will always be rooted in the love and rage of blue-skinned gods and goddesses, even as it can find peace under the quiet frescoes of a village church.

But the one thing that will never change despite growing up in the West, that is fundamentally Indian about me, is my understanding that older women are to be respected and honoured. These women are often fierce and hold together the strands of their family and their community.

In the Western world, particularly the UK and US, there is a huge ageism bias. Dr Pragya Agarwal says in her book *Sway*: 'As a society we are used to dehumanising old people, seeing old age as a second childhood where the individual becomes dependent once again and loses their economic and social capital. In Greek, Native American, South Asian cultures, old age is a sign of wisdom, revered and respected. In Korea, sixtieth and seventieth birthdays are celebrated as positive occasions at which children celebrate their parents' transition into old age.'

Older women get the brunt of ageism, she adds, because of how the ageing process is perceived. 'Older women are called "hags" while men are still virile and called "silver fox" as they grow older.' Women in entertainment, whether it's music, film or TV, often have much shorter careers and narrower roles available to them than their male counterparts.

Using a set of cues – such as grey hair, wrinkled skin, posture, pace of movement – we create stereotypes about older people that we assume are absolute, based on perceptions of frailty, fragility and dependence. We make assumptions about how 'useful' a person is based on their age and that can have some shocking impacts on policies and things like the medical care an older person may (or may not) receive.

Worse, old-age stereotypes are self-fulfilling, writes Dr

Agarwal. 'Older people stereotype themselves,' she wrote, 'which tends to shape their own identities, so they are likely to be much more explicitly biased against other people in the same age group compared to other people around them.'

This has a huge impact on something like physical fitness. Search for 'older people' and 'fitness' in any stock image library and the results are terrible. You'll see people wearing pastel joggers going for a gentle walk or doing yoga, and that's it. The need to slow down is so ingrained in how we depict and treat our older people, regardless of their health and cognitive function, which is bizarre given that we are one of the very few creatures to have significant lifespans beyond our ability to bear children.

Humans are the only primates that don't die within a few years of our fertility ending. We are on par with female killer whales, which reproduce between the ages of 12 and 40 and can go on to live to 90. Elephants don't go through menopause but they are a matriarchal society and the presence and status of older females has been shown to increase the survival rates of herds. Similarly, in ancient humans, anthropologists believe that the knowledge of older females – from where food is located to recognising danger – protected the group. They would also improve survival rates by helping to look after the babies of other females.

Older females, therefore, seem critical to our success as a species. How then have older women become one of the most disempowered groups in human society?

It seems to me that if you feel sound of mind and body, the whole purpose of this extra time is to live your life to its absolute fullest. Who says there is an expiry date on doing certain things – whether that's getting a tattoo or starting to lift weights, cycling across the country or selling your home to go and live somewhere fun and different? Who says young people have the monopoly on any of that? Beyond certain biological functions and processes, there is nothing that you are too old for. Sure, you may have physical limitations depending on your health, and there are greater risks around disease and mortality when you get older, but it isn't a foregone conclusion that it means you're frail. Younger people have health problems too.

None of us know how much time we have left from the moment we take that first breath outside of our mother's body. We don't spend the majority of our life not taking chances because we're worried about dying. So why does it become a way of living when we're older, when, if anything, time is even more precious and seizing those chances is even more important?

'I want to be a strong old lady,' wrote Tig in the survey. 'I see my nan struggling to reach for things and putting her back out and that's not a life I want.'

I will never forget something Tyrone said in the early days of lifting. It was when I was doing a set of deadlifts and was finding it hard. I can't remember the circumstances but I was grumpy and tired and, because I look young for my age, I wanted to remind him that I wasn't in my twenties but a then-36-year-old.

'Tyrone, I'm not a spring chicken, you know,' I said.

He laughed. 'And? Age has got nothing to do with it. Come on, let's go.'

I couldn't believe I wasn't receiving sympathy from him but he was right and I did complete the set. Every time I want to grumble about how I can't do something, I remember that moment and how it's mostly all in my head.

I'm lucky to have parents who embody the ethos of 'you

have to do what you want, and live and be happy'. It makes me proud that the two of them get comments in the gym about how amazing it is that they work out hard. But I also know that ageing is a big deal for the both of them and I can see exactly where it has come from.

It's from the million little cues we get on television, where being told how youthful you look is a compliment and how old you look is an insult. It's from not seeing older women and men in fitness campaigns or working as personal trainers in gyms.

'We are a generation who have been taught that it's all downhill after 50,' says Jo Moseley, 'and we need to challenge that message both within ourselves and in society. It is easy to think, "oh I'm too old for this" or "how silly would a woman my age look doing boxfit or kettlebells or paddling across the country". But by doing these activities we can overturn the stories we tell ourselves and encourage others to change the narrative too.'

I interviewed the ageism bias activist and photojournalist Alex Rotas, whose main subjects are older athletes in their sixties, seventies, eighties and nineties, and who has made it her mission to dismantle the unhelpful ideas of what we think ageing is about. Many of her athletes are ordinary people who took up sport later in life. Alex told me about one lady who is in her early eighties and uses her washing line in her back garden to practise hurdles: 'Who'd want to get old if what awaits is a time of passivity, the life-force drained out of you while you are slumped in a chair? No one. But who'd want to get old if opportunities continue to open up, and you can enjoy new experiences with more freedom than you've felt before? Quite a lot of us, I'd say.'

*

Mum and Dad live in a small leafy village in Kent, surrounded by meadows and fields of wheat. It is worth driving through the hellscape of the M25 just to exit into a warren of tiny country lanes and cottages with thatched roofs, and breathe a sigh of relief at the prettiness and slowness of it all.

One weekend, the three of us were sitting out in the garden drinking prosecco. We were talking about grey hair. Mum has an unusual collection of genes that she has passed down to Priya and me. For a start, she is like a naked mole rat – she has almost zero body hair; none on her arms or legs. The second is that she didn't start getting grey hair until she was in her sixties. Even the grey hair she has now, as someone a few months away from turning 70, is a smattering at best. Dad started going grey in his forties and the Just For Men dye box has been a permanent fixture in their bathroom ever since. They both want to look young because it matches their youthful spirit but I don't think they fully appreciate that they already look about 10 to 15 years younger than their actual age.

'Would you like it if I dyed my hair?' my mother asked me. We were a fair few glasses of prosecco in and I couldn't quite understand the question.

'How do you mean?'

'Well,' she said, 'would you like it if your mother looked more youthful?'

'You mean by dyeing your hair?' I said and she nodded.

Mum is one of five siblings and as a baby she was 'butt ugly'. (Her words, not mine.) Most of her baby photos were mysteriously lost, which we used to tease her about, but the very few that remain showed that her looks didn't exactly improve into childhood.

But when she hit 20, she turned from a mushroom into a rose – the transformation was ridiculous. Her 100-kilowatt smile, beautiful nose and long glossy hair. She was, and is, beautiful and, more than that, her personality is so bubbly and effusive that it amplifies her entire presence but I think part of her has never let go of her mushroom self.

'I think you should do whatever you want to do, Mum,' I said. 'You look beautiful and if I were you, I wouldn't care about what other people think. Getting older or looking older is nothing to be scared of.'

It got me thinking.

Most of my last book, *In Search of Silence*, was about reconfiguring your relationships with the people you love, especially your parents. I talked a bit about how a lot of us get exasperated with them and don't actually ask them questions about their lives. That crucial part of what makes us respect our elders, the knowledge they have to pass on, gets lost.

I realised that while I'd asked Mum a lot about her childhood, I'd never really asked her about her experience with her own body and how it related to fitness. I had a vague sense, based on what I saw her do in the gym or how she talks about herself (I think she fat-shames herself and I am forever trying to break her out of the habit). Given that Mum had a hole in the heart that dramatically shaped her childhood in a way that it didn't do in mine, I wanted to know more.

I knew she was naturally quite strong – she'd always had strong arms, for instance – and while she didn't weightlift, she did bicep curls and other things as part of her training. We'd also had a conversation around her arms getting bigger. She loves doing weights but doesn't want her shoulders and arms to get too big and, although I did tell her it shouldn't matter, I held off from saying anything because my words are not going to be able to cut through decades of social conditioning and her exposure to the diet culture of the 1980s and 90s. She has to feel good about her body and it's not my right or my place to tell her what that should be.

When I asked her about what physical fitness meant to her and why it was important, her answers surprised me and were proof of how we form an idea around our parents without actually really knowing the truth because we don't bother to ask them. 'My being physically fit gives me the ability to do almost anything I want,' she told me, 'and also enjoy my life the way I want, therefore giving me a quality of life that I thought I would never have. I have good upper body strength and rarely have to ask your dad to help me lift anything in the garden for instance.'

This was news to me because I always thought Mum mainly did exercise to maintain her weight. But she said she doesn't associate weight loss with exercise, rather the amount of food she eats. She also said that doing exercise helps her with stress. Again, I had no idea.

I was diagnosed with a hole in the heart at 31, so I didn't have to deal with being a sick child and all the problems that come with that. But Mum did. She wasn't properly diagnosed until she was in her teens. As a child, she knew she couldn't do as much physically as her siblings but didn't understand why.

'I was able to do things like ride a bike (not too far or fast though), learn to swim (although I couldn't swim far) and play games like hopscotch but not anything really boisterous like running, or climbing trees. It was hard to stand on the sidelines and watch my siblings playing games such as hockey and generally chase each other around. I always felt inadequate as though I was not good enough. I knew that I had something wrong with me but, true to the ways parents treated children back then, it was never explained to me exactly what was wrong with me and how my body could not cope with strenuous exercise. In their defence, I suppose they did not know much about heart illness.'

After her operation to fix her hole in the heart, Mum described feeling as if a coiled spring in her body had been released and that's how I felt too. But Mum's recovery was a lot more complicated than mine. For a start, she had open heart surgery while I had keyhole, and she contracted pneumonia afterwards which damaged her lungs and gave her a condition called bronchiectasis.

Once she fully recovered, she took up badminton, table tennis and tennis. After we moved to England, I remember her having Jane Fonda's videos and the Reebok step-up box (which I tried once but the instructor in the accompanying video and her eye-wateringly high-waisted leotard creeped me out) but I didn't realise that it was also at this time that she joined her first gym.

She mainly joined to use the swimming pool and credits a female neighbour of ours with encouraging her to use the other parts of the gym too. That then led to her hiring a trainer named Julie, who is passionate about training older women, and they've been training together for years. Mum's favourite activity is boxing and she says it's great for releasing her aggression.

Although Mum is self-deprecating about her weight, she says she knows she is in decent shape for her age and she does feel a sense of pride when people comment on her strength. Earlier this year, she was with her two sisters Indu and Meera in India, staying in their brother Ashok's flat. You can't just drink water out of the tap in India because of the impurities and Ashok has a watercooler. One day, the water had been finished and he wasn't around to change the heavy and unwieldy bottle. Mum managed to lift it up and put it on the stand. She told me that Indu said: 'Only she could have lifted it.' It made her feel really proud.

Mum said to me: 'With so many things wrong with me, such as my damaged lungs and arthritis, I see physical activity as providing me with a challenge to prove to myself that I am not done yet.'

The cutesie-fication of older people, particularly women, has to stop if we are going to dismantle ageism bias. That means not saying things like 'old people are adorable' or 'I love old people, they're such darlings.' If you don't see the problem, then replace the word 'old' with another word such as 'Asian' or 'women' – sounds wrong, right? That's because we are much more aware of race and gender bias than we are our own ageism bias.

If an older person is an athlete or is really into fitness, it means not saying things like 'it's impressive for their age' because what we're saying there is that the default of being old is weak and useless. 'But it's a compliment,' someone will chirp. It's not a compliment. Saying someone is impressive is a compliment. You don't need to bring age into it. It's like saying you did that really well 'for a woman'. Even though it is well intentioned, you are using the bias of ageism to frame their achievement and it's unnecessary.

Instagram has been a gamechanger in terms of giving older women in fitness a platform because it isn't constrained by the same rigidity of advertising and print media. The conversation can be conducted in an authentic, unedited way because, unlike the 'classic' influencer – young, usually white, perhaps cosmetically enhanced and slim – older women influence just by virtue of being visibly fit and older, because they are subverting the status quo.

There is a limit to its success in terms of women inspiring their peers though, because the majority of older women are not on Instagram – only 2.3 per cent of women who use the platform are aged between 55 and 64, while 1.3 per cent are 65 and older according to Statista.[1]

However, what it does do is change the perception of ageing and fitness for girls and women under 50, which will eventually have a positive long-term effect when we do reach that age. And, even if our mothers and aunts aren't on Instagram – as is the case with my family – I still share stories of women I come across on Instagram that my mum might find relatable or interesting.

One of the first women I came across was Michelle Franklin, who goes by the handle This Granny Can. Michelle, 54, is a powerlifter and previously had a fairly non-existent relationship with fitness. Now, she competes for British Powerlifting nationally and the International Powerlifting Federation internationally.

She'd tried aqua aerobics and running but nothing really stuck or felt right. There was also a weight-loss component to her journey – previously she was a UK size 22 and, after seeing a photo of herself at her daughter's dance graduation, decided she wanted to lose weight. She had lost about 30kg when she came across powerlifting completely by random on Facebook in 2015, via a blog written by a young female coach. Something made her click on it, she says, and she contacted the coach and went along for a female-only lifters session.

'For some women, age is another label we have to wear,' she says. 'I still get comments like "what do you want to be doing that for?" but anyone who knows me knows exactly what I am doing it for – it's for me.' Powerlifting, she says, mentally elates her, grounds her, physically exhausts her and has made her understand the role rest, food and recovery play in how her body feels.

If there is just one lesson I want every woman reading to take away from this book, it's around reconnecting the circuitry between your mind and body. I see my own mum running herself into the ground, then feeling indescribably tired and not realising it's because she hasn't eaten much that day. Or other women going into a workout feeling fatigued because they are starving themselves and then hating the exercise because it feels hard.

Some sports make you realise that connection whether you like it or not and powerlifting is one of those. I've been guilty of trying to cheat the system, or think I know better, and I've seen my teammates do the same, where we've clung on to old ways of eating or working out and it has meant that our lifting has gone to hell because we haven't fuelled enough or we wanted to squeeze in an extra run to burn off some calories.

'There is so much focus on losing weight,' says Michelle, 'that my answer for anyone wanting to get fitter is to go lift some weights first and see how strong you can be. The great thing about the barbell is it does not care how old you are or what you weigh. Personally, I find Instagram and Facebook still mainly promote females and cardio but I think the trend is starting to change as more women get into lifting.'

Michelle says that one thing that would help encourage older women – and athletes in general – is sponsorship and that is something brands can help with if they are serious about being truly diverse. Even something small like having brand ambassadors who aren't exclusively in their twenties and thirties would make a difference.

While a lot of local communities do classes for older people, this often lumps together quite a broad age range of people. There is a huge distinction between being 50 and 65, for instance. There's also a stigma attached to 'seniors' classes because they tend to be advertised as sedate and gentle. Even the NHS website, as well-intentioned as it is, places a lot of emphasis on gentle exercise and stretching.

'I don't very often read fitness articles in the media,' wrote Jean in the survey, 'but I do think there's a tendency to patronise women as they get older. We expect to live until we're 90, but we're "seniors" as soon as we hit 50 – that's a whole 40 years in a very broad category. If I registered for a new class now, I might even be tempted to lie about my age, saying I was in my forties, so that I wasn't treated like a frail, bone-brittle old lady.'

Women's Health published a feature on exercises for women over 50 and not only chose an image of an older woman clutching tiny 1kg dumbbells, but also used the word gentle a lot. Maybe some people want that but not every person does. My dad, for instance, in his seventies, does some of the high-intensity Les Mills classes that are marketed at people in their twenties and thirties. A more natural integration of age within fitness would be more effective. Parkrun, the free, weekly community five-kilometre running event, is a great example of that. It's super inclusive, open to different ages and doesn't make you feel like you're being othered because of your age.

One week, I was visiting my parents with Priya and her family, who had come over from Spain. Priya and I had planned to do a resistance band workout in the garden and I asked Mum if she'd like to join us. She said she'd like to and she kept pace with both of us. Had I offered her more gentle options just because of her age without even bothering to find out what she was capable of, it would have been incredibly patronising but also unnecessary as she was clearly capable of keeping up.

A broader range of representation is important, says Heather Smith from Women in Sport, to show the whole scale of what women in their forties and older are choosing to do in the fitness sphere. 'There are some incredible women like Iron Nun (the 86-year-old nun Madonna Buder who is currently the oldest woman to have completed the endurance event ironman), but in terms of getting your average woman active, they need something much more relatable.'

An influencer who I think represents the middle ground of fitness and strength in a good way, is Joan MacDonald. Joan is 74 and has nearly one million followers on Instagram and yet she only really started in the fitness world when she turned 70. Her physique is amazing and makes you do a double take (or at least I did when I first saw a picture of her and her glorious bum) because you don't often see older women look like that. She has muscle but she's not a competing athlete and, most wonderfully, looks her age.

When I called her to ask her about her journey, she said that she'd been active over the course of her life but never in an organised way. She'd had a PT in the gym at one point but where she struggled was around food and just not knowing how much to eat and what to eat. When she decided to get fit, she was around 90kg at a height of five foot three and was on a variety of medication for high blood pressure, acid reflux and cholesterol.

'I was huffing and puffing taking the stairs one at a time,' she says, 'and my face was always flushed.' Her daughter Michelle, who is a bodybuilder, ex-competitive powerlifter and specialises in training women over 40, found out that Joan was on all this medication and that doctors were saying she'd have to increase her dosage or change her lifestyle.

Michelle was upset and said she didn't want her mother to

be in a home, unable to function. She gave her a challenge and offered to train her, as well as teach her about macronutrients and how to eat to support her training.

'I told her I didn't want to lose weight fast but that I would rather lose it slower and hope that it stays off,' Joan said. 'It was having a realistic goal. Take it in chunks. Don't look at it every day. Three months in with Michelle, my blood pressure came down. By autumn of the year I started, I was off all meds.' Her doctors had previously said she'd be on meds for life.

It took two years for Joan to get to her current weight. Although it initially started as a way to lose weight, she loved the unexpected definition in her body. She trains five days in the gym and does a mixture of strength and cardio. 'I would keep getting compliments from women and men,' she said. 'They said I was getting shredded and I said "Really? I can't see what you're seeing," so they started taking pictures of me.'

Being strong is important to her because she says there is a lot of gardening to do, and she wants to be able to carry on.

She does sometimes find that when people know her age they ask her why she's doing all of this fitness stuff but she says: 'It's actually a put-down because they don't want to do the work you're doing. I look good in my clothes and I get admiring looks when I'm out and that's a good incentive. It's a good feeling to be strong. I'm not one of these women who are "poor little me and men can do it for me" – a lot of us are capable and women in their forties and upwards are starting to think like that.'

Joan says that a lot of the blockers people have for themselves are usually in their heads. For instance, someone looking at Joan squatting might say, 'Well I'd love to do that but I can't because I have knee problems.' But Joan has arthritis and has had a knee replacement. It doesn't mean her knee problems aren't significant but rather, she's not going to let it stop her doing what she wants. She just uses different variations that work around her capabilities and she wears a knee brace.

The problem with ageism bias and the stereotypes we have in the West around older people isn't just that it whitewashes an entire chunk of society. It's that it creates mountains in one's own head about overcoming the problems that arise from getting older.

For anyone thinking about following in Joan's footsteps, she recommends starting off with light weights and increasing them when they start to feel easy. But also, she says in an Instagram post, if you do get a personal trainer and you are an older woman make sure you find someone who can teach you good form and not patronise you. 'I see a lot of chit-chat going on in general between trainers and their older female clients, and not much effort,' she writes on her page. 'I imagine trainers must think we can't be pushed and we are there to mark time and not accomplish much. [My trainer] always tells me: whether you're young or old, all bodies respond to the same technique of proper exercise selection, proper volume and progressive overload. If you dumb it down just because you're older you won't get the results you are looking for. Don't be taken advantage of my dears. If you really want to make changes, decide to become strong and decide that you're worth the effort.'

While I was still reflecting on what Joan said, I couldn't help thinking back to my chat with Mum. It made me think about my own grandmothers – Parvathy was my paternal grandmother and Nagaveni was my maternal grandmother. My first memories of them were from when we moved to India in 1987, even though they'd made trips to England when I was a baby. They were completely different characters. Parvathy wore red lipstick and was outgoing and liked a few drinks while Nagaveni was quieter and calmer. I loved them both and felt loved by them, but I knew them more by their mental resilience and strength.

Parvathy lost her husband at a young age and raised four children by herself, while Nagaveni navigated two different continents with her children and husband. Both of them had love marriages rather than arranged marriages, which was really unusual back then.

I remember knowing, in my bones, that my family was filled with strong women and these were two of the strongest. I'm South Indian and my family name is Shetty, and our society is matriarchal, unlike other Indian communities which may be patriarchal. It means that while women still may be subject to oppression and traditional gender roles, there is a legitimacy in our power, in terms of the rules around how women inherit land and money.

There is no doubt that this strength has been passed through our mother and onto Priya and myself. We know it soul-deep. We owe the women who came before us, made of our blood, who shelved their own dreams, who sacrificed and fought so that we would have it better than they did.

What we owe the generations before us isn't just respect. It isn't enough. I think we owe it to them to take the time to ask them questions and listen. We owe it to them to support their life choices and not ask them to slow down or make safer decisions. I also think we owe it to them to give them the confidence to overcome that mountain that has built up in their heads over time. If we would not hesitate to build up our peers and our children, to encourage them to be brave, bold and fearless, why do we hesitate when it comes to the older women in our lives?

No one's relationship is perfect, certainly not the ones we have with our mothers or aunts, because there are so many power dynamics at play as we jostle to be heard, respected, seen, understood. But my mother is one of the biggest loves of my life. She has, at times, sacrificed so much for us in ways that I cannot imagine. She has dealt with things so we didn't have to.

When I sometimes hear the way she talks about herself, even small things like her saying proper skincare isn't worth bothering with because her skin is older and therefore less important or valued, it makes me indescribably sad. This is a woman who has overcome a hole in the heart, damaged lungs, arthritis, another hole in the heart, a pacemaker and had two kids when she was told she wouldn't have children due to her heart issues as well as a career, and is still one of the fiercest, bravest, most energetic souls I know. But I see where society has done its work and I see the doubts and the gaps when she talks about her body or face, or getting older.

And as I work to create a better world for Leela, I see how important it is to look to the women who raised us, and take a small piece of our power that we wouldn't even possess if not for their sacrifice, that was purchased with their love and toil, and hand it back to them.

Just over ten years ago, when she was in her fifties, Alex Rotas was looking for photos of older athletes for her MA. At first, she couldn't find any and the ones she did find fed into what she calls the 'frailty narrative'.

'In these photos,' she told me, 'the older person was either sitting in what looked like a care home setting or, if they were a bit more lively, they might be sitting in a chair with a carer standing over them and the person would be gratefully smiling up. These images associated the older person with frailty, dependence, lack of goals, passivity and a general emptying out of what makes us human.'

In other words, she says, a dependency relationship. Alex knew that was only part of the story of getting older, not the whole story. 'Younger people need to see the other side,' she says, 'because everyone is so depressed about the ageing trajectory. The more I delve into it, and the more I progress into it as I myself get older, it can be the most joyful, wonderful, liberating time when your horizons can grow and expand.'

A fire was lit, and this was the start of Alex's rebirth as an anti-ageism activist. 'I wanted to overturn the idea that ageing was something to be feared. The imagery around ageing in the media is awful. Those ghastly images just of wrinkly hands for example – individual body parts that are somehow meant to stand for the whole person – are dehumanising, depressing and insulting.'

Deciding she wanted to take her own photographs to fill the gap, Alex sought out events she could take pictures at and came across Masters athletics, which includes a whole range of sports from heptathlon to pole vaulting, shot put to sprinting. 'Masters' is the category for older athletes, so in powerlifting that might be from 40 years old, in athletics it could be as young as 35, and you then compete within your own age category.

Her first event was in Lignano, Italy, and her reaction to seeing all of these older athletes made her realise her own ageism bias. 'It surprised me in a good way. It was gloriously liberating to see older women so comfortable in their bodies, especially in track and field athletics. They wear very skimpy kit so you get to see the musculature but you also get to see the wrinkles and see how wonderful that combination is.'

When I was chatting to Alex, she told me about Dorothy McLennan who took up running in her fifties, switched to pole vaulting until she was 79, and then switched to pentathlon. She also mentioned Olga Kotelko, who took up track and field when she was 77, and Rosa Pederson, who is the current long jump world champion in the 90+ age category.

My brain was trying to keep up. 'But Alex,' I said hesitantly, trying to word it delicately without sounding like a patronising twerp, 'aren't they, you know, worried about injuring themselves?'

'Well,' said Alex, 'there is this prevailing view that if an older person falls and goes onto their wrists, they'll inevitably break their wrists because it's assumed they must have osteoporosis. And they don't, at least not necessarily. Take for instance long jump where you deliberately have to fall onto the sand. I've seen 95-year-old women doing it. Yes, they have all the same sorts of issues that other older people have – heart issues, cancer, ligaments, etc. But it's just they have a different attitude. For instance, before I had to have hip surgery, I met an Irish woman who competed in the hurdle event and she's had two hip replacements in the last two years. I was looking at my own hip issue as an impassable mountain but for her, it was just a mountain to climb and then you get to the other side and you go back to doing what you love.'

Alex's photos capture the joy and fluidity of movement in her athletes but also tell a story of freedom within one's own body. When these women are doing high jump, for instance, they jump legs akimbo and land on the mats.

'These are elderly women,' she says, 'and they must have been brought up to feel you have to keep your knees together, with all these rules of what makes you feminine and a girl. Yet they are beautifully comfortable in flinging their bodies around.

You might not actually see a lot of younger women who feel that comfortable and free in their bodies.'

Also, she says, if we are likely to live to our nineties, it shouldn't be surprising if you take up something new in your sixties and seventies.

Alex introduced me to Dorothy McClennan, a retired bank cashier, who is Irish but lives in England with her husband. She has had three children. She used to do one of the most daring athletics sports – pole vaulting until she was 79. I can't even imagine the chutzpah it takes for anyone to launch themselves up into the air via a pole, knowing they could potentially flip backwards and that they are definitely going to fall down.

When I say this to her, she laughs. 'You're concentrating so much on what you're doing, whether it's your position on the pole, when you have to jump up and then you have to keep going. That's the sensation. You don't think "Am I brave enough to do it?" You think, "I'm doing this and I'll do this properly."'

Dorothy says that when she was younger, women like her didn't do athletics. Along with her twin sister Sheila, she would go out on bikes and play badminton. In 1984, she saw an 82-year-old man running the marathon and thought, 'If he can do it, so I can I.' At the time, she was 50.

She started running on her own but, as anyone new to running will know, it feels like you're dying most of the time. One day, a friend of her daughter asked to go on a run with her. Off they went, chatting as they ran and then she realised that she'd actually run for a mile and half without stopping. That made her think that she'd like to run with other people so she joined her local jogging club and learned how to pace herself. She did her first marathon in Dublin that year.

She was doing a 5,000-metre race at an athletics competition abroad with her sister when a male athlete suggested she try one of the newer sports that were coming out. Hammer throwing was one, pole vaulting was another.

She started off with a beginners' class, once a month indoors, at a venue in Crystal Palace. She then did her first competition at the World Championships in 1991. A few years ago, she gave up pole vaulting because she couldn't quite get the speed needed to launch herself safely over the pole and switched to pentathlon instead. She does some form of physical activity every day and, because she recently injured her knee, she's been doing stretching and conditioning at home.

I found Dorothy's story fascinating – not just because she took up fitness later in life but because it is evident that, every step of the way, she had just followed through with what she wanted to do, rather than thinking about her age or her gender.

It tracks with what Alex says about the athletes she photographs. 'It's not that they're fearless. They just think beyond the fear. One of the lessons I've learned is that as you get older, it becomes more about who you are, what motivates you and what you want to do.'

One thing that insulates older athletes from the 'aren't you too old to be doing that?' brigade is the community they belong to. This community validates their choices, celebrates them and provides a supportive space to help them just do what they love doing, without othering them as 'old people'. For instance, it wouldn't even occur to them to wear different clothing than younger athletes, Alex says, because if you're thinking about your training and your performance, then that's what's more important. You want to look like an athlete, so you wear the kit that athletes wear.

The other invaluable aspect of the community is that it is where people can meet and connect with other like-minded individuals, make friends and feel like they belong to something much bigger than themselves. In the fight against loneliness, the sense of community through sport and fitness can be incredibly powerful.

Loneliness isn't just something older people experience but Age UK says that there are 1.4 million chronically lonely older people.[2] The way they measure it is by asking people how often they feel lonely, whether they lack companionship and whether they feel left out.

As someone who is not yet an older person, I've experienced deep loneliness for significant periods twice in my life. The first was when Rob was going through a severe bout of depression as well as struggling with recovery from heroin. For around two to three years, while I was trying to help him and keep our household going, I felt like I couldn't really talk to people about what was going on. At certain points, Rob was emotionally unavailable because he wasn't well. That experience taught me a lot about how loneliness isn't just about the proximity to other people but about communication and being understood by others.

The second significant period was after he passed away. Not only did I miss him intensely, I felt no one around me knew the depth of that grief or how it felt. I felt it lessen whenever I spoke to someone else who had lost a spouse in that way and when I went on the Widowed and Young forum.

At the heart of loneliness is the absence of being able to communicate the deepest parts of yourself. Introvert or extrovert, the need to be recognised, seen and truly heard by others is fundamentally human.

When you are older, the world often tells you that your opinion no longer matters much. You don't see people that look like you on TV or films – or at least not in a way that reflects how you might feel inside. You don't see people with wrinkles and muscle running, leaping, throwing, yelling, pushing, jumping with everything their body can give. You are also going through a state of transition. Maybe your friends and family are getting ill, or moving away, or dying. Where in all of this, then, do you see yourself reflected?

I asked Alex about commonalities she had noticed, in the athletes she photographed. I wanted to know what made them so special; what made them able to throw off the stifling, suffocating Western narrative of ageing. She said it was likely the friendship and community.

'They train in their local clubs and then they see all their buddies at the national and international events. It works because they are with people who get them and understand what they are doing. No one there is going to tell them they're bonkers for pole vaulting or doing long jump in their eighties, which their family might do.'

The beauty of this community is that it's also peer-to-peer support and friendship. My previous understanding about loneliness and older people was pretty ignorant; I just assumed it was about having human contact with anyone. While that is true in some cases, of course the quality of the contact matters. Being able to socialise with people who understand your reference points, don't patronise you and, more importantly share your interests, matters a lot.

Getting older also comprises many different types of life transitions, whether that's health issues, losing friends and family, gaining grandchildren, retiring and so on. Having a community like this helps to navigate some of the uncertainty that these experiences can bring about and means you aren't so reliant on your old network of friends and family.

No matter what your age, it's a valuable lesson for all of us to learn. Having friends who reflect your current set of interests and who lead a similar lifestyle to you is critical to navigating life changes and feeling seen and heard. It's a lesson I learned only recently when I was philosophising about friendships and how they evolve.

For most of my life, I have held on probably too hard to my friendships and expected too much from them. It has been particularly painful while going through periods of transition. Looking back, the significant ones were leaving university, mates starting to settle down when we were in our twenties, getting married at 30 and then becoming a widow and more recently watching all my friends have kids and realising that I probably don't want any of my own.

In each transition, I wanted so much from them and I don't know that my expectations were always realistic or fair. Now, however, I feel the most satisfied and the most seen in all my friendships at a time when, actually, I'm going through a huge transition around children and turning 40.

While being older and less tolerant of toxic behaviour has something to do with that, a huge part of it is due to my being part of the powerlifting community, my team Barfight and Jack and Aga. My set of friends from childhood and university are amazing, and they are the historians of my life. But our friendships were also forged in a time when we were in the trenches, figuring ourselves out and not yet certain of who we were. Expecting my friends with children, for instance, to have the same amount of time for me, or even to understand my life, is not realistic. Rather than feeling resentful or bitter around parenthood, which is something that gives them immense joy and I'm not sure I want for myself, I would much rather expand my heart and allow myself to form new friendships with people who mirror my lifestyle.

Finding friends along the way to reflect who you are – which evolves and changes throughout a lifetime depending on your circumstances or personal growth – means you are understood but also that you don't navigate transitions alone. The same is true for parents, as well as women going through the menopause, after menopause or any other significant life change.

Physical fitness and sport can be a powerful gateway to people who connect with you and, most importantly, understand you. I've seen how the commonality of women who lift weights instantly dissolves any hesitations I might have about opening up or being friendly. When I went on a business trip to Guernsey a few months ago, my point of contact, Maddy, told me that she lifted weights and did I want to do a session with her? My immediate reply was yes and I can't say I would have done that in any other scenario. Lifting is a language I immediately understand and can use to connect with someone.

I have seen time and again, no matter where or what the activity, how vital friendship and community are. Sea swimming in Brighton, pole dancing in Peckham. Cycling clubs in Scotland, walking groups in Wales. They have helped women through trauma, to feel a sense of belonging, a connection to the outdoors and the universe and beyond. We need it at every stage and every age of our lives because the need for connection remains a constant.

When Rob died, I was lucky that I had friends and family who caught me in their nets, a million strands of love wrapped around me, each one a lifeline leading back to an existence I felt so detached and removed from. But as time went on, they couldn't fill the gap in my life all the time and, mighty as my love is for them, they didn't reflect where my life was, or where it was going.

I don't believe 'everything happens for a reason' because I

lost my husband to suicide and there will never, ever be a good enough reason for why he only got to live for 39 years or why he was dealt a hand of such mental suffering. But the steps that led me to Jack, which led me to a community that have saved me in countless ways, who make me finally feel like I belong somewhere, have felt like a counterweight to some of the grief I have experienced.

On the day of my first powerlifting competition, when I realised my team – who back then were practically strangers – would show up for me and support me, it was something I wanted to give back with an open heart. It made me feel useful, needed, wanted, but also showed that whatever I needed from them, I just had to ask and it would happen. It has also meant that I have learned something valuable about friendship. Making new friends is like a muscle and using it with my powerlifting team has given me the strength and confidence to try it with other people unrelated to sport.

Someone asked me once if I could ever see myself living with someone again, or getting married, and I said: 'When I love someone, every door in my heart is open to them. So if I love them, then yes, of course.'

I've applied that principle to friendships as well. It's not about quantity but quality. I don't want or need superficial connections with people. My measure of friendship is actually comfort and trust – feeling like I can fall asleep on their sofa or root around in their cupboard and make myself a cup of tea. In other words, a person who feels like home.

The other day, I went to Jack and Aga's for dinner. Aga is an incredible cook and we were lying on the sofa, bellies full of homemade gnocchi, drinking glasses of prosecco and just chatting. The evening was warm, the final lance of sunlight drawing away from the room and I felt drowsy. I knew in that moment that I could ask them if I could stay the night and one of them would pull a blanket over me or show me to the spare room and I would sleep like a baby. It never fails to amaze me how effortless a friendship it is. Given that we come from such different cultures, we share the same ethics, sense of humour, even crappy films.

When my love life is going in the toilet, I always rail against the universe and say that I deserve to meet someone decent given that the love of my life was taken from me. But I think I've been given something much, much bigger.

As we approach the end of this book together, I am going to leave you with one final story about strength.

The first international competition I did was the AWPC Euros in 2019, which took place in Ireland. We were all taking part in it, including Jack and Lindsay, and the plan was to hire three cottages, and spend the week out there as not all of us were competing on the same day.

It was always going to be tough for a couple of reasons. I'd been powerlifting for less than a year and to compete in an international competition, you need to do a national qualifying competition first.

Two months before a competition you go into what's called 'peaking', which is when you steadily build up your strength so that on competition day, you are primed to hit the biggest numbers you can possibly do. The training is full-on, though. You have to sleep and eat properly and you can't miss your days of training or it ends up setting your numbers back. By the end of it, the physical exhaustion is immense and mentally it takes its toll.

My qualifying competition was so close to Euros that there just hadn't been enough time to recover between my two peaking phases. So, when it came time to compete, my body was absolutely fried. Mentally, I had also been through the mill because the competition was just after I'd done the publicity for my second book, which involved talking a lot about Rob and grief, and it took place just a week after the anniversary of his death.

On the day, I failed one of my squats, then one of my bench press. The time then came to do my final deadlift. I had secretly hoped that being able to succeed in this competition would lighten my grief. In my mind, it was a literal weight and I thought that if I could lift it, then somehow I would free myself of it.

When I could barely get that barbell off the ground – maybe an inch – and had to drop it back down, it wasn't just a failed lift, it felt like a failure to push through and be bigger than my grief. Being truthful with myself, I now know I failed because my body was beaten and tired but also because my motivation was wrong. I wanted success to fix things, to fix me and prove that I wasn't broken and I could be stronger than my grief. I didn't understand that sometimes fighting against it is like pushing against the ocean. I had to move with it, make it part of me.

Six months later, I find myself in North Devon with my team-mates who I've gotten to know much better, some of whom have become friends outside of our training sessions. From the tiny spark of what made him happy and granted him sanity and purpose, Jack has created a team that, in 12 months, expanded to include 34 lifters, 27 of whom are women.

A lot has changed. I have learned how to take failure and use it to become wiser, more patient and thoughtful.

We've hired a massive house for a big group of us to stay in. Part of why I love competitions is the little wolf pack we travel in. It reminds me of being a student, well, minus the weird smells and questionable hygiene.

It is competition day and everyone has already gone to the venue. Ameesha and I are the only ones yet to leave and we are getting ready together in the house while listening to Rihanna, singing along, our friendship a newly minted but already an intense and comfortable thing.

We head to the draughty venue, where the men are just finishing up with their part of the competition. We start to warm up, eat cookies, glug energy drinks, eat peanut M&Ms, sausage rolls from Greggs – everything to keep our strength at maximum levels.

The time comes and, although my entire body floods with adrenaline, I close my eyes and breathe deep. It's not about being brave or beating grief, it's about feeling every single part of my life. The sound of my parents' laughter. The scent of sea water when I stood knee deep in the ocean calling out to Rob, falling apart with grief. Leela's face pressing close to mine in an Eskimo kiss. Priya's arms around me.

But also, feeling the shape of the life I have built for myself. Navigating that loss. Allowing that fury, allowing that rage. Becoming bigger, becoming more. Understanding that grief and loss are not things to be afraid of. Understanding that you don't have to listen to what people say you should be. Understanding that it shouldn't have to take losing everything to realise this.

I get all of my squats and hit a personal best. I hit all of my bench press and hit a personal best. I get my first two deadlifts. My third deadlift attempt is the weight I failed at Euros – 130kg.

Jack talks to me before I go on as he does with every one of our lifters.

When we first started becoming friends, one thing we always

joked about was the fact that both of us love potatoes. I mean LOVE potatoes. My name is called. Before I go on, he yells: 'ATTACK THE BAR LIKE IT STOLE YOUR POTATOES!' Everyone's face says *huh?* But I know what my brother means.

I walk over to the bar with purpose. I feel the chalk on my hands, I place my hands on the bar.

Grief is simply untethered love. It is love that has no home, no place to go because the person it connected us to has gone.

I take that love and I tether it to Jack. I tether it to Aga. To Lindsay. To my teammates. To every person who sees me start to lift that bar and shouts at me to keep going, as I struggle to keep raising it upwards. I tether it to every person in my life who might not understand why I do what I do but wants this for me and is proud of me. Who isn't jealous of this new family of mine but grateful that the net that catches me is now even bigger.

Stronger.

The roar of their voices is like the sound of the ocean and it carries me forward.

At the point of lock out, I am filled to the brim with my life: I am someone who was loved and I am someone who is loved. I fought so fucking hard for this life. To exist, to be seen, to be heard.

When it's time for the medals, we all go and collect ours and then the best lifter is announced. Emma says my name and I think it's a mistake. 'Is it a Miss Congeniality type of prize?' I ask Jack.

'No,' he laughs. 'It's because you lifted the most weight.'

Emma hands me my prize and says: 'I don't think I've seen you without a huge smile on your face throughout this whole competition.'

I look at the trophy. It is a statue of Leonidas the Spartan clutching a wobbly spear that looks like a hazard for a child or a drunk person.

It is the most beautiful thing I have ever seen.

Epilogue

'What would Rob think of you lifting weights?'

This is a question I get asked a lot in interviews when it comes to weight training, and it is paradoxical.

I would not be a powerlifter if Rob were still alive because the need to get physically strong was carved from the deepest cavern of loss. It is not a place I would have naturally arrived at, or even something I would have thought of doing if he were still here.

If the choice were between having him here or being physically strong, then there is no galaxy, no universe, no plane of existence where I don't choose him. But this is the reality I find myself in. Rob is not here. He has walked through a doorway to a place I don't want to visit for a very long time.

A better question would be: what would Rob have wanted for you?

And that, I can answer in a heartbeat because I know the size and shape of the love we shared. Rob would have wanted me to have survived his death but not just that, he would have wanted me to have had a full life. It is the same thing I wanted for him. To be happy, to be loved, to be safe and to live a long life, filled with good people.

Along with his best friend Jesse, he was such a massive believer in a thing they called the Big Family, which was that no matter where you were in the world, they'd find someone they knew in that city and get them to help you out, whether that was meeting you for a drink or putting you up for the night. He would have loved that I was part of a team and a community who would look out for me and protect me. Yes, he would have been proud of what I have achieved but he always was, anyway.

And I want that full, long life. I want decades filled with adventure and freedom. I want to still be squeezing into a singlet in my older years and lifting iron. I want to cycle fast down hills, swim in the wildest of waters, kayak into still, quiet places. I want every single moment to be filled with the possibility of what I can be and for that sense of freedom to only intensify the older I grow.

The journey to finding my own sense of what makes me feel strong has changed my life forever. It's not about the weight I can lift or the miles I can walk. It's about knowing that whatever life throws at me, however heavy the burden, I can lift it. If someone feels the need to comment on my body or what I'm doing, I now have armour to protect the land I occupy, and an army behind me.

In many religions and cultures, from Hinduism to Zoroastrianism, from Native American tribes to Judaism, there is the idea of the eternal flame. Sometimes they happen naturally and sometimes they are manmade but they tend to be either in places of worship where people go to find strength and feel connected to a deeper power or they are reminders of when indomitable spirit and bravery were shown.

The way that I feel about my strength is that it is an eternal flame: it may get smaller or bigger but the spark of it never extinguishes.

Perhaps you started reading this book not feeling very strong. But I am willing to bet that you have been strong in ways you never imagined. You have probably survived things you didn't believe you could, until it happened. All of this is evidence of what your potential is, and what you're capable of doing.

You are strong. I already knew that about you. But if you want it, there is limitless potential for you to be stronger.

This is a truth I know.

Acknowledgements

Not in all my years of being a writer, did I ever dream I would get to write a book like this – for so many reasons, but one is that I didn't know if people were ready to change their minds about what women's strength really looks like, and the second is that I just didn't think of myself, a brown Indian woman, as being someone who could write about it. But here we are. None of this would be possible without Jack, who has changed not just my life but the lives of so many of my teammates, in helping us discover and redefine what strength is. But also, huge thanks to Aga, Lindsay, Lu, Ameesha, Neha, Kirsty and the rest of my Barfight family who have been part of this journey.

Thanks also go to my incredible family – my mother Jaya, my father Ashok, who have inspired me and set a good example in countless ways but have also been with me on this current journey. My big sister Priya who is one of the most phenomenal women I know, a role model and someone who has overcome so much. My in-laws Prue and David – thank you always for your love, for giving me Rob, and for being so supportive when I write about him. Mal, thank you for being the best friend and cheerleader – you kept me sane while writing this book during a pandemic – no mean feat! I also want to thank my brother-in-law Shabby, as well as my three home boys, Kumaran, Ahmed and Niaz.

Thank you hugely Rowan, for being the best agent and for helping me believe this could be a book when I wasn't sure. And to the whole team at Bluebird – Carole, I knew I loved you the moment I met you, but what a privilege it is to work with you on this. To Grainne and Sarah at Siren, you are amazing and make it possible for me to do all that I do. To my See My Strong community who are filled with the best kind of humans, who lift each other up and are the flame of courage others carry into spaces when they feel small – thank you for all of it. To everyone who gave up their time and allowed me to interview you for this book, I see you and appreciate you. To all who I didn't get to mention but you do so much to change the narrative for girls and women, and you create joy around movement – thank you. And for Rob, whose love is with me always. The world changes, the world turns, and we are all a part of that, together.

References

CHAPTER ONE

1. telegraph.co.uk/womens-sport/2019/03/21/sport-england-discover-early-gender-gap-attitudes-participation/

CHAPTER TWO

1. barbie.mattel.com/en-us/about/dream-gap.html
2. drjen.com/mind-the-dream-gap/
3. nytimes.com/2018/10/01/well/family/confidence-gap-teen-girls-tips-parents.html
4. thelancet.com/journals/eclinm/article/PIIS2589-5370(18)30060-9/fulltext#%20
5. sciencedirect.com/science/article/pii/S174014451730517X#!
6. sportengland.org/news/this-girl-can-returns-with-new-tv-advert
7. sportforbusiness.com/state-of-the-nation-on-teenage-sport/

CHAPTER FIVE

1. sciencedirect.com/science/article/pii/S2210261212001940
2. obesity.imedpub.com/extreme-obesity-and-its-associations-with-victimization-ptsd-major-depression-and-eating-disorders-in-a-national-sample-of-women.php?aid=7740
3. bmj.com/content/369/bmj.m696
4. pubmed.ncbi.nlm.nih.gov/21829159/
5. who.int/news-room/fact-sheets/detail/obesity-and-overweight

CHAPTER SIX

1. prnewswire.com/news-releases/female-executives-say-participation-in-sport-helps-accelerate-leadership-and-career-potential-278614041.html
2. telegraph.co.uk/science/2018/11/16/weight-lifting-better-heart-health-running-new-study-finds/
3. ncbi.nlm.nih.gov/pmc/articles/PMC5380170/

CHAPTER EIGHT

1. runnersworld.com/training/a18848270/running-while-female/#survey
2. pubmed.ncbi.nlm.nih.gov/29127850/
3. beateatingdisorders.org.uk/media-centre/eating-disorder-statistics
4. eatingdisorderhope.com/blog/transgender-people-likely-develop-eating-disorder
5. nature.com/articles/s41598-020-74608-6

CHAPTER TEN

1. sciencedaily.com/releases/2018/08/180808193656.htm
2. thelancet.com/journals/lancet/article/PIIS0140-6736(10)61462-6/fulltext
3. ons.gov.uk/peoplepopulationandcommunity/crimeand justice/bulletins/domesticabuseinenglandandwalesoverview/ november2019
4. rapecrisis.org.uk/get-informed/about-sexual-violence/ statistics-sexual-violence/

CHAPTER ELEVEN

1. sportengland.org/news/sport-for-all
2. ons.gov.uk/employmentandlabourmarket/peopleinwork/ earningsandworkinghours/articles/ethnicitypaygapsin-greatbritain/2018
3. custom.shutterstock.com/blog/2018/1/11/diversity-in-advertising-visuals
4. bbc.co.uk/sport/swimming/51664922

CHAPTER THIRTEEN

1. mumsnet.com/campaigns/gps-and-menopause-survey
2. jamanetwork.com/journals/jama/fullarticle/2653735

CHAPTER FOURTEEN

1. statista.com/statistics/248769/age-distribution-of-worldwide-instagram-users/
2. ageuk.org.uk/our-impact/policy-research/loneliness-research-and-resources/

Resources

BOOKS

Am I Ugly? Michelle Elman
Eat Sweat Play, Anna Kessel
Eat Up: Food, Appetite and Eating What You Want, Ruby Tandoh
Fattily Ever After, Stephanie Yeboah
In Their Shoes, Jamie Windust
Just Eat It, Laura Thomas
Lift Yourself, Laura Hoggins
Sway, Dr Pragya Agarwal
Train Happy, Tally Rye

INFLUENCERS/AWESOME PEOPLE TO FOLLOW

CHAPTER 1 DIARY OF A RUNT

Bryony Gordon: Instagram @bryonygordon
See My Strong: Instagram @seemystrong
This Girl Can: Instagram @thisgirlcanuk

CHAPTER 2 DEATH TO GYM KNICKERS

Abi Burton: Instagram @abi_burton
Mini Mermaid Running Club: Instagram @minimermaiduk,
    website: minimermaiduk.com
Street Games: Twitter @streetgames, website: streetgames.org

CHAPTER 3 ROLE MODELS: THE GOOD, THE BAD, THE NON-EXISTENT

We Are Girls in Sport: Instagram @wearegirlsinsport, website:
    wearegirlsinsport.com

Anna Panna: Instagram @Annaxpanna
Yomi Adegoke: Twitter @yomiadegoke Instagram @yomi.adegoke
Jessica Fostekew: Instagram @jessicafostekew
Dr Pragya Agarwal: Twitter and Instagram @drpragyaagarwal
Nicola Adams: Instagram @nicolaadams
Megan Rapinoe: Twitter @mpinoe Instagram @mrapinoe
Ayah Abduldaim: Twitter @Ayah_abdul1
Goals 4 Girls: Twitter @goals4girlsuk Instagram @goals4girls

CHAPTER 4 YOUR BODY IS YOUR LAND

Christy Harrison: Twitter and Instagram @chr1styharrison,
       website: christyharrison.com
Laura Thomas: Instagram @laurathomasphd
Ruby Tandoh: Instagram @ruby.tandoh
Rhiannon Lambert: Instagram @rhitrition
Tally Rye: Instagram @tallyrye @trainhappypodcast
Stephanie Yeboah: @stephanieyeboah
Kelechi Okafor: Twitter and Instagram: @kelechnekoff, website:
       kelechnekoff.com

CHAPTER 5 STRONG IS NOT A SIZE

Michelle Elman: Instagram @scarrednotscared, website:
       michelleelman.com
Megan Crabbe: Instagram @bodyposipanda
Latoya Shauntay Snell: Instagram @iamlshauntay @runningfatchef
       Artika Gunathasan: Instagram @arti.speaks
Suhani Gandhi: Instagram @suhani_strongwoman

CHAPTER 6 BECOMING MY STRONGEST SELF

Ban Hass: Instagram @banhass
Jack Toczydlowski: Instagram @jacked_t @barfight_team
Aleem Majid: @mr_hencherz
Maariyah Tahir: @ms_hencherz
Stacy Burr: @bamaburr @thechampionmindset
The School of Hard Knocks: Instagram @sohkcharity website:
       schoolofhardknocks.org.uk

CHAPTER 7 NO ONE HAS THE MONOPOLY ON STRENGTH

Project Fearless: Instagram @project.fearless website:
    projectfearless.org
You Look Like A Man: Instagram: @you.look.like.a.man
Kortney Olson: Instagram @kortney.olson
Grrrl: Instagram @grrrl_clothing website grrrl.com

CHAPTER 8 GYMS, R U OK, HUN?

Becky Scott: Instagram @missfitsworkout
Dr Stephanie Coen: Twitter @steph_coen
Jamie Windust: Instagram @jamie_windust
Farrah Herbert: Instagram @farrahherbert
Pride Sports: Instagram @pridesportsuk website; pridesports.org.uk
Grl Gym: Instagram @grl.gym
The Underdog Gym: Instagram @theunderdoggym
Hope Virgo: Twitter @hopevirgo
Shannon Murray: Instagram @shannonigans_murray

CHAPTER 9 AN ODE TO BODIES, IN SICKNESS AND IN HEALTH

Team Phoenix Foundation: Twitter @teamphoenixuk website:
    teamphoenixfoundation.co.uk
Coppafeel: Instagram @coppafeelpeople website: coppafeel.org
Kris Hallenga: Instagram @howtoglitteraturd
Anoushé Husain: Instagram @anoushehusain @paraclimbin-
    glondon

CHAPTER 10 LET'S TALK ABOUT MENTAL HEALTH

Stephanie Nimmo: website: stephnimmo.com
Good Gym: Instagram @goodgym website: www.goodgym.org
Girls on Hills: Instagram @girlsonhillsuk website: girlsonhills.com

CHAPTER 11 WOMEN IN COLOUR

Bani J: Instagram @BaniJ
Mantra Surf Club: Instagram @surfingindia
Tanvi Jagadish: Instagram @indiansurfergirl

Karenjeet Kaur Bains: Instagram @karenjeet_bains
Bhavna Tokekar: Instagram @bhavnatokekar
Onna Ju Jitsu: Twitter @onnajujitsuclub website:
    onnajujitsuclub.com
Zainab Alema: Instagram @zeealema
Zeina Nassar: Instagram @zeina.boxer
Ibtihaj Muhammad: Instagram @ibtihajmuhammad
Nouf Alosaimi: Instagram @pinkbubblesdivers
Muslim Girls Fence: website: muslimgirlsfence.org
Donna Noble: Instagram @donnanobleyoga
Black Girls Hike: Instagram @bgh_uk website: bghuk.com
Boarders Without Borders: Instagram @boarderswithoutborders_
Ebony Horse Club: Instagram @ebonyhorseclubbrixton
Khadijah Mellah: Instagram @khadijah_mellah
Swim Dem Crew: Instagram @swimdemcrew

CHAPTER 12 THE POWER OF PERIODS AND WEREWOLF MOTHERS

Clare Bourne: Instagram @clarebournephysio
Charlie Barker: Instagram @bumpsandburpees
Wendy Searle: Instagram @betweensnowandsky

CHAPTER 13 EVERYONE SHOULD READ THIS CHAPTER ABOUT THE MENOPAUSE (I MEAN EVERYONE)

Dr Shahzadi Harper: website: theharperclinic.com
        Women in Sport: website: womeninsport.org
Jane Dowling: Instagram @menoandme website: menoandme.com
Jo Moseley: Instagram @healthyhappy50 website: jomoseley.com
Nicola McPhun: Instagram @invisible.to.invincible
Meg Matthews: website: megsmenopause.com
Mita Mistry: website: mitamistry.co.uk

CHAPTER 14 STRONG HAS NO AGE LIMIT

Alex Rotas: Instagram @alexrotasphotography website:
    alexrotasphotography.co.uk
This Granny Can: Instagram @thisgrannycan
Train With Joan: Instagram @trainwithjoan